CROSSROADS
Time & Space /
Tradition & Modernity in
Hispanic Worlds

In *Crossroads: Time & Space/ Tradition & Modernity in Hispanic Worlds*, art and science converge, as well as past and present, in a combination of topics and authors, attractively-balanced by Debra D. Andrist. The book is a kaleidoscope that invites people so interested (not only Hispanics, Latinxs or Chicanxs) from inside the United States, as well as outside, to look through it as a sample of how the *crisol* of cultures enriches social life in various countries.

Jesús Ruíz Flores, PhD, Director of the Centro de Estudios Sociales y Regionales, Departamento de Política y Sociedad, Universidad de Guadalajara/Centro Universitario de la Ciénega, Guadalajara, México

This new book offers a very well integrated collection of essays addressing a multitude of crossroads in numerous Hispanic contexts across the intersections of time & space/tradition & modernity. Almost as if these crossroads were composed of innumerable grids of differing sizes overlaid ad infinitum, these intersections become logarithmic and inform much of the content of the book. Grouped in four sections, the 15 chapters in the books examine a wide variety of topics ranging from visual architectural time & space/tradition & modernity, the history of "Hispanic" religious and social organizations in Texas, cosmopolitanism and nativism in the U.S, and the cultural and gender crossroads defining Mexican American/Chicana/Latina writers like Sandra Cisneros. The authors of this collection ask questions about cultural and social intersections and overlaps, offering remarkable insights on how the Hispanic world is an extraordinarily vivid place to explore these crossroads.

Francisco Lara-Valencia, PhD, Southwest Borderland Scholar & Program Director, Program for Transborder Communities, School of Liberal Arts & Sciences and Associate, School of Geographic Sciences & Urban Planning, Arizona State University, Tempe, Arizona

Crossroads indeed! The Hispanic influence evolves, grows and permeates through our communities, bursting at the seams with heritage and history. Andrist pieces together a fascinating portrait of Hispanic art in our global community.

> Andy Kaufman, Director, Conversa Language Schools,
> Santa Ana, Costa Rica

Understanding the complexity of a culture that encompasses different traditions, belief, practices, and even languages across more than 20 countries, such as the Hispanic cultures, requires abandoning the idea of monolithic categories, and embracing the liminality of cultural and social expressions. Debra D. Andrist's *Crossroads: Time & Space/Tradition & Modernity* takes on this challenge examining a variety of topics, including arts, literature, social and political sciences. Recognizing the interconnected, overlapped, and interdependent nature of social and cultural categorizations, the essays collected in this book shed light from innovative angles on meaningful social and cultural aspects of the "Hispanic World."

> Andrés F. Ruíz-Olaya, PhD, Assistant Professor, University of Mary,
> Advisory Board for "Society: Americas" for the *Routledge Encyclopedia of the Renaissance World*

CROSSROADS

Time & Space / Tradition & Modernity in Hispanic Worlds

Edited by
Debra D. Andrist

sussex
ACADEMIC
PRESS
Brighton • Chicago • Toronto

Copyright © Sussex Academic Press 2020; Introductions and editorial organization of this volume copyright © Debra D. Andrist.

The right of Debra D. Andrist to be identified as Editor of this work has been asserted in accordance with the Copyright, Designs and Patents Act 1988.

2 4 6 8 10 9 7 5 3 1

First published in Great Britain in 2020 by
SUSSEX ACADEMIC PRESS
PO Box 139, Eastbourne BN24 9BP

Distributed in North America by
SUSSEX ACADEMIC PRESS
Independent Publishers Group
814 N. Franklin Street
Chicago, IL 60610

All rights reserved. Except for the quotation of short passages for the purposes of criticism and review, no part of this publication may be reproduced, stored in a retrieval system, or transmitted, in any form or by any means, electronic, mechanical, photocopying, recording or otherwise, without the prior permission of the publisher.

British Library Cataloguing in Publication Data
A CIP catalogue record for this book is available from the British Library.

Library of Congress Cataloging-in-Publication Data
To be applied for.

Hardcover ISBN 978-1-78976-019-4

MIX
Paper from responsible sources
FSC www.fsc.org FSC® C013056

Typeset & designed by Sussex Academic Press, Brighton & Eastbourne.
Printed by TJ International, Padstow, Cornwall.

Contents

Preface ix
Acknowledgments xiv

Part I Physical Crossroads of Time & Space/Tradition & Modernity

1 Spain's Wine Museums: Where Age-Old Oenological Tradition Intersects with Contemporary Design and Modern Technology 3
   Kimberly A. Habegger

2 Twentieth-Century Pyramid: Vestiges of Dictatorship in a Democracy—Spain's Valley of the Fallen 19
   Kimberly A. Habegger

3 Home, Sweet and Not-So-Sweet, Home: The Museum of Fine Art/Houston (MFAH) and Latin American Art 32
   Debra D. Andrist

4 Architecture and the Constant Hispanic Postmodern Project 46
   Elizabeth White Coscio

Part II Social, Artistic, Religious & Political Crossroads

5 Representation of the Absent Object: Pictorial Mysticism in El Greco and Pablo Picasso 71
   Enrique Mallén

6 Transmogrifying Traditions: *el guadalupanismo*. The History of *Sociedades Guadalupanas* and Other Hispanic Organizations in Texas, Especially in Houston 87
   Debra D. Andrist

7 *Mestizaje* as Lateral Universality: Moving In-Between Elitist Cosmopolitanism and Populist Tribalism 106
   John Francis Burke

viii | Contents

Part III Crossroads of Social & Literary Time & Space, Not to Mention Tradition & Modernity, in Spain

8 Pablo Picasso's Semantically-Complex Visual Poetry Through Modern Technology 127
   Enrique Mallén & Luis Meneses

9 Ramón J. Sender's Sublime Visions of Freedom in *Relatos fronterizos* (1970) 162
   Montse Feu

10 Pérez Reverte at the Early Twenty-First Century Crossroads of Spanish History and Literature 179
   Stephen Miller

Part IV Crossroads of Social, Gender, Artistic, Literary & Cinematic Time & Space, Not to Mention Tradition & Modernity, in Latin/Latino(x) America

11 Time, Space and Creativity 195
   Rose Mary Salum

12 Why Can't a Feminist be Sexy? Sandra Cisneros' *My Wicked, Wicked Ways* 199
   Gwendolyn Díaz-Ridgeway

13 Confrontations on All Fronts: *The War of the End of the World* by Mario Vargas Llosa 205
   Jorge Chavarro

14 The Many Homes: A Reading of Marina Perezagua's *The Story of H* 212
   Eduardo Cerdán

15 China and *Chinago*: Globalization of the Kung Fu Genre and the Interpretation of Hero and History 220
   Haiqing Sun

Conclusions 230

The Editor and Contributors 232
Index 239

Preface

Crossroads! Intersections—physical and/or metaphorical—demand processes of consideration, determination, decision and commitment. Stasis is no longer an option where convergence is poised before the unknown. Where categories such as gender, culture (particularly visual art and literature), ethnicity, socio-economic status, philosophy and religion clash, the multivariate process can reach such complexity that literary, sociological and psychological tools may offer widely-differing interpretations. Real-life intersections range from the mundane (choosing among food items on a menu according to taste preferences) to survival-determinants (evaluating the efficacy of various medical procedures). But such intersections are at the two ends of a very long continuum that takes in issues of form/function, and traditional versus "modern." Both physical constructions and their purposes evolve over time, whether public spaces like museums and monuments or private spaces like a dwelling. For example, the concept of "home" may be defined as both a physical place and/or a mental construct. In more esoteric contexts, artists chiefly known for visual production, representing their ideas with color and form, not infrequently cross media to "paint" with words. Philosophy, religion, art and literature cross paths via symbols and other visual and linguistic constructs. Writers deal with how and where their own or their characters' multiple identities intersect. The Hispanic world is an extraordinarily vivid place to explore these crossroads. This collection of essays addresses a multitude of crossroads in numerous Hispanic contexts across the intersections of time & space/tradition & modernity. Almost as if these crossroads were composed of innumerable grids of differing sizes overlaid ad infinitum, these intersections become logarithmic and inform much of the content of this book overall.

The contexts and interpretations are wide-ranging; e.g., in Part I, Kimberly A. Habegger traces visual architectural time & space/tradition & modernity via how Spain's age-old oenological tradition meets modern technology and, in a second chapter, how the vestiges of long-term dictatorship lurk in the architectural spaces of Spain's democracy. I examine how a particular groundbreaking museum has addressed both diversity and philosophical concepts of place in exhibits over its lifetime. Elizabeth Coscio relates the intersections between architecture and literary philosophy and production to each other in Latin America.

In Part II, Enrique Mallén recognizes how the works of Spanish Renaissance/Baroque painter, El Greco, and those of 20th century artist, Pablo Picasso, share similar religious intersections in terms of mysticism. I trace the history of "Hispanic" religious and social organizations over time in a socio-historically inhospitable area of Texas (in spite of and/or due to its geographic history as part of Mexico and the state's changing demographics). Political scientist, John Francis Burke, examines the seemingly irreconcilably opposed worldviews of Cosmopolitan Elitism and Nativist Populism among U.S. residents and proposes *Mestizaje* (the concept itself being a genetic/ethnic/cultural crossroads) as a Lateral Universality.

Continuing with how space/architecture and art/literature/technology cross, this time in Spain, inform the chapters of Part III. Detailing a particularly-apt methodology for the 21st century double world of real and virtual, the latter a kind of fourth dimension, if you will—and a still-unique in the majority of Hispanist critique—Enrique Mallén and Luis Meneses bridge the cultural "real" world and the virtual one as they scrutinize the literary works of Spanish painter, Pablo Picasso, using tools from the technological world. Montse Feu's chapter on activities and writings of Spanish Civil War (1936–9) political self-exile to the U.S., Ramón Sender, bridges even more than the overt cultures and categories of politics and journalism. Along the same lines, Stephen Miller's treatise on Spanish war correspondent, later novelist, Arturo Pérez Reverte, illuminates the writer's crossroad of career transformation, as well as evolved/evolving canonical reactions to his fictional works as a result, over the last century into the current one.

The five chapters of Part IV focus on Latin America, including the Latinx[1] world in the U.S. recognized as the fifth-largest Spanish-speaking country in the Americas. Similar to how the real and the virtual worlds intersect currently, the 15th and 16th century *encuentro/encounter* between European and indigenous American worlds, formerly—and xenophobically—identified as the "Discovery," but accurately also as the Conquest, was so dramatic a contrast for both sides that the two originally geographically-separated cultures must have seemed "unreal" to each other, fragmenting each group's own concepts of time and space. Frankly, I contend that the *choque/shock* therein foretells that quintessential Latin American 20th century movement, magical realism, in which products of the twentieth century Latin American artistic movements defy nature, science, time and space.

While many producers of creative artistic works are primarily known publicly for their works in only one particular (sub)genre, like painting, and generally for one period of time and/or style, like twentieth century or cubism, and most frequently are home-based in one place, like their birth country, some actually create across not only across artistic genres, and not just across the semi-expected sub-genres like painting/sculpting, but across time & space and tradition & modernity—adding the virtual world to that of the physical one. These artists, traditionally, pre-social media, were not so frequently known for their personal lives, in addition to being painters and sculptors and writers and composers and designers, etc., sometimes concurrently, sometimes sequentially. For an especially well-known example (and exception), the aforementioned world-famous Spaniard, Pablo Picasso, worked in every studio specialty, crossed numerous stylistic boundaries, produced over many decades, whether in later self-imposed political exile in France or elsewhere, as well as wrote all sorts of poetry and prose and certainly was (in)famous for his prodigious love life, pre-social media.

In a brief nod to Mexican artist, Frida Kahlo, about whom I've written in other publications, exemplifying creative productions which cross the visual to the written, I call attention to the fact that she both painted—and it's not so well known as with Picasso—wrote poetry and prose. She was traditionally known initially for her unfortunate relationship with her (negative) muse husband, Diego Rivera, rather than for her own production—though he and that relationship constitute a good deal of the subject matter of both her painting and her writing. That perception and evaluation changed dramatically—but decades after her death! Her life was her art in all contexts.

Creative women like Kahlo and so many others, who exemplify identities and productions at crossroads, offer insights into their processes, as well as illuminating gender and cultural phenomena. They mix their identities and production across all these categories, plus their multiple identities as homemakers, wives, mothers, victims, activists, etc. For example, Mexican-Lebanese writer now living in the U.S., RoseMary Salum, introduces a different approach from the rest of the chapters in this book. She contributes an autobiographical short story in itself, which segues to Part IV as the first chapter, illuminating the personal links and intersections in her creative processes: between space, i.e., her father's library, and over time, i.e., as she grows older and matures intellectually.

Gwen Díaz highlights how Mexican American/Chicana/Latina

writer, Sandra Cisneros, demands the right to claim herself not only a feminist philosophically, but as a woman physically, the cover of her *My Wicked, Wicked Ways* serving as case-in-point. Jorge Chavarro contrasts the roles of female characters as in Vargas Llosa's *The War of the End of the World,* particularly in terms of biblical precedents for female behavior. He illuminates the cultural and gender crossroads in the novel by the Peruvian writer, Mario Vargas Llosa. The fictional town, Canudos, in Brazil, is distinctly not a Hispanic country but, thanks to the sixteenth-century pope, a Portuguese one; the inspiration for the cross-cultural site is from actual late 19th century Brazilian history.

Echoing back to the concept of "home," Eduardo Cerdán bridges the gaps between East and West, male and female, in his essay on Marina Perezagua's *The Story of H,* not to mention that this novel details ramifications of the continuing Japan/U.S. history during and post-World War II. Continuing with the East/West intersections and citing a traditionally recognized genre movie intended for (warrior) males, Haiqing Sun points out the strikingly discordant cultural disconnects in the Mexican *Kung Fu* movie, *Chinago*, which twists Chinese martial arts and philosophy almost out of recognition.

Overall, as Hispanists, we contributors not only examine grids within categories, but across them, for remarkable insights in the crossroads and intersections that are the overriding theme of this collection. At the same time, those grids are so overlaid, sometimes so interlocking, that it is difficult to "tease out" specifics. For this reason, so many seemingly divergent essays on initial consideration are brought together in this collection. The division of four parts helps to segue each grouping of essays from one main general topic to the next, while the titles of the same parts tie them together more specifically, even though they may emphasize different aspects of any particular topic, whether physical, gender, intellectual, artistic, literary, cinematic, but all cultural with Hispanic worlds as the focus.

Note

1 To emphasis the multitude of intersections in "naming" alone in the worlds addressed in this collection, I quote from the footnotes to my own essay on ethnic terminology in the *Western Social Science Association Newsletter* of Spring 2019: "*Hispanic* refers more to linguistic & cultural origins, frequently via the last name, and however long-ago, at least partially of Spanish descent (Spain), who may, or may not, actually speak the language; may both be from Spain or from, or descended from, those born in the Americas which were conquered by the Spanish (Spain). *Hispanic American* refers to the same linguistic & cultural descent but

does NOT include those actually from Spain, only emphasizes those who are, or are descended from, those born in the Americas, which were conquered by the Spanish (Spain). *Latin American* refers to those whose linguistic & cultural descent has to do with the Latin-based languages and/or cultures: Spanish, Portuguese, French, Italian or Romanian AND who are from, or descended from, those same who were born or live in the Americas. According to the popular culture web source, *Wikipedia*, *Latinx* is a gender-neutral term sometimes used in lieu of *Latino* or *Latina*. The plural is *Latinxs*. The "x" replaces the standard "o" and "a" of gender-specific suffixes in Spanish, Portuguese and related languages, which form nouns of the masculine and feminine genders, respectively. The term is a politicized neologism that has gained traction among advocacy groups intersectionally combining the identity politics of race and gender. Other forms such as *Latin@* and *Latine* are also used. Continuing with *Wikipedia*: *Latino* is a term often used in the U.S. to refer to people with cultural ties to Latin America, in contrast to *Hispanic*, which is a demonym that includes Spaniards and other speakers of the Spanish language-but *Latino* as a category used in the United States may be understood as a shorthand for the Spanish word *latinoamericano* (Latin American in English) or the Portuguese phrase, *latino americano*, thus excluding speakers of Spanish or Portuguese from Europe. Both *Hispanic* and *Latino* are generally used to denote people living in the United States, so much so that "Outside the United States, we don't speak of Latinos; we speak of Mexicans, Colombians, Peruvians, and so forth." In Latin America, the term *latino* is not a common endonym and its usage in Spanish as a demonym is restricted to the Latin American-descended population of the United States. *Chicano* or *Chicana* is a chosen identity of some Mexican Americans in the United States. The term, *Chicano*, is sometimes used interchangeably with Mexican-American. Both names are chosen identities within the Mexican-American community in the United States; however, these terms have a wide range of meanings in various parts of the Southwest. The term became widely used during the *Chicano* Movement by Mexican Americans to express pride in a shared cultural, ethnic and community identity."

Acknowledgments

All translations are by the chapter authors themselves unless otherwise indicated. All Spanish-to-English and French-to-English translations in Debra D. Andrist's whole-chapter translations of "The Other Protagonists in *The War of the End of the World*" by Mario Vargas Llosa, by Jorge Chavarro; and "The Many Homes: A Reading of Marina Perezagua's *The Story of H*" by Eduardo Cerdán, are by Andrist.

Photos illustrating "Spain's Wine Museums: Where Age-Old Oenological Tradition Intersects with Contemporary Design and Modern Technology" by Kimberly A. Habegger are from her personal collection, taken on visits to said spaces.

All references to exhibitions and illustrations of art in "Home, Sweet and Not-So-Sweet, Home: The Museum of Fine Art/Houston (MFAH) & Latin American Art" by Debra D. Andrist are from the MFAH website, https://www.mfah.org/

All references to illustrations of artworks by Picasso in "Pablo Picasso's Semantically-Complex Visual Poetry" by Enrique Mallén and Luis Meneses and to those by El Greco and Picasso in "Representation of the Absent Object: Pictorial Mysticism in El Greco and Pablo Picasso" by Enrique Mallén are from *The On-Line Picasso Project* founded and edited by Mallén, authorized by the Picasso Foundation. Request a password at https://picasso.shsu.edu/

CROSSROADS

Time & Space /
Tradition & Modernity in
Hispanic Worlds

PART I

Physical Crossroads of Time & Space/Tradition & Modernity

CHAPTER

1

Spain's Wine Museums: Where Age-Old Oenological Tradition Intersects with Contemporary Design and Modern Technology

KIMBERLY A. HABEGGER

Since approximately the year 2000, innovative contemporary architecture has been incorporated into the creation and renovation of wineries in Spain. This tendency is part of a planned effort to differentiate Spain's wineries and their wines to a world market through a growing emphasis on wine tourism. Many distinguished architects of international acclaim have contributed to this redesign of the Spanish wine country, including Frank Gehry, Jesús Mario Pascual, Zaha Hadid, Richard Rogers, Santiago Calatrava, Rafael Moneo, and Norman Foster, among others.

Enhancing the wine tasting and architectural experiences, a number of the *bodegas* have given visitors access to valuable and unique collections that educate guests and enhance their overall experience as they lean about the wines produced on the grounds. The collections complement the visitors' experience by showcasing the family-curated specimens. Artefacts range from contemporary sculpture, botanical specimens, historical wine making tools and drinking vessels, architectural structures and traditional and contemporary paintings.

In a continuing effort to display artefacts and educate the public on oenological topics, a proliferation of wine museums has accompanied the appearance of design-oriented wineries. The website www.museosdelvino.es lists twenty-seven different wine museums in Spain at present. Some of these museums reflect the creative architecture of the new winery buildings while others place the contemporary museum interior into important pre-existing historical structures. While some museums are part of a private winery, others are sponsored by local governments to highlight wine culture and to educate visitors on the wines of their specific region. A theme common to the museums and the wineries is the juxtaposition of tradition and innovation in the wine industry in Spain today and the museum spaces explored in this monograph attempt to illustrate and explain this juxtaposition (Habegger).

Wine museums are an important tool in the wine tourism promotion and said museums may contribute in different ways: through highlighting the history of wine in the region; through a portrayal of wine culture in general; or by allowing visitors the opportunity to explore the many facets of wine appreciation and tasting. The success of these spaces is explained in part by J.B. Jackson's concept of "a sense of place." Jackson observes that we are drawn to localities that give us "a certain indefinable sense of well-being and which we want to return to, time and again. Therefore, the original notion of the ritual, of repeated celebration or reverence, is inherent in the phrase. It is not a temporary response, for it persists and brings us back, reminding us of previous visits" (158). Jackson further notes that this "sense of place" has become increasingly rare in our contemporary society that prioritizes the "sense of time" in the organization of the landscape. A "sense of place" provides "a lively awareness of the familiar environment, a ritual repetition, a sense of fellowship based on shared experience" (159). Through the blending of both highly original and historical architecture, different sensorial experiences, and the opportunity to share wine and food with others, a "sense of place" enhances the visitors' experience of these museums.

Michel Foucault's concept of "heterotopias" provides an alternative approach to assist in defining the character of these complex spaces. Foucault explains that the study of heterotopias serves as a "simultaneously mythic and real contestation of the space in which we live" (4) and aids in revealing the layers of meaning and relationships in a space that are not easily discernable. Of the several types of heterotopias he delineates, the "heterotopias of time" reflect the nature of museums and libraries in general as they attempt "to accumulate time . . . in one place . . . outside of time and inaccessible to its ravages" (7). Nevertheless, wine museums also share traits of a different class of heterotopia, one linked to time in its most flowing, transitory, precarious aspect, to time in the "mode of festival." This mode is discernable through the events and social activities hosted by the wine museum: tastings, lectures, tours, festivals, and varied dining options. Functioning both as heterotopias "of the festival and of the eternity of accumulating time" (7) wine museums require architecture that is highly functional and adaptable.

The Cambridge Dictionary defines a museum as "A building where objects of historical, scientific, or artistic interest are kept." To this definition, we should add the museum's critical function or not merely storing, but displaying said objects for a particular audience. In Spain today, some wineries or *bodegas* serve as museums in addition to their primary winemaking function in their display of notable collections of art and historical artefacts as seen at Bodegas Otazu with their collection of contemporary sculpture and the former Bodegas Darien known for its collection of historic wine vessels, as examples. Due to their originality and captivating architectural design, other *bodegas* "feel like" or are experienced as contemporary museum spaces such as Bodegas Portia and Bodegas Protos in Ribera del Duero and Bodegas Marqués de Riscal and Bodegas Ysios in Rioja. Finally, some museums are structures dedicated to wine education and appreciation without the winemaking function or the purpose of promoting the wine of a specific vineyard.

The wine museum itself is of increasing importance around the world and its linkage to the wine industry and the wine tourism effort has been described and analyzed extensively, ranging from the cases of the Aragón Wine Museum and the Chilean Wine Museum (Zamora) to the d'Arenberg Cube in Australia's McLaren Vale (Llewellyn). In this study, we will address museums about wine, some of which are connected to specific wineries and others that are independent or publicly supported. The museums to be studied are found in three different wine areas in northern Spain and will include the Museo de la Cultura del Vino at the Bodegas Vivanco in Rioja, the Museo del Vino in Valladolid, the Museo de la Cultura del Rioja, and the intimate wine museum at the Bodegas Fariña in the town of Toro in the Toro D.O. in western Spain. These three wine areas are acclaimed for the quality of Spanish red wines, particularly those produced from the *tempranillo* grape, also known by other names according to the region.

Museo de la Cultura del Vino at Dinastía Vivanco

The Museo de la Cultura del Vino (figs. 1–2) is part of the Dinastía Vivanco winery located in Briones, Rioja, designed by architect Jesús Marino Pascual. Dedicated in 2004, Dinastía Vivanco offers wine tourists an incredible array of wine-related experiences. This obligatory stop on the Rioja wine trail provides the many expansive spaces required to accommodate these experiences as well: the facility includes ample parking, an excellent restaurant, a spacious gift store, a wine bar with *tapas*, beautifully planned gardens, a historical archive containing 5000 books on wine (accessible by appointment) and a world-class museum exploring wine culture around the world. Structurally, the museum and the winery are combined into one large complex consisting of multiple volumes. Architect Marino Pascual has created a number of other viniculture-oriented spaces in Spain: Bodega Antión and Bodega Darien are both located in Rioja, as is the Centro del la Cultura del Rioja in Logroño that we will discuss later. In addition, Bodegas Irius in Somontano is a spectacular example of Marino Pascual's work.

Approaching Dinastía Vivanco from some distance, the observer notes that the overall design consists of a number of inter-locking volumes reflecting some neoclassical influences through details such as a large rotunda placed towards the center of the complex and a square-shaped entry area, both crowned with lantern-like structures (the appendage over the entry actually functions as a chimney providing natural ventilation). In contrast with the neoclassical influences, a more contemporary sensibility is felt in the manner in which these volumes and others are varying dimensions are connected with trellises and walkways of large, square cement pavers. Despite the contemporary feel, the grouping of these architectural volumes actually is characteristic of vernacular *bodega* structures and is reflective of the complexity of the winemaking process to be revealed through exploring this museum (Divisare).

The exterior materials, including oxidized copper, glass, and colored concrete (waves of purple on the perimeter wall and terracotta-toned areas of concrete on the building exterior) echo the colors of the landscape and the wine itself, all replicated by reflecting pools. In addition, the golden stone ashlar employed in the structure is indigenous to the Rioja Alta region thus further linking the *bodega* to its environment. The grounds surrounding the winery/museum display a garden of over 200 varietals (said to be one of the most significant private ampelographic collections in the world) and the well-manicured grounds and patios showcase statuary that pays homage to wine culture ranging from classical representations of Bacchus to a copious, stylized handful of grapes. This second sculpture is located to the side of a large open frame that features a superb view of the vineyards themselves with a vintage tractor visible in the distance. The entire vignette seems to honor the concepts of labor, nature, and abundance that constitute the process of creating wine.

Mostly underground, the interior of the winery, the museum space, and the social spaces are spacious and contemporary leading the visitor on a multi-sensorial exploration of wine, wine making and wine appreciation. The collection of art and archaeology spanning from Antiquity to the present complement the educational experience of visitors as they proceed through the museum: historical implements used in the cultivation of grapes and the processing of wine, a collection of over 4000 corkscrews and accessories and vessels for serving wine. The third floor houses the fine art and significant historical artefacts one would find in an archaeological museum such as an Egyptian frieze and original Picassos—all portraying some aspect of wine culture. In addition to the collections of objects, there are stops in the museum where guests learn about barrel making and the oaks used in their manufacture and how the use of glass and cork allow for the proper storage and aging of wine. Visitors also have access to experiential opportunities available through stations where the qualities of wine color and aroma are displayed and guests are invited to test their abilities to distinguish the different nuances. Several videos placed throughout the museum dramatize aspects of the growing seasons and their corresponding vinicultural activities.

Owner, Pedro Vivanco, began safeguarding the family's traditional winemaking equipment as the *bodega* modernized; these implements would serve as the starting point for the museum that is the result of 40 years of artefact accumulation (Robinson) now curated by son, Santiago Vivanco. Pedro Vivanco has expressed the intention of the public display of the collection, observing that the family feels compelled to "give back to wine what wine has given us" (Dinastía Vivanco). As an offering to Bacchus or as a gift to contemporary wine consumers that have contributed to the success of Bodegas Dinastía Vivanco, the collections of the winery reward both the gods and mortals alike.

So, in fact, this carefully curated collection was originally a family collection of tools of the trade of wine production and artistic works inspired by the final product of the family's labor, the wine itself. In his observations on the nature of collecting, critic, Greg Noble, reminds us that collected objects make our cultural world concrete, that objects are mnemonics for a complex world, and that our private acts of consumption are indeed profoundly social (235). The items in Dinastía Vivanco's Museo de la Cultura del Vino both reflect and are tangible fruits of the family's endeavors across several generations. Yet their public display insures that society is the beneficiary of the Vivanco's desire to "give back to wine what wine has given us." This cycle of labor resulting in wealth to be shared with those who contributed to the creation of this wealth is both an act of thanks and an investment in the future. Visitors should become consumers better informed about and more appreciate of wine culture who, in turn, should enthusiastically support the wine industry through the consumption of wine and the participation in wine tourism activities.

Museo del Vino de Valladolid

The Museo del Vino (figs. 3–4), located in the town of Peñafiel, was designed by architect, Roberto Valle, in 1999. The museum is a contemporary space that has been placed into the cellar of the Medieval Castle of Peñafiel, located in the renowned Ribera del Duero wine- producing area in the state of Valladolid in northern Spain. Visitors may purchase a tour of the Castle, a ticket for the museum, or both spaces can be experienced at a reduced price. The Castle is placed prominently on a hill that enabled domination of both the Duero and the Duratón rivers and this location allows for remarkable views both of the castle from a distance and from the castle as one surveys the town of Peñafiel and the neighboring vineyards and villages. The historic structure has its origins in the ninth century, although the present manifestation is attributed largely to Don Pedro Téllez Girónsu in the fifteenth century.

In order to access the museum, one must descend to the lower level of the castle arriving at a landing where a contemporary work of sculpture constructed of metal ribbons suggesting grapes greets visitors. Moving through the museum interior, the juxtaposition of contemporary and historical architectural elements reminds guests of both the history and the innovation of wine in Spain today. The open floor plan allows easy passage through the exhibit space while also enhancing those historical architectural elements such as the stone walls and the original carved apertures for the castle's structural beams. The museum contains sections dedicated to aspects of wine production and wine tasting (including professional tasting rooms)—at the same time, many exhibits are clearly intended to illustrate the history and the characteristics of wine from the five DOs (denominación de origen) of Valladolid: Tierra de León, Ribera del Duero, Cigales, Toro, and Rueda and to the wines classified as Vinos de la Tierra de Castilla y León. One particularly-unique display features garments and wine accessories used by the historic organizations of wine growers of the region over centuries while another showcases the bottles labels of many of the famous wineries of Valladolid including examples from the prestigious Vega Sicilia. Visitors can explore nine different sections such as "History," "Procedures," and those featuring types of wine presses, tools, bottles, and the specifics of wine tasting. The museum space also includes smaller spaces that multiply the possibilities for visitor experiences such as the professional tasting room, the library, the shop and the auditorium. Interactive displays demonstrating wine traits and multiple audiovisual stations allow guests to process information through multiple avenues.

The Museo del Vino is clearly more than an area for display of historical artefacts and wine-related equipment, the province of Valladolid uses to museum to promote the wine not only of the acclaimed Ribera de Duero, but also of the other DOs mentioned previously. The Valladolid website expands on the mission with the following: "This unique museum space promotes the understanding, through the world of wine, of the province of Valladolid culturally and geographically as wine tourism has the ability to structure and connect all of the area's resources: landscape and nature, artistic patrimony, traditional arts, sport and leisure, festival and traditions, and of course, gastronomy" (www.provinciadevalladolid.com). The museum philosophy recognizes that viniculture influences and is molded by many different cultural aspects and therefore successfully demonstrates the interconnectivity between wine, history, and contemporary culture in Valladolid.

El Centro de la Cultura del Rioja

The Centro de la Cultura del Rioja in Logroño (figs. 5–6) was designed by Jesús Marino Pascual from 2008–2011. Situated in the historic center of Logroño, political capital of the state of Rioja, the museum occupies an entire block between Mercaderes, Ruavieja, and Marqués de San Nicolás streets. The original historical building was a sixteenth-century palace of the Yanguas family that has been a historical center of winemaking activities in the city. As in the case of Valladolid, this structure features the wines of the local area, and houses multiple wine-tasting purposes: wine store and bar, professional tasting rooms, temporary and permanent exhibits, all in significant historical buildings repurposed and reinterpreted by contemporary architecture.

The various spaces of the museum are situated amongst four levels of the building to include the cellar. The open area on the ground floor allows for only smaller, L-shaped exhibit spaces on the two floors overhead. The expansiveness and abundant natural light augmented by contemporary fenestration render the entire floor quite appealing as other inviting spaces such as the shop and the wine bar greet visitors and promise the opportunity to savor local wines and culinary delicacies after the tour. The contrast between the historical architectural elements and those added by Marino Pascual are often delineated by the use of a wine-colored plaster application as seen in both interior and exterior views. A stairway original to the Renaissance palace has been carefully restored as it serves as the connection between the themes of the different floors; the staircases serves as a metaphor for the museum linking tradition with contemporary innovation. One display of particular interest is the original wine-aging cellar to the palace that was unearthed during the recent renovation work. A very distinct experience is that of a monumental metal sculpture of a bottle of wine that serves as the nucleus of the permanent exhibition space. Connecting the entire experience, a kind of computerized game queries visitors about their food and wine preferences at stations throughout the museum. The program makes a final wine recommendation and the end of the visit—conveniently as guests return to the ground floor's wine and epicurean shop.

Dedicated to the wine culture and gastronomy of Rioja, the Center hopes that visitors "can breathe history, tradition, innovation, design, and the wine of Rioja in a building of historical interest that combines exceptional architecture, artistic patrimony, history and innovation, design and tradition, wine and gastronomy" (El Centro). It is interesting to note a small linguistic detail: the word, "wine," does not appear in the museum's name, although it is most definitely a wine museum. A visitor might expect some kind of general anthropological museum instead of one delving into numerous facets of wine cultivation, production, and appreciation. However, the part of the Museum's name: the Center for the Culture "del Rioja" references the celebrated wine of Rioja as opposed to the culture of Rioja in more generic terms.

Bodegas Fariña

Other less-elaborate forms of wine museums also are found, among those is the Bodegas Fariña (figs. 7–8) located in Toro, a wine-producing DO in Castilla y León to the west of the more prominent Ribera del Duero. Toro (both a town and a DO) is a picturesque area with a growing wine industry that continues to receive increasing recognition for the quality of its product. Founded in 1942, shortly after the grueling years of the Civil War, Bodegas Fariña is the oldest established winery in the area and consists of 300 hectors of wine featuring the varietal "tinta de Toro," a variation on the *tempranillo* grape. The winery offers tours, tastings, and an opportunity to visit

1,2 Dinastía Vivanco

3,4 Museo de Valladolid

5,6 El Centro de la Cultura del Rioja

7,8 Bodegas Fariña

their intimate wine museum. The museum space is located in a spacious agricultural structure modified to allow significant natural light and interesting construction details in the exposed roof frame. The objects in the museum include historical tools and wine presses formerly used in wine production and the most recent collection of paintings that are in competition to be selected as the image for the wine label of the current year's harvest. A large wine-tasting bar complements the space and supplements an additional bar in the tasting room where purchases are made. The colorful bar in the tasting room displays the labels produced as a result of previous painting contests; the collection illustrates the variety, creativity, and quality of the artwork chosen since the inception of the competition. The museum offers a special treat for guests as they tour the winery grounds, offering insights into the process of winemaking and the values and passions of the vintners.

Conclusions

The innovative design of these museum spaces, coupled with the multiple functions these spaces serve, invite the question that Larry Shiner poses around the issue of aesthetic significance and functionality in the assessment of architectural design, particularly in the evaluation of museum architecture. While there is critical agreement on the importance of both aesthetic relevance and practical functionalism in architectural criticism, how can these both be addressed without resorting either to a "separatist" perspective or to a position of "functional beauty" that renders aesthetic appreciation directly reliant on a building satisfying its "proper" function? Shiner proposes an approach of "moderate functionalism" that "leads to a continuing discussion about how successfully a museum's various functions have been integrated into the overall design." Shiner reminds us that there are two poles within this range: some works are so aesthetically exceptional that we can overlook limited practical shortcomings (as in the case of Frank Gehry's Guggenheim in Bilbao); and yet, no single function should be "the sole determining criterion in the overall aesthetic judgement of a museum design" (Shiner).

Certainly a primary function for wine museums is the promotion of the industry of wine tourism which can be analyzed from three distinct perspectives: i) as a strategy through which destinations develop and wine-related attractions are marketed; ii) as a form of consumer behavior that motivates wine lovers to travel to preferred destinations of wine production; iii) as an opportunity for wineries and wine merchants to sell directly to consumers (Staging Experiences). As seen in this essay, the four wine museums featured contribute to the promotion of wine tourism in unique and compelling ways. The availability of interactive experiences and the focus on engaging the five senses in wine education are key to the success of museums dedicated to the development of wine appreciation and to the understanding of wine-producing cultures.

Many secondary functions are facilitated though the complex designed environment that allow the visitors to experience specific facets of wine culture in varied and engaging ways promoting the wine from specific vineyards, certain DOs, or promoting wine culture in broad terms. In addition, these wine appreciation experiences are not limited to structures representative of a specific aesthetic; the architecture styles include the reinterpreted classicism of Dinastía Vivanco, the juxtaposition of historic ruin and contemporary functionality of Museo del Vino de Valladolid and the Museo de la Cultura del Rioja, and the agrarian functionalism of Bodegas Fariña.

The success of the wine museum model has manifested itself in other types of museums as well. Architectural critic, David Cohen, reviews a museum by Barcelona architect, Toni Gironès, in the small village of Seró as a "small archaeological museum and the settlement's only social centre, with a multi-purpose room and a would-be bar featuring wine and other local products" (2). Cohen emphasizes the transformative and spiritual aspects of the exhibit and the visitor experience of the megalithic sculptures found nearby in 2007, remarking on how the architect successfully creates spaces allowing for experiences both "sacred and the profane." Seemingly too profane, as the local head of cultural affairs determined that this social space not be used as a bar, as such uses were "undignified for a museum" (3).

This sacred or awe-inspiring aspect of the past century of museum design is evoked by architectural critics in reviews of museums ranging from Modern (Louis Kahn's Kimbell Museum in Fort Worth Texas) to the "spectacular" of more recent structures such as Gehry's masterpiece building, the Guggenheim Museum in Bilbao, Spain, and Santiago Calatrava's addition to the Milwaukee Art Museum. Gretchen Buggelin notes the recent emphasis on the creation of awe "seems to be more of a priority even than creating spaces that are functionally-effective places to show art" (39) seemingly questioning the emphasis on the "spectacular" more than Shiner. The wine museums reviewed in this study avoid the spectacular, while still displaying innovative and thought-provoking architecture capable of housing the functions that are intended for these spaces. The iconic architecture of three of the examples, the Museo de la Cultura del Vino, the Museo del Vino in Peñafiel and the Centro de la Cultura del Rioja, aligns with the critical acclaim of the design of numerous *bodegas* constructed in recent years and reflects a consistent theme of pairing the traditions of wine culture with technological and artistic innovations in contemporary Spain and all four destinations successfully blend art, architecture, and wine to create memorable experiences.

Note
The photos were taken by the author.

Works Cited
Bodegas Fariña. https://www.bodegasfarina.com
Buggelin, Gretchen. "Museum Space and the Experience of the Sacred." *Material Religion*. Vol. II., pp. 30–51. Valparaiso University. Print.
Cambridge Dictionary. https://dictionary.cambridge.org/us/
Cohen, David. "Sacred and Profane." *Architectural Review*. 00038611X, Mar. 2015, Vol. 237, no. 1417. Web.
Dinastía Vivanco. https://vivancoculturadevino.es
Divisare. https://divisare.com website closed Dec. 15, 2018.
El Centro de la Cultura de la Rioja. www.centrodelaculturadelrioja.es/
Foucault, Michel. "Of other spaces: Utopias and Heterotopias." Trans. Jay Miskowiec. *Architecture/Mouvement/Continuité*. Oct. 1984. Web.
Habegger, Kimberly. "Architecture Meets Viniculture: The Iconic Structures of Spain's Rioja and Ribera del Duero Regions." *The International Journal of Architectonic Spatial, and Environmental Design*. Vol. 6, no. 4, 2012–2013. Print.
Jackson, John Brinckerhoff. *A Sense of place, a Sense of Time*. New Haven and London: Yale University Press, 1994. Print.
Llewellyn, Marc. "Inside the Extraordinary d'Arenberg Cube." *Good Food*. www.goodfood.com.au. June 16, 2017. Web.
Museos del Vino. www.museosdelvino.es
Noble, Greg. "Accumulating Being." *International Journal of Cultural Studies."* London: Sage Publications, 2004, pp. 233–256. Web.
Provincia de Valladolid. www.provinciadevalladolid.com/enoturismygastronomia/museoprovincialdelvino
Pikkemaat, Birgit, Mike Peters, Philip Boksberger & Manuela Secco (2009). "The Staging of Experiences in Wine Tourism." *Journal of Hospitality Marketing & Management* 18: 2–3, pp. 237–253. Web.
Robinson, Zev. "Making the Dinastia Vivanco Documentary." Feb. 16, 2011. http://zevrobinson.com/video/making-the-dinastia-vivanco-documentary. Web.
Shiner, Larry. "On Aesthetics and Function in Architecture: The Case of the "Spectacle" Art Museum." *The American Society for Aesthetics*. 2011, pp. 31–41. Web.

Zamora, Jorge & Pablo Lacoste. "Tourism and Wine: A Marriage of Convenience or True Love?" *Journal of Wine Research*. 2007. Vol. 18. no. 2, pp. 121–123. Web.

CHAPTER
2

Twentieth-Century Pyramid: Vestiges of Dictatorship in a Democracy—Spain's Valley of the Fallen

KIMBERLY A. HABEGGER

Decreed by Francisco Franco in 1940 but not completed until 1959, the Valley of the Fallen was designed by architects Pedro Muguruza and Diego Méndez. Located in San Lorenzo de El Escorial, the monument officially commemorated the sacrifices of the Civil War (1936–1939) of both the Francoist victors and the vanquished Republicans. From its inception, many Spaniards questioned the official mission of the monument as both the imagery implemented and the devotees to the monument hailed from the political right. Nevertheless, criticism of the government was prohibited during Franco's regime until more open expression came about after Franco's death in 1975. Since the dictator's passing up until the present day, opposition to the monument has become increasingly pronounced, as the Spanish public now understands the monument from a very different historical perspective.

This study will analyze the meaning intended at the time of construction as reflected in the imagery found in the architecture and the significance of the siting of the monument. With this foundation, we will proceed to examine the complex meanings of the Valley of Fallen to the contemporary Spanish populace. Historian, John Crow, in *Spain: The Root and the Flower*, written in 1963, prophetically anticipates the change of meaning of the monument that will evolve in the post-Franco era:

When this generation passes away, and the Franco regime is forgotten, all of the old hatreds will be focused on this spot, and it will either be destroyed or altered so that it no longer represents what it does today. I do not see how future generations can act otherwise. Perhaps the monument will come to symbolize where a whole Spanish epoch is buried. (348)

With the recent plans to remove Franco's remains from the site after much contentious debate, it appears that the implications of this site have developed significantly.

Meaning Transmitted through Design

According to the official propaganda of the Franco regime, the Valley of the Fallen commemorates the losses from both sides of the Spanish Civil War. In his decree of April 2, 1940, Franco reframes the Civil War as a "crusade" which demanded extreme sacrifice from all its citizens. The *Generalísimo* proceeds to call for a monument that has "the perennial grandeur of the ancient monuments." He further elaborates that the stones of its construction will "defy time" and that the site will become "a perennial place of pilgrimage" (Cuelgamuros). The rhetoric employed in this brief document clearly reflects the imperial and Catholic ideals so dear to the recently-established dictator. In addition to the hollow sound of this rhetoric, two other realities that will occur during and after construction of the monument further weakened Franco's conciliatory claims. The first was the use of forced labor of Republican prisoners of war in the monument's construction and the second was the exhumation and relocation of victims of the war from both sides without consent of the families.

The Valley of the Fallen is a structure charged with conflicting meanings from its inception in part due to serving multiple functions: commemorative monument, basilica in the custody of Benedictine fathers, crypt of anonymous victims of the war, and tomb featuring the prominent placement of the hero of Francoism, Antonio Primo de Rivera, and ultimately of Franco himself after his death in 1975. Design decisions made by the architects and the dictator visually reflect the values of tradition, Catholicism, and empire through the selection of the specific site of the monument and the stylistic elements and the art employed in the design of the interior and exterior of the monument. This symbolism that unites the portrayal of the glory of God with victory over the defunct Republic is further evidence that the monument exalts the victors instead of reconciling the opponents of a shattered country.

The monument was positioned in the mountainous terrain in close proximity to another famous structure founded some 400 years earlier, the Escorial by King Phillip II of Spain. This monarch in particular has been a favorite of the Spanish Right for his deep religious devotion, his expansion of the Spanish/Catholic Empire, and his ability to further entangle the institutions of church and state in Spain. The parallels between these two structures in physical terms are numerous: they both function as monasteries even today; the décor of both sites is strikingly austere; the scale of the spaces is massive; and both serve as crypts for Spain's rulers: the Escorial contains the remains of the kings of Spain starting with Phillip's father Carlos I of Spain. The physical proximity and these additional similarities between the two memorials reflect Franco's fondness for Phillip II and the glory of the imperial past the dictator hoped to resuscitate.

The Valley of the Fallen also incorporates elements reminiscent of two architectural styles favored some 20 years before construction was initiated in Spain. The first model is found in the Italian monumental classicism of the Mussolini era as seen in works by Marcello Piacentini and Innocenzo Sabbatini (designers of the EUR in Rome planned for 1942 to celebrate 20 years of fascist Italy); the architectural projects of Albert Speer in Nazi Germany serve as the second standard. In fascist Italy, certainly the Roman Empire provided the ideal inspiration both politically and visually for the building projects of *Il Duce*, invoking memories of the awesome power and grandeur of the Italian peninsula. In Germany, Speer himself describes this "Theory of Ruin Value" that holds that "by using special materials and by applying certain principles of statistics, we should be able to build structures which even in a state of decay, after hundreds of years or (such were our reckonings) thousands of years, would more or less resemble Roman models" (56), thus both schools favored Roman architectural traits. Speer further explains that the impulse behind such structures is to inspire pride and nationalism in future generations, even if the empire has fallen into decline. Some of the common characteristics of this type of mid-century neo-classical fascist architecture are the use of massive scale in order to make the public feel subordinate to the power structure. In addition, there is a preference for architectural elements that are somewhat streamlined and simplified versions of the Classical originals such as Roman arches, great domes, the use of stone, walkways flanked by statuary, etc.

Isolated from the Western democracies, the devastated Spain of Franco was not able to commit to many grand and symbolic construction projects, yet Franco seized the opportunity of the construction of Valley of the Fallen to symbolically express political ideals that paralleled, in many ways, those of their Italian and German allies during the Civil War. Ironically, in the years immediately following the war in Spain, Italy and Germany had also been ravaged and defeated in war by the Allies, which presents the perplexing question of why Franco and his architects would have continued to consider Roman models an inspiring option by the late 1940s.

In the Valley of the Fallen, the basic traits of this earlier fascist architecture are punctuated with strong Catholic symbolism, as would be expected, particularly in a commemorative and religious structure. In the description that follows, we will see that the majority of this Catholic symbolism is delivered through powerful works of art, in particular, statuary. Through the artistic imagery, the human experiences of death, suffering, sacrifice, and revenge take center stage.

The most dramatic element of the exterior of the monument is the imposing cross measuring 150 meters that tops the summit and dominates the surroundings. At the base of the cross, large statues of the four evangelists carved by Juan de Ávalos visually anchor the cross. Below the evangelists and above an opening in the mountain that serves as entrance into the monument, a large *pietá*[1] made of some 115 blocks of stone weighing 1500 kilos each reminds visitors of the sacrifice and suffering embodied in this structure. Visitors enter and proceed past an arcade of commanding Roman arches to access the huge nave of 88 meters that were all drilled into the rock of the mountain. As visitors move through the nave, they are watched over by what appears to be a series of avenging angels placed in towering niches also executed by de Ávalos. Their imposing stances and their general demeanor approximates the stylized, almost robotic appearance found in some examples of Art Deco statuary. Apart from these angels, there is little ornamentation until arrival to the altar above which rises an elaborate cupola. The overall mood is indeed dark and somber and to some, threatening. Once visitors enter the space, there is virtually no natural light; this, of course, contrasts with almost all-Christian religious architecture since the appearance of Gothic architecture. Most importantly, the remains of the many nameless victims housed in the monument are located in crypts hidden along the sides of the nave, while the altar was flanked by the tombs of the two champions of Nationalist Spain, Antonio Primo de Rivera and Francisco Franco, as mentioned previously.

Meaning for the Contemporary Public

It is through this religious statuary where in 2010, we see our first example of how its powerful political symbolism has survived into the 21st century. The government decided that the *pietá* needed to be temporarily deconstructed in order to properly clean and restore it. As the Spanish daily, *El Mundo*, describes this process, the comments to the online report reflect that many readers were concerned that the liberal government at the time was actually using the restoration as a ruse and that the statue would never be returned to the site. The previous talk of "depoliticizing" the Valley of the Fallen convinced a segment to the population that the removal of the *pietá* was merely the first step (*El desmontaje*). With the victory of the conservative Popular Party in 2012, the limitations that had been placed on visitors due to safely concerns were reversed, much to the pleasure of the monument's supporters. The subsequent reopening was welcomed, although there was much speculation that the increase from five to nine euros for entrance would discourage future visitors.

As we have seen, the architecture, the siting, and the visual symbols of the Valley of the Fallen were chosen to reinforce Franco's understanding of the war, religion, and Spanish history. During the dictatorship, the monument was either received enthusiastically or with silent disapproval because for the former the monument represented their ultimate victory and for the latter, their absolute defeat and subjugation. Since the establishment of democracy in 1978, the Spanish people have felt increasingly free to censure the site; the events of recent years indicate that negative associations now seem to dominate the public consciousness and the people are demanding modifications to the monument as others challenge its right to continue to exist. In general terms, theses changes in attitudes are owed to more progressive political leanings in addition to indignation about the deteriorating conditions of the massive crypts. In addition, the protestors of the status quo address historical injustices such as: 1) the forced transfer of remains of the fallen regardless of the families' desires; 2) the use of forced labor of Republican prisoners in the construction of the monument; and 3) the continued presence and prominent placement of the graves of Franco and Primo de Rivera.

Exhumations and Transfer to the Crypts

Passions run high among Spaniards of all persuasions regarding the graves founds in the monument's crypts. In response to the finding of a commission on the monument's future, a December 4, 2011 post by Carlos Escudier comments:

> More disturbing still is that the commission follows Francoist propaganda proposing that the Valley of the Fallen should endure as a monument to reconciliation, when it in fact should be (considered) one of the horrors of the Dictatorship. Franco wanted to be buried only with his own. The reason for the transfer of thousands murdered by the regime was the opposition of the Nationals (Francoists) and of many local officials to emptying their cemeteries and leaving only the Reds. (17)

The massive exhumations that occurred some twenty years after the war's conclusion have outraged families affected on both sides, although the Republican families understandably have expressed the greatest opposition. The forced exhumations and subsequent transfer of the remains, together with the poorly-kept crypts, have more recently motivated many families to request a transfer of the remains of their ancestor to the family or village cemetery from which they were removed. Many poignant stories have been recorded by surviving family members that explain the initial exhumation and the families' legal challenges as they have struggled to have their ancestor's remains returned to family plots (Barcala).

Forced Labor

The fact that Republican prisoners of war and political prisoners were used as virtually free labor in the construction of the Valley of the Fallen also fuels anti-monument sentiment. Estimates indicate that the regime saved some 780 million euros by employing this method of forced labor. Influential Spaniards such as Nicolás Sánchez-Albornoz, director of the Cervantes Institute from 1991 to 1996, have described the brutal treatment they received as "rented workers" in the construction of the monument. The government paid 10.5 pesetas per day per worker and the workers received .5 pesetas of that sum for dangerous and physically-exhausting labor. Today, the internet serves as a vehicle to expose the ties that current companies have with those that benefited from this forced labor in the fifties: an example being present-day Obrascón-Huarte-Laín (OHL), offspring of the company Huarte that employed 141 battalions of Republican prisoners. Websites such as *La memoria viva* remind readers of and/or reveal not only the past of certain companies, but the Francoist connections that some high-level politicians and business executives might rather ignore, such as recent president, José María Aznar's grandfather, Manuel Aznar Zubigarary, who served as the ambassador from Spain for the United Nations and in several other countries during the regime (Torrús).

Franco's Tomb

Not surprisingly, the main demand of those opposed to the monument was the removal of Franco's remains. In a 2011 interview, renowned Spanish historian, Juan Pablo Fusi Aizpúrua, was asked his opinion regarding the possible transfer of Franco's remains. Fusi responded: "the presence of Franco's remains define any issue that we may attempt to give to the Valley of the Fallen, If I were his family, I would have taken him to a distinguished private cemetery (Ojeda). Carlos Escudier express his views more passionately: "As offensive as Franco remaining in the Valley and that his mummy has not been returned to his family, is that the commission establishes as a requirement for transfer the authorization of the same Church that previously (supported him)" (Escudier 17). Of course, the head of the Franco Foundation, who is also Franco's daughter, objected to transferring Franco's remains to lie beside his wife. A *BBC News* article from 2011 quoted Franco supporter, Jaime Alonso's position: "You can't move Franco without his family's permission—that would be desecration. You have to be careful with history in Spain. You can't demonize one part of society and praise the other. That's wrong and achieves nothing" (Rainsford).

Meaning to Defenders of the Regime

Nevertheless, the monument continues to receive avid support in reiterating Alonso's position and the Asociación para la Defensa del Valle de los Caídos represents this stance. The publication statement found on its website declares that the monument commemorates all of the losses of the Civil War: "Hablamos de monumento cultural creado en otros tiempos y otras personas para recordar quienes perdieron la vida en un fratricida enfrentamiento entre españoles para que las diferencias que siempre podrá haber entre nosotros nunca más nos lleven a choques violentos/we're talking about a cultural monument created in different times and [by] other people to remember who lost their lives in a confrontation between brothers among Spaniards in order that the differences that always will be among us never again take us to violent clashes" (Asociación, Feb. 26, 2011). The website claims that the monument represents the diversity of Spain "ya que está dedicado a todos los españoles, los de todas las tierras, todas las ideologías y todos los tiempos. Patrimonio de España. Y de ahí, si se quiere del mundo entero/since it is already dedicated to all Spaniards, those of all lands, all ideologies and all times. Spanish patrimony. And, from there, if you like, the whole world" (Asociación, Feb. 26, 2011). It also declares that it will only disseminate information that supports the monument in its current manifestation: "la Asociación para la Defensa del Valle de los Caídos nunca será plataforma para los que atacan el Valle y lo que él representa. Y tampoco para quienes desearían que fuera otra cosa/the Association for the Defense of the Valley of the Fallen will never be a platform for those who attack the Valley and what it represents. Nor is it for those who would wish it were something else" (Asociación, Nov. 7, 2017). From this perspective, the Valley continues to represent the values enunciated by Franco, yet it simultaneously attempts to contextualize the monument on the contemporary world stage through claims of diversity and inclusiveness.

Summary of events of the opposition

Let us now summarize selected events of the past ten years to note how the overall public response to the monument has evolved. While there were few changes during the first thirty years of democracy, significant legal decisions and political positions have coalesced to transform the site as an increased pace.

On October 31, 2007, the Law of Historical Memory officially recognized the rights of the victims of the Civil War and the dictatorship, and the rights of their descendants as well. In addition, the act formally condemned the regime and prohibited that "political events" take place on the grounds of the memorial since the site had been a favorite among Franco-inspired groups. This measure indicated a radical change of perspective with regard to any crimes committed during the Franco regime. Such crimes have been virtually ignored as a result of the compromises made to achieve a peaceful transition to democracy in 1978. Known as the "Pact of Forgetting," this tacit agreement was seen as a way of moving beyond Civil War and dictatorship.

On November 29, 2011, a commission established to study the future of the Valley of the Fallen recommended that Franco's remains be transferred to another site. During the next couple of years, protestors demanded "que pongan fin a ese lugar de culto fascista, símbolo de la impunidad del franquismo/that they put an end to that place of the Fascist cult, a symbol of the impunity of Francoism" (Reclaman). In addition, in February of 2014, the United Nations suggested the Spanish government contextualize the monument for visitors "in favor of truth and memory with a preventive purpose" (La ONU).

The president of the Patrimonio Nacional (the custodian of the Valley of the Fallen), José Rodríguez Spiteri, resigned from the post in the summer of 2015. This departure was celebrated by the pro-monument group, as they had been unhappy with decisions such as the visitor's price increase. Of course, the anti-monument coalition continued to be frustrated with the continuing presence of Franco's grave and the shameful neglect of the remains interned on the site (Barcala).

The most recent and significant event in this episode played out in September of 2018 when Spain's new socialist government led by Pedro Sánchez decided to remove Franco's remains by the end of the year. While the government's plans developed, Franco's seven grandchildren declared their opposition to the transfer because the family "felt persecuted and mistreated and they were not disposed to (allowing) their grandfather's cadaver to be played with" (Casqueiro). In addition, the Abbot of the Basilica of the Valley of the Fallen, Santiago Cantera, has stated that he will not allow this transfer to take place. The government maintains that the exhumation is irrevocable and is currently in negotiations with Church officials in order to arrive at a solution. Every day, new actions are being taken in this evolving conflict; it will be interesting to observe how the recent elections of April 2019 effect the development of events.

Conclusions

Product of an absolutist ideology, the meanings imbedded in this structure have evolved dramatically in the past twenty years, nevertheless, there remain those who cling to antiquated understandings. The discomfort towards the monument that many have experienced even prior to recent events seems largely due to the fact that both the constructed symbols and the historical facts prove that the purpose of the monument was not to mourn the all the deaths caused by the Civil War but instead to glorify the victors. Divisive in concept; divisive in design through symbolic architectural style and intentional site selection; divisive by means of construction; and divisive through serving as resting place for the remains of tens of thousands of loved ones of unwilling surviving family members, the majority of Spaniards demand some modifications of this structure. The current use of popular metaphors such as "the theme park of fascism" and the "site of the fascist cult" emphasizes this dissatisfaction.

Architecture enables the construction of narratives that contribute to our social identity. In contrast with a purely aesthetic evaluation, an authentic understanding of the built environment requires familiarity with the surroundings and some knowledge of the historical context of the structure: the meaning of a built space cannot be deciphered based merely on limited contact with the space. The often-discussed relationship between functionality and architecture typically refers to the structure's response to the physical needs of its inhabitants; yet one might argue that the social understanding of a public space figures prominently among the many functions that architecture serves.

Historian Rudy Koshar elaborates on how buildings have pasts "because human beings create narratives that tell readers when a building was erected, what historical events it endured, who lived in it, and how it has been used (216). Koshar continues:

> The point of using the built environment . . . has been to invent . . . identities, to stress the sameness of individuals who, because they are engaged in multiple social relations, are in fact marked by difference. This process consists of discursively using building-pasts to 'build' those collective pasts that give continuity, stability, and familiarity to particular historical contexts. (216)

While these observations may apply to all types of structures, they are more deeply applicable to commemorative architecture that has been purposely conceived, designed, constructed and managed to reinforce this concept of the collective past.

Yet in Spain, from the postwar to democracy, the ideologically unreconciled parties of the Spanish Civil War have rendered any type of memorial problematic given that the objective of commemoration lies primarily in the construction of common identities that stress sameness— an identity that the Right was willing to impose and the Left continues to oppose. Instead of a sense of unity, this and other commemorative sites "occasionally emerge as contact zones between contesting factions of our society" (Redman).

In his *Sites of Memory, Sites of Mourning*, Jay Winter offers an additional insight that is useful in understanding the dissonance that the Valley of the Fallen has for many people. In his analysis of traditional versus modern languages of mourning, Winter explains that the traditional language of bereavement emphasizes the glory of battle and the sanctity of the war dead: "in sum, the sentimentality and lies of wartime propaganda" (2). In contrast, the modern language of bereavement has other aims ranging from the exploration and reconfiguration of traditional ideals to the iconoclastic attack on prevailing conventions (3–4). Winter posits that World War I commemoration was essentially a mixture of traditional and modern languages, while the modern language did not dominate until World War II commemorative structures surfaced.

Completed in 1959 while commemorating the sacrifices of 1936–30, The Valley of the Fallen is unique. The layers of semiotics contained in this structure reveal the underlying tension: this historically modern monument clearly speaks a traditional language (Winter 8).

Symbolism glorifying empire and proclaiming victory in a sense render the Valley anachronistic not only today but from its inception. This anachronism has apparently alienated almost all those who do not closely share the Franco vision of Spain and its history.

Since the establishment of democracy in Spain in 1978, most Spanish governments have been attempting to distance themselves from the Valley of the Fallen but the process has been too slow for a number of citizens who consider the monument a symbol of ideology incompatible with democracy. The question of the meaning of the monument was addressed in recent years by the PP (the right-leaning Popular Party) on December 17, 2014. In a response to an initiative of the opposing PSOE (Spanish Socialist Workers' Party) to convert the monument so that it no longer exists "as a symbol of grievance and exclusion to a large part of the citizenry," the PP rejected the initiative and concluded that the Valley "has no political meaning" and implored the opposition to "let the dead rest" (*Europa*). Clearly the record indicates that from inception to its use in political events, the monument has always had political meaning and any claim to the contrary is at least naïve and at worst, cynical.

While it appears imminent that Franco's remains will be transferred, will the removal of this icon alter the meaning of the space in a meaningful manner? Is the removal of Franco a superficial solution? Considering the built-in symbolism of the monument, is it more appropriate that Franco stay behind in his crypt while assisting opposing families in the transfer of the remains of their ancestors (thus fulfilling Crow's prophecy of the monument symbolizing where a whole Spanish epoch is buried)? What other modifications to the structure shall follow if the political will so determines? Does the current space have value as a historical document? Such decisions about this space and others built in different periods in different cultures continue to challenge contemporary societies as we adopt evolving social norms around commemoration and acquire more nuanced understandings of history.

Note

1 A *pietá* (pity) refers to a representation of the Virgin Mary with the body of the crucified Christ draped across her lap. The best-known example is Michelangelo's statue in the Vatican.

Works Cited

Asociación para la Defensa del Valle de los Caídos. Feb. 26, 2011, Nov. 7, 2017, & Aug. 7, 2015. www.elvalledeloscaidos.es. Web.

Barcala, Diego. "Mi padre está en la caja 198, en la cripta derecha." *Público*. 13/10/2010. www.publico.es. Web.

Casqueiro, Javier. "El folletín de la exhumación de Franco." *El País*. 6 enero 2019. www.elpais.com. Web.

Crow, John. *Spain: The Root and the Flower: An Interpretation of Spain and the Spanish People*. Berkeley: *University* of California Press, 2005. Print.

Cuelgamuros. El Valle de los Caídos. www.cuelgamuros.com

"El desmontaje de 'La Piedad' del Valle de los Caídos, a 'mazazo limpio.'" *El Mundo* 23/04/2010. www.elmundo.es

"El PP proclama que el Valle de los Caídos no tiene 'significación política' y pide dejar descansar a los muertos." *Europa Press Nacional*. 17/12/2014. 20:25:34. Web.

Escudier, Juan Carlos. "Franco se saldrá con la suya . . . " *La memoria viva*. https://lamemoriaviva.worldpress.com. 2011/12/04. Web.

Europa Press Nacional. "*El PP proclama que el Valle de los Caídos no tiene 'significación política' y pide dejar descansar a los muertos*." 17/12/2014 20:25:34. Web.

Franco, Francisco. Decreto de 1 abril 1940. Asociación para la Defensa del Valle de los Caídos. www.elvalledeloscaidos.es. Web.

Koshar, Rudy. *Commemorations: The Politics of National Identity*. Princeton: Princeton University Press, 1994. Print.

La memoria viva. https://lamemoriaviva.worldclass.com. Web.

"La ONU pide reinventar el Valle de los Caídos y anular la Ley de Amnistía de 1977." *El Mundo* 03/02/2014. www.elmundo.es

Ojeda, Alberto. "No hay urgencias amenazantes para reformar la constitución." *El Cultural*. 06/12/2011. www.Elcultural.es

Rainsford, Sarah. "Fate of Franco's Valley of the Fallen Reopens Spain (sic) Wounds." *BBC Europe*. July 18, 2011. Web.

"Reclaman transformar el Valle de los Caídos en un memorial para las víctimas de la dictadura." Nov. 24, 2013. https://lamemoriaviva.worldclass.com. Web.

Redman, Samuel J. "The US National WWII Memorial and the 2013 Federal

Shutdown: Politics, Culture, and Public History." Oct. 9, 2013. www.umasshistory.worldpress.com
Speer, Albert. *Inside the Third Reich: Memoirs by Albert Speer.* Trans. Richard & Clara Winston. New York: The MacMillan CO., 1970. Print.
Torrús, Alejandro. "Del Valle de los Caídos al Ibex 35." Nov. 18, 2012. https://lamemoriaviva.worldclass.com. Web.
Winter, Jay. *Sites of Memory, Sites of Mourning: The Great War in European Cultural History.* Cambridge: Cambridge University Press, 1995. Print.

CHAPTER

3

Home, Sweet and Not-So-Sweet, Home: The Museum of Fine Art/Houston (MFAH) and Latin American Art

DEBRA D. ANDRIST

Where is, what is *hom*e—and why is the concept so integral to human experience?

The *Bing Search* and *Merriam-Webster Dictionary* list at least five general definitions of the word, various grammar categories from noun to adjective to adverb to verb, each with numerous synonyms and examples, including at least four *wheres* and a couple of *whos* (with some overlap between where and who). The *Thought Catalog* blogger observes "that the-concept-of-home-its-a-feeling-not-a-place." So, as the writer of a *Washington Post* article of December 27, 2012 remarks,

> [thus the] Concept of 'home' gives rise to artistic differences . . . Multiple ideas of domesticity quarrel or concur in exhibitions at Heiner Contemporary and the District of Columbia Arts Center. The Heiner show, *Housebound*, tends toward the cozily domestic, while the other, *A/way Home*, is rather less comfortable. But both include works that look at "home" from the outside.

This last brings us to the theme of the 2017–18 Museum of Fine Arts/Houston exhibition, *Home—So Different, So Appealing*, which inspired the title and focus of this essay. As a sociologist, one of whose specialties is visual art, particularly that of the Hispanic worlds, I am particularly interested in the MFAH, as it was the first in the U.S. to hire a full-time curator of Latin American art, Mari Carmen Ramírez, in 2001. In addition to on-going exhibitions like Home, the permanent collections now include five (permanent) Special Collections, in addition to the approximately seven dozen exhibitions dedicated to Latin American art since 1927.

Adolpho Leirner Collection of Brazilian Constructive Art

The cornerstone of the Museum's Constructive art holdings is the Adolpho Leirner Collection of Brazilian Constructive Art, acquired in 2007. This world-renowned collection consists of more than 100 extraordinary examples by Concrete and Neo-Concrete groups that flourished in São Paulo and Rio de Janeiro between 1950 and 1965. Featured prominently in the Leirner Collection is the innovative production by the leaders of these two groups—Lygia Clark, Waldemar Cordeiro, and Hélio Oiticica—as well as works by independent artists such as Milton Dacosta, Mira Schendel, and Alfredo Volpi. The Leirner Collection is featured on the MFAH website.

The Brillembourg Capriles Collection of Latin American Art

Assembled over the last thirty years by Venezuelan philanthropist, Tanya Capriles de Brillembourg, this extraordinary collection on long-term loan to the MFAH features over one hundred works by Latin American masters of the first half of the twentieth century. Concentrations of master works by Emilio Pettoruti, Diego Rivera, David Alfaro Siqueiros, Joaquín Torres-García, Armando Reverón, Wifredo Lam, and Matta showcase avant-garde achievements across the Spanish-speaking region. The collection also includes emblematic paintings by Fernando Botero, Rufino Tamayo, Armando Morales, and Antonio Segui produced at the height of their respective careers. In the last decade, the collection has grown to include pioneering constructivist works by Loló de Soldevilla, Sandú Darié, Carlos Rojas, as well as contemporary kinetic installations by Elias Crespin, many of which were featured in the 2013 MFAH exhibition, *Intersecting Modernities: The Brillembourg Capriles Collection.*

Caribbean Art Fund Collection

In 2011, the Museum established an accessions fund with Fundación Gego, Caracas, to acquire works from Venezuela, Colombia, Central America, and the Caribbean. The Caribbean Art Fund has allowed the Museum to gather a broad range of innovative works in all media by artists born in these countries after 1960. Among the artists included in this collection are Tanya Bruguera, Johana Calle, Yoan Capote, Los Carpinteros, José Gabriel Fernández, Juan Iribarren, and Roberto Obregón. Through the Caribbean Art Fund, the Museum also has begun to build an outstanding collection of video installations by leading exponents of this medium, such as Magdalena Fernández, Óscar Muñoz, Javier Tellez, José Alejandro Restrepo, and Miguel Ángel Rojas.

Cruz-Diez Foundation Collection at the Museum of Fine Arts, Houston

The Cruz-Diez Foundation is a non-profit organization founded in Houston in 2005 in collaboration with the MFAH and committed to preserving, developing, exhibiting, and researching the artistic and conceptual legacy of Franco-Venezuelan artist Carlos Cruz-Diez (b. 1924), one of the twentieth century's seminal thinkers in the field of color. Over one hundred key works owned by the foundation, including paintings, silk-screen prints, innovative chromatic structures, and room-size chromatic environments, are housed at the museum, which promotes their study, exhibition, and maintenance. The MFAH—Cruz-Diez partnership has been fundamental to documenting the artist's investigations into optical phenomena, kineticism, and color theory, and strives to make accessible to the public and lending institutions its research as well as the opportunity to experience Cruz-Diez's most pioneering accomplishments.

Fundación Gego Collection at the Museum of Fine Arts, Houston

Since 2003, the Museum has served as leading center for scholarship, exhibition, and care of work by German-born Venezuelan artist, Gego (Gertrud Goldschmidt). As part of a long-term partnership with Fundación Gego, the Museum houses more than 400 Gego works, from her early drawings, prints, and three-dimensional stainless-steel constructions of the late 1950s to her distinctive wire drawings—*dibujos sin papel* (drawings without paper)—and *tejeduras* (weavings) of the late 1970s and 1980s. The MFAH/Fundación Gego partnership has also produced two exhibitions and four books.

And, some of those aforementioned dozens of "show" exhibitions include works based on geographical areas, or on artists, or on mediums, etc., in the so-called "Hispanic" worlds of Latin America:[1]

1927	Modern Mexican Art
1930	Drawings and Lithographs by José Clemente Orozco
1930	Work of Students of the Mexican Free School
1932	Oils, Watercolors, Drawings, Prints by Roberto Montenegro
1932	Mexican Arts
1941	Oils of the Southwest and Mexico
1941	75 Latin-American Prints
1942	Contemporary Latin American Art
1943	Modern Mexican Art
1943	Inter-American Photographic Salon
1943	Sculpture by Juan José Calandria and Challis Walker
1947	Prints by Federico Cantú
1947	Paintings by Pedro Figari
1949	Mexican Prints from the Permanent Collection
1951	Oils and Watercolors by Diego Rivera
1952	Latin American Paintings by Mildred Dixon
1953	Pan-American Exhibition
1956	Rufino Tamayo Exhibition
1956	Gulf-Caribbean Art Exhibition
1956	Armando Reverón Exhibition
1956	Robert K. Winn Collection of Mexican Folk Art
1963	The Olmec Tradition
1967	Our Mexican Heritage
1975	Mexican Prints in the Collection
1976	Selections from the Primitive Collections
1979	Covered Faces: The Mask Through the Ages
1983	Works on Paper: Mexican Prints and Drawings of the 20th Century
1985	Faces of Mexico: Masks from the Cordry Collection
1987	Torres-García: Grid-Pattern-Sign, Paris–Montevideo,1929–1949
1990	God, Man, and Animal: Pre-Columbian Art from Private Collections in Houston and Austin
1992	On the Edge of the Maya World: Stone Vases from the Ulúa Valley, Honduras

1992	Contemporary Mexican Photography
1993	Mexico's Holiest Shrine: Treasures from the Basilica of Guadalupe
1993	The World of Frida Kahlo
1994	Royal Tombs of Sipán, Peru
1995	Tina Modotti: Photographs
1996	The Olmec World: Ritual and Rulership
1997	Portrait of a Decade: David Alfaro Siqueiros, 1930–1940
1999	From Playful Pups to Feathered Serpents: Animals in Ancient Mesoamerican Art
1999	Diego Rivera: Art and Revolution
2001	Recent Photography from the Latin American Collection of the MFAH
2002	Questioning the Line: Gego, A Selection, 1955–90
2002	Cultural Exchange: Linking Houston and Mexico City
2002	The Grandeur of Viceregal Mexico: Treasures from the Museo Franz Mayer
2002	Americanos: Latino Life in the United States
2003	Upstairs Projects: Chemi Rosado Seijo — "El Cerro"
2004	Inverted Utopias: Avant-Garde Art in Latin America
2005	Gego, Between Transparency and the Invisible
2005	Brought to Light: Recent Accessions in Latin American Art
2006	Xul Solar: Visions and Revelations
2006	Hélio Oiticica: The Body of Color
2006	Past, Present, Future: Documenting Latin American Art at the MFAH
2007	Constructing a Poetic Universe: The Diane and Bruce Halle Collection of Latin American Art
2007	Dimensions of Constructive Art in Brazil: The Adolpho Leirner Collection
2007	Gráficas Políticas: Mexican Prints, 1900–1950
2009	North Looks South: Building the Latin American Art Collection
2009	Torres-García: Houston Collections
2009	The Adolpho Leirner Collection
2010	Cosmopolitan Routes: Houston Collects Latin American Art
2011	Carlos Cruz-Diez: Color in Space and Time
2012	Modern and Contemporary Masterpieces from Malba — Fundación Costantini
2012	Constructed Dialogues: Concrete, Geometric, and Kinetic Art from the Latin American Art Collection
2013	Intersecting Modernities: Latin American Art from The Brillembourg Capriles Collection

2014   Soto: The Houston Penetrable
2014   Fangs, Feathers, and Fins: Sacred Creatures in Ancient American Art
2015   Cosmic Dialogues: Selections from the Latin American Art Collection
2015   Contingent Beauty: Contemporary Art from Latin America

And, in the last few years,

The Glamour and Romance of Oscar de la Renta (October 8, 2017–March 18, 2018)
Monuments: 276 Views of the U.S.–Mexico Border by David Taylor (December 5, 2017–January 31, 2018)
HOME—So Different, So Appealing (November 17, 2017–January 21, 2018)
Paint the Revolution: Mexican Modernism, 1910–1950 (June 25, 2017–October 1, 2017)
Off-site *Exhibition Rain: Magdalena Fernández at the Houston Cistern* (December 10, 2016–June 25, 2017)
Cuban Photography after 1980: Selections from the Museum's Collection (February 7, 2017–June 4, 2017)
Adiós Utopia: Dreams and Deceptions in Cuban Art Since 1950 (March 5, 2017–May 21, 2017)

But, back "home" at the MFAH itself, as it has become the home of one of the preeminent collections and exhibiters of Latin American art . . .

The original MFAH building was the first art museum to be built in the state and only the third in the South. Houston architect, William Ward Watkin, designed it as a "temple for art," in the neoclassical style favored at the time. Watkin collaborated with then-director, James Chillman, Jr., who, like Watkin, was a professor at nearby Rice University. Watkin envisioned a pure exhibition space, but Chillman's perspective brought practicality to Watkin's design conventions by ensuring that the added wings accommodated administrative offices, storage, and meeting rooms.

Additional wings were completed in 1926, at which time Chillman presented American paintings from Grand Central Art Galleries in New York, a show that included work by renowned artist, John Singer Sargent. With this significant exhibition, the MFAH established itself as a cultural gem in the young city of Houston. This building is a part of what is now the Museum's Caroline Wiess Building, with its original façade still visible from the South Lawn.

Because of the Great Depression and World War II, the MFAH paused for nearly 30 years until resources for a much-needed expansion of the galleries became available. In 1952, the Museum received a gift from Camilla Davis and John H. Blaffer to build a wing dedicated to the memory of Robert Lee Blaffer, cofounder of Humble Oil & Refining Co. Kenneth Franzheim, the architect who had designed the Blaffers' Chicago home, was named to the job. Franzheim had collaborated on the design of three of Houston's tallest skyscrapers and received national recognition for his design of the downtown Foley's department store, which, at the time, represented state-of-the-art retail design. These new galleries were intended to house the growing MFAH permanent collection. Franzheim began with ambitious plans to renovate the existing Museum building by making it more accessible, following other modernized museums that took advantage of conveniences such as incandescent lighting and air conditioning to allow less reliance on open air and natural light. He proposed a three-story building that extended to Bissonnet Street but, for undocumented reasons, the board rejected these plans and limited his work to what would become the Blaffer Memorial Wing—still a part of the current Caroline Wiess Law Building.

In 1953, Nina J. Cullinan made an extraordinary gift to the Museum for a building addition that would be a memorial to her parents. She stipulated that an architect of "outstanding reputation and wide experience" design the building. The MFAH trustees turned to Ludwig Mies van der Rohe, one of the great figures of 20th-century modern architecture, for the commission. Arriving in Houston on a hot summer day to initiate planning, Mies van der Rohe is said to have remarked, "But in this climate you cannot want an open patio." His eventual design was predicated on a curved, glass-enclosed space, fully visible from the street. Ignoring the standard of an open-air courtyard, Mies van der Rohe rejected conventional museum design in favor of Modernism. As Ann Holmes, fine arts editor of the *Houston Chronicle*, wrote, "entering Cullinan Hall was like walking from inside to the out-of-doors." The free-span exhibition space featured flexible walls and lighting and an addition of office spaces and expanded areas for shipping and storage. With an expanse of lawn in front of the entrance to showcase large-scale sculpture, the new pavilion, set back on a long path through the green lawn, beckoned guests to explore the treasures inside. Cullinan Hall is still the central feature of what is now the Caroline Wiess Law Building.

In 1961, James Johnson Sweeney, founding director of the Guggenheim Museum and a former curator at the Museum of Modern Art, became director of the MFAH. A close friend of Mies van der

Rohe's and an admirer of Cullinan Hall, Sweeney determined that the Museum needed an expansion accessible from Bissonnet Street that would serve as a new entrance lobby, as well as an expansive gallery on the second floor. A theater, now called Brown Auditorium Theater and one of few Mies van der Rohe-designed theaters still in use today, comprised the lower level, along with expanded galleries and office spaces. Plans were drawn up for what would become Brown Pavilion, but neither Sweeney nor Mies van der Rohe would see the project through to completion. Sweeney left the Museum in 1967; his successor, Philippe de Montebello, began work in 1969, the year Mies van der Rohe passed away. From the beginning of his tenure, de Montebello supported the design and was determined to raise money for the construction of both the Mies van der Rohe pavilion and a new building for the Museum school. When complete, Brown Pavilion had the same modern details and finishes as Cullinan Hall: white plaster walls, suspended ceiling panels, and exposed steel columns. With the 1974 dedication of Brown Pavilion—named for The Brown Foundation, Inc., supported by brothers Herman and George R. Brown, founders of a gas pipeline network—the Museum more than doubled its space. Paul Goldberger, writing in the *New York Times*, declared it "one of Mies van der Rohe's most stunning spaces." The Brown Pavilion still serves as the Bissonnet Street entrance to what is now the Caroline Wiess Law Building.

By the mid-1970s, the Museum needed a new facility for its school of art to accommodate the growing student body. Under the guidance of Museum director, William C. Agee, and with a generous donation from Alfred Glassell, Jr., a plan for an approximately 42,000-square-foot building was drawn up by architects Eugene Aubry and R. Nolen Willis of prominent Houston firm S. I. Morris and Associates. The building—a two-story space made from concrete and glass block, and located one block north of the Museum—represented the first time the school had a home of its own in its 52-year history. The Glassell School of Art opened to the public on January 13, 1979. The structure has since been replaced by a structure designed by Steven Holl Architects.

In 1978, funds were provided by The Brown Foundation, Inc. for the purchase of a one-acre tract next to the new Glassell School of Art, then under construction. The commission for the site's sculpture garden—named the Lillie and Hugh Roy Cullen Sculpture Garden for the independent oilman and philanthropist and his wife—was awarded to Isamu Noguchi in the same year. Initiated under director, William C. Agee, the garden was completed under director, Peter C. Marzio, who worked closely on the planning with Noguchi and undertook acquisitions for the garden. Born in Los Angeles in 1904, the son of an American mother and Japanese poet father, Noguchi was interested in sculpture out-of-doors rather than within building galleries. "I had a revelation of the earth outdoors as a new way of conceiving sculpture," Noguchi once wrote, and he described his gardens as "sculpture for sculpture." For his entire career, Noguchi focused on the spatial domain that sculpture could evoke. His design for Cullen Sculpture Garden is a modern approach to the traditional idea of a garden—framed by concrete walls ranging in height, the works of sculpture within it are set among broken curves and abrupt angles. Spread out on a long, horizontal plane, the sculpture garden is meant, not for quick consumption, but for thoughtful and contemplative exploration. A unique and tranquil oasis of art and nature at the corner of Bissonnet and Montrose, Cullen Sculpture Garden showcases masterworks of 20th- and 21st-century sculpture by artists including Louise Bourgeois, Dan Graham, Henri Matisse, Auguste Rodin, and David Smith.

After the Glassell School of Art opened in 1979, participation in art education classes grew exponentially. The growth of the school was mirrored in the growth of the Museum's central administration and, with this progress, came the need for expanded space.

Museum director, Peter C. Marzio, enlisted the expertise of award-winning Houston architect, Carlos Jiménez, to create a new administration building with an attached space for the Junior School of the Glassell School of Art. The 42,270-square-foot, L-shaped plan Jiménez designed for the new Administration and Junior School Building mirrors the Glassell School directly across Montrose Boulevard. The Junior School portion comprises two stories, with ample windows to allow northern light into the classrooms and exhibition gallery. The building uses the same limestone, metal, glass block, and insulated glass materials as other buildings on the MFAH campus.

Spanish architect, Rafael Moneo, was enlisted in 1992 to design the next MFAH expansion, to be named for Museum patron, Audrey Jones Beck. The Beck Building was created to hold the Museum's collections of masterworks of European art; Renaissance and Baroque art from the Blaffer Foundation; the John A. and Audrey Jones Beck Collection of Impressionist and Post-Impressionist Art; prints, drawings, and photographs; and American paintings, sculpture, and decorative arts before 1945. The building is situated directly across Main Street from the Ludwig Mies van der Rohe-designed Caroline Wiess Law Building. Moneo determined that instead of emulating an architectural style similar to the Museum's other buildings, the new structure would allow the MFAH campus to be seen as an eclectic compilation of fine architectural design. Moneo's design created an urban, three-story structure with a 192,447-square-foot footprint, housing more than 85,000 square feet dedicated to gallery space. The outside of the building is clad in Indiana limestone, similar to the other MFAH buildings, and the roof is covered with a series of skylight lanterns—a signature feature of the project—which use natural light to illuminate second-floor galleries. The street-level entrance to the building is meant to extend the feel of the city, with an active area for the information desk, ticket counter, and shop that leads into gallery spaces. From the lower level, visitors can easily walk between the Law and Beck buildings through the Wilson Tunnel, a site-specific passageway of light commissioned from artist James Turrell and titled *The Light Inside.*

An aside, this description of the home(s) of the MFAH does not include spaces in other parts of Houston dedicated to other foci in art, neither Bayou Bend, Miss Ima Hogg's paean to American decorative arts, nor Rienzi, the Mastersons' Italian palazzo, dedicated to European decorative arts, homes though they were before being bequeathed to the MFAH—but not associated with the Latin American focus at the MFAH.

Quite possibly in a preemptive response to the 2000 U.S. Census finally officially recognizing the large Hispanic population in the city, in 2001 and for decades after, the first—and only—major U.S. museum to feature a curator dedicated to Latin American art in all its locations and variations and media, was the Museum of Fine Arts/Houston. In the interim, as that demographic has swelled, the MFAH has mounted those numerous exhibitions of—and procured—many artworks from Spain, from the countries of Hispanic America and by U.S. Chicano/Latino/Hispanic artists.

In addition to the concept of "home" overall at the MFAH itself, I've mentioned that this presentation highlights the aforementioned overview of works and artists from several of those exhibitions, but focuses on the second-to-latest, *HOME—So Different, So Appealing*, which features U.S. Latino/x and Latin American artists from the late 1950s to the present who use the universal concept of "home" as a lens through which to view socioeconomic and political changes in the Americas over the past seven decades. More than 100 works by 39 artists explore the differences and similarities within art related to topics not always so sweet, immigration and political repression; dislocation and diaspora; and personal memory and utopian ideals.

Ironically and not-so-sweet, this exhibition is not one of my personal favorites conceptually . . . though it features wide-ranging thematic foci addressing nearly all of the definitions I offered at the beginning of this essay (and attempted to mimic via the chosen visualizations of the architectural history of the museum itself, including models, archaeology, mapping, recycling, form, embodied entities, (troubled, so not-so-sweet) homeland and going home. It *is* an amazing exhibition in terms of the culmination of a decade of collaboration among three institutions (UCLA Chicano Studies Research Center, Los Angeles County Museum of Art and the MFAH) and, more unusual and another no-so-sweet, among three curators, one of whom is the original and current curator at the MFAH, whose professional history was the topic of a lengthy article in the *New York Times Magazine* as being "endowed with a self-confidence that her critics call grandiosity or arrogance." But, referring back to the *Washington Post* article cited initially in this presentation, the "concept of home [does give] rise to artistic differences . . . "

Quoting from the *Introduction* to the catalog for the exhibition, which cites geographer Theano Terkenli,

> [home] is the conceptual site for locating self within multiple and interconnected social contexts from family to community to nation to region and world, [it articulates] a sense of belonging . . . is inherently transportable . . . not tied to place [but] gives rise to 'personal geographies' that map the interface between self and world through 'the dichotomy between us and them.'

Home has been constantly recurring theme in MFAH acquisitions, 444 of them, quite apart from Latin American art, e.g.:

Thomas Nast, American, 1840–1902, *"Home, Sweet Home. There's No Place Like Home"*
   www.mfah.org/art/detail/13498- Work of Art 89.689.2
Bert L. Long, Jr., American, 1940–2013, *Home Sweet Home*
   www.mfah.org/art/detail/27035- Work of Art 94.714
Dora Maar at Home
   www.mfah.org/fellowships/doramaarhouse/dora-maar-home/- Page
   "in the village where, following her painful breakup with Pablo Picasso, she lived each summer from near the end of World War II until her death on July 16, 1997. In this house, the spirit of Dora Maar is always present. She remains at **home** . . . . "
Unknown, At Home Dress
   www.mfah.org/art/detail/38984 - Work of Art 98.423
The Eskimo at Home.
   www.mfah.org/art/detail/76709 - Work of Art 2004.1222.110

HOME—So Different, So Appealing
www.mfah.org/exhibitions/home-so-different-so-appealing- Exhibition
Información en español sobre la exposición "A truly astonishing show"—says the Huffington Post—"*HOME—So Different, So Appealing* features U.S. Latino and Latin American . . . "
Exploring Art and Creativity at Home
www.mfah.org/research/kinder-foundation-education-center/EACH/- Page
"These parent workshops include learning about art in the MFAH collections, art projects, and activities to do at home. Each workshop includes exploring works of art, including context, style, and artist biography . . . "
HOME—So Different, So Appealing
www.mfah.org/visit/homeso-different-so-appealing-espanol/- Page 17 *de noviembre de 2017 al 21 de enero de 2018 Esta exposición presenta rótulos en español e inglés.* "Learn more about the exhibition (English) *HOME—So Different, So* . . . "
Elisabeth Sunday, American, born 1958, *Home*
www.mfah.org/art/detail/113101- Work of Art 2012.586.3
Eastman Johnson, American, 1824–1906, *Home and Warmth*
www.mfah.org/art/detail/4203- Work of Art 77.336
Robert Frank, American, born Switzerland, 1924, *Home Improvements*
www.mfah.org/art/detail/9820—Work of Art 86.154
Tina Leser, American, 1910–1986, *At Home Dress*
www.mfah.org/art/detail/40181—Work of Art 99.137. A, B
John Thomson, Scottish, 1837–1921, *A Convicts' Home*
www.mfah.org/art/detail/57661—Work of Art 2004.701
Robert Clark, American, born 1961, *Home Game*
www.mfah.org/art/detail/62838—Work of Art 2003.369
Fazal Sheikh, American, born 1965, *Zubris Home*
www.mfah.org/art/detail/73840—Work of Art 2002.2245
Constantino Arias, Cuban, 1920–1991, *Untitled (Home Products)*
www.mfah.org/art/detail/83737—Work of Art 2006.468
John R. Gossage, American, born 1946, *Home, Maryland*
www.mfah.org/art/detail/6316—Work of Art 82.346
André Kertész, American, 1894–1985, *Homing Ship*
www.mfah.org/art/detail/4431—Work of Art 78.112.6
Thomas Nast, American, 1840–1902, "Home-Stretched"
www.mfah.org/art/detail/13277—Work of Art 89.589.1
William Home Lizars, Scottish, 1788–1859, *Wild Turkey*
www.mfah.org/art/detail/28887—Work of Art B.73.3

Robert Frank, American, born Switzerland, 1924, *Home Improvements*
www.mfah.org/art/detail/31679—Work of Art 91.12.A-.G
Lawrence Carroll, American, born Australia, 1954, *Towards Home*
www.mfah.org/art/detail/39816—Work of Art 98.313
Adriana Groisman, Argentinean, born 1959, *Osvaldo at Home*
www.mfah.org/art/detail/66641—Work of Art 2004.1413
Esther Bubley, American, 1921–1998, *Blythedale Convalescent Home*
www.mfah.org/art/detail/108312—Work of Art 2010.1872
Conflict at "HOME": Miguel Ángel Rojas & "Nowadays"
www.mfah.org/blogs/inside-mfah/conflict-at-home-miguel-angel-rojas-nowadays- Blog
"When you enter the first gallery of **HOME**—*So Different, So Appealing*, you're greeted with large letters on the wall: "Just what is it that makes today's **homes** so different, so appealing . . . "
Adrian Piper, American, born 1948, *Close to Home*
www.mfah.org/art/detail/18806—Work of Art 92.111.1-.15
Josef Sudek, Czech, 1896–1976, *At Janàcek's Home*
www.mfah.org/art/detail/70960—Work of Art 2002.2387
A Miner's home at Cape Nome, Alaska.
www.mfah.org/art/detail/76719—Work of Art 2004.1222.120
Tony Schanuel, American, born 1952, *Going Home*
www.mfah.org/art/detail/88756—Work of Art 2007.1758
Jessie Spiess, American, born 1986, *Impressions of Home*
www.mfah.org/art/detail/106594—Work of Art 2010.1629

Thus, the particular exhibition which drives this essay, *HOME— So Different, So Appealing*, at this particular museum at this particular time, reiterates not only the universality of the importance of "home," whether sweet or not-so-sweet, to humans, allowing for all the possible definitions and interpretations, but also culminates the efforts of the MFAH to recognize and celebrate its role in the incredible diversity of Houston ethnically and culturally, as well as to underscore the decision to diversify holdings and exhibitions in general, while especially acknowledging and appreciating the Hispanic heritage of the area and inhabitants.

Note

1   For the most part, only exhibitions featuring Latin American artworks from Spanish-dominant countries, or indigenous art from those same countries, or Chicano/Latino/Hispanic works from the U.S. as the fifth-largest "Spanish-speaking country in the Americas," are included, with a few exceptions for Brazil (Portuguese), due to the gifts to, and holdings in,

the MFAH. No exhibitions that address(ed) art from any other-language-dominant areas of Latin America, e.g., Haiti (French/Creole), etc.—or even the multitude of exhibitions addressing art from the so-called *madre patria*/mother country, "Hispanic" Spain, in Europe, are cited among these examples of exhibitions. This focus in exhibitions is quite apart from what art is included in a later list of MFAH acquisitions that address the concept of "home."

Works Consulted

Fox, Stephen for *The Museum of Fine Arts, Houston: An Architectural History 1924–1986*. Houston: The Museum of Fine Arts, Houston. 1992. Print.

https://www.merriam-webster.com/thesaurus/home

https://www.mfah.org/exhibitions

https://www.nytimes.com/2008/03/23/magazine/23ramirez-t.html

https://thoughtcatalog.com/trisha-velarmino/2015/02/the-concept-of-home-its-a-feeling-not-a-place/

https://www.washingtonpost.com/entertainment/museums/concept-of-home-gives-rise-to-artistic-differences/2012/12/27/d36ac176-4f97-11e2-839d-d54cc6e49b63_story.html?utm_term=.b9f27ed54d75

CHAPTER
4
Architecture and the Constant Hispanic Postmodern Project

ELIZABETH WHITE COSCIO

The parallelism between architecture and the poetic is not new; rather, it is a reciprocal relationship constantly present within the confines of cultural theory, philosophy, sociology and other disciplines. Actually, in the world of construction itself, projects are rendered that are never built, so do those projects become "fictional?" The purpose of architecture is to improve our experience in the world of construction, to move beyond just a battle of different styles, it has more to do with the way ideas, vocabulary and structure are combined. Novelties, be they new construction materials or forms in space that may be translated into fiction as certain types of figurative language or literary tropes, are always going to change.

Neil Leach has noted the twentieth century began with optimism and visions of a utopian future for the Americas and ended on a note of critical reflection of past architecture. His commentary applies perfectly to the dilemma of modernism/postmodernism in Latin American literature. Leach compares what Fredric Jameson has called an "inverted millenarianism," which instead of projecting towards the future, reconsidered the past in terms of a failure of certain basic accepted notions. He described this representation as the same "crisis of legitimacy" that Jürgen Habermas had noted about modernity being an incomplete project (Habermas in *Anti-esthetic* 3). There is a reciprocal relationship between literature and architecture evidenced by the constant presence of both in the domain of cultural theory, philosophy, sociology and other disciplines in general.

Kenneth Frampton proposes six points of reference for an architecture of resistance to the tendency of universalization so common in all art in general by way of a critical regionalism. Using the term "universalization," according to Paul Ricoeur in *History and Truth,* who calls it the paradox of the so-called underdeveloped nations, the same question can be asked about all Latin American art, including architecture and literature: How does one revive a native civilization so present in Latin America but not yet completely developed or active, at the same time taking part in all the scientific, rational, technical and political universal progress civilization has to offer?

Actually, it was the reading of the articles edited by Hal Foster in *The Anti Aesthetic: Essays on Postmodern Culture* that provided the impetus to write these musings. My final take-away from those texts is a suggestion to resist the kind of negativity that a definition of modernity or postmodernity as a concept or practice, local style, a new epoch or a polemical economic phase can engender. The question of when, how and what are the forms and effects of postmodernism in Latin American are simply difficult questions. In the preface, Foster comments more than thirty-five years ago that postmodernism in architecture was a return to tradition.

Some time ago, the critical regionalism of which Frampton spoke became the official representation. At least there are a number of representative works. Even twenty-five years ago, we were considering the superficiality of the vanguard, the problems of pastiche, pseudo-history or kitsch in all artistic endeavors. By the mid-twentieth century, in the years of the classic Latin American literary master narratives Carlos Fuentes spoke of, we already see the beginnings of doubt in the great project of humanity.

Perhaps, as Habermas advised, we do not have to scream revolution nor react but only return to pick up the narrative where it dropped off (Leach 225). So returning to the Latin American master narrative, the proposal of this essay is an analysis of the architectonic allegory in *Los pasos perdidos (The Lost Steps)*[1] in relation to Latin American literature in the first half of the twentieth century, analyzing a representative literary monument that reflects some of the same causes, conditions or possibilities of space in postmodern art

The first two decades of the 1900s saw the rise of important vanguard modern art movements in Latin America. Meanwhile, Latin American literary Realism rebelled against Romanticism, and so on through Modernism, Surrealism through Magic Realism and that amorphous postmodernism label begins to appear as early as the middle to late twentieth century in relationship to all artistic trends in the tradition of Baudelaire's reinvention of modern man.

Several large building projects were undertaken in different parts of Latin America during the same period. A group of more than 150 architects, including Juan O'Gorman and Félix Candela, designed the

University of Mexico in 1950–53. It combines modern architecture with the work of Mexican muralists. Similarly, the University City in Caracas, Venezuela, integrates modern buildings with works by artists. Carlos Raúl Villanueva built it in 1950–57. Ignacio Artismuño recognizes the period from the thirties to the sixties as a time of innovative progress in modern architecture, ending with the building of an urban city in the jungle, Brasilia. He blames the seventies dictators who promoted and were associated with these progressive works and the social and economic instability they provoked for the downfall of new postmodern ideas. Critical regionalism is the answer and he mentions the Mexican architect, Luis Barragán, and the Brazilian, Roberto Burl Marx, whose works have been imitated outside of Latin America (Artismuño 2).

As Terri Eagleton said, the postmodern is contradictory; it is radical and conservative; libertarian and authoritarian; hedonistic and repressive; multiple and monolithic (132). With that kind of a definition, an investigation into a field or system with those contrasting hierarchies, allows for a step aside from chronology or thirty year literary generations to look at postmodern works that see art as a consumer's or reader's material reality. There are no boundaries of high and low culture and the ultimate goal could be compared to Antonio Gaudi's columns in Güell Park in Barcelona. In the Hypostyle Room, designed to be the market place for this utopian hillside development that is now a famous park, there are 86 striated columns inspired by the Doric order. I remember standing in amazement, as so many others have, to note in the guidebook that the outermost columns refuse to follow the interior, resulting in an undulating movement completely contrary to classical composition, but all the while retaining some awareness of their structural role in the whole.

Rosalind Krauss, writing in 1979 about the new postmodern esthetic in the world of sculpture and painting, looked to provide some kind of structure and meaning to these changes in that art world. She showed no desire to return to the positivist critics of the past century that she compared to elaborate genealogical trees that searched the millennia for comparisons of anything to legitimize works as sculpture. She refuted the notion that Stonehenge and Toltec ball courts were sculpture and insisted those critics had universalized the category of sculpture by leaving out the particulars of history.

Literary monuments of the past century, codified into a "Latin American Boom" canon, are similar to a historical vision that accepts that certain definite ruptures that can be identified and analyzed. The definition of "monument" as a public structure, erected in memory of a person or event of historic or cultural value, helps to distinguish such offerings once they have been encapsulated in what Kraus and others called the logic of the past century.

The same type of universalization in the world of literary criticism today has become an archaeological and/or anthropological search for literary, historical and/or political significance in order to define literature. The search for meaning somewhat resembles working a crossword puzzle. The researcher must employ primary sources as varied as chronicles, testimonials, diaries, various types of religious and civil records, diverse prose and verse narratives and works including travel tales, music and theatre. All of these forms are considered valid as literature in the twenty-first century, revealing the same type of universalization referred to by Krauss.

Here should be a simple definition of allegory, but even the term itself in Western literary terminology eludes a strict definition. It has been applied since ancient times to such diverse form: as a literary trope, a sustained metaphor, or simply ironic discourse. Some critics even apply the term to any reformulation in altered terminology. It is possible to conceive the term as a concept, as part of history, a reflection of conscience, or literary structure.

Ancient Greek and Roman scholars applied a very specific rhetorical meaning to allegory. Originally, allegory meant a brief trope but Schlegel expanded the concept of a general tension in literary language. Such expansion in scope of meaning demonstrates how literary works always aspire to express that which cannot be expressed, even to the commentary of De Man, that narratives can even betray their own system of values.

Current trends allow for varying degrees of allegorical expression. The fictional autonomy of the text and how many different ambient factors point to another set of principles, actions or circumstances, both important considerations. Ambivalence in allegorical language is an artistic sign in composition that the text will allow for different interpretations. An allegorical interpretation helps preserve the author's intent and in a sense, it canonizes it. Historically, allegorical strategy resulted in the exegesis of a text not as mythology but rather as sacred text. The relationship of allegory to sacred texts provided an authority, at the same time as a vision of the future yet to be written, only in prophesy.

By the end of the Middle Ages, there were more and more apocalyptic forms. By the Renaissance and Neoclassic periods, those changes between fiction and fact became a rather formal design. At that point, how one text related to another was revealed in the relationship of imaginative language to formal structure. Structural decorum reigned and the sixteenth century Italian critics, under the influence of Aristotle's *Poetics*, insisted on the formalities of composition including unity and credibility. The allegory was reserved precisely to give credibility to the fantastic back then. Afterwards, in the eighteenth and nineteenth centuries, critics like Vico maintained that an image could separate from its abstract concept, preferring symbols and myth over the allegory. By the time of Freud, Jung and Frazer, myth critics and psychoanalysts employed their psychological and anthropological theories to explain the myths and symbols as deep structures. Walter Benjamin points out that the romantic symbol obscured the effect of time and impeded the unity of the ephemeral object with an eternal idea, a kind of dead allegory.

That preconscious level was not exploited in structuralism literary criticism, although it provided a unique system in the form of a grid to judge literary works. The arbitrary nature of the sign, as postulated in De Saussure's *Course in General Linguistics*, was the basis for the modern structuralism movement. Since a structure is a system of differences, studied independently of what it or its parts might mean outside of the system, a structuralism appears to view words only in their differential relationship to other words on anthropological or linguistic terms.

Choosing to move beyond a particular critical reading, such as a structuralism one, to a rather eclectic set of theoretical underpinnings allows an allegory to emerge. The use of allegory results in a rather formal ideology or discourse that is ritualized with symbolic values. We can follow Plato's description of poetry as an imitation of an imitation, twice removed from the truth, to Saussure's writings couched in Western metaphysics, which presumed *logos* as Webster's philosophical definition of the 'rational principle that governs and develops the universe,' based on the Greek translation of *logo* as word. The transcendental signifier, which revealed the power of *a priori* knowledge), *parole* was prioritized over *langue*, leaving writing a displaced second. Deconstruction as a literary critical method is identified with the French philosopher Jacques Derrida. The critical readings in this work owe much to Derrida's theory of *Grammatology*, which implied critical readings can make a work exist.

Derrida showed that speech was subject to the same logic as writing, extending Saussure's arbitrary nature of the sign to speech, which must be inscribed as the signifier of the signified absent to both systems. He then proceeded to deconstruct that tradition of logocentric metaphysics (always assigning origin of truth to *logos*, the spoken word, and voice of reason or word of God) by means of a new science called "grammatology," foregrounding writing in preference to speech for tracing the displacement of signifiers. Derrida chose to deconstruct the value of voice over the mute signs of writing, reversing the binary historical and cultural oppositions common to phono-centrism. In that way, such concepts as voice/writing, sound/silence, being/nonbeing, reality/image, thing/sign, truth/lie, presence/absence, signified/signifier were reversed.

Derrida imagined a science before it even became one, presenting grammatology as a radical challenge to structuralism. Jacques Derrida also found the analogy of the differential sign in describing myths as bundles of relations or differences in the work of Claude Lévi-Strauss. The author's interest in advancing the argument of writing over speech could be revealed through his reading of Lévi-Strauss. In *Structure, Sign and Play in the Discourse of the Human Sciences,* Derrida focused on the peculiar idea of structure as a totalization for any system, presuming to give closure and coherence, which he said could not work with the element of play in the signifier.

A structure was generated, then repressed, by the requirement of closure; this was possible since a logical relation cannot be separated from its political oppositions as in the case of censorship. Closure then becomes a type of repression, particularly the origin concerning genesis of any given structure. Also amplifying on the analysis of Claude Lévi-Strauss begun in *Structure, Sign and Play,* Derrida proposed in *De la grammatologie* to explain how the contradictions of classic logic drafted modern concepts in the social sciences, and linguistics in particular. The logical oppositions in the novels provide for an open critical reading of the historical and political traces through allegory.

Supplement, as used by Lévi-Strauss, possessed a double meaning, to supply the missing, as well as supplying another something. In that manner, there was always something more to be understood. Derrida described this process as a floating one, emphasizing the double direction of the process taking it back to Saussure. "The strange structure of the *supplement* appears . . . by delayed reaction, a possibility produces that to which it is said to be added on" (Harland 130). Such philosophers as Frederick Nietzsche and Martin Heidegger also reviewed that ontological dilemma.

Perhaps Derrida's strongest argument for his claim that writing precedes speech rested upon his rejection of the German philosopher, Edmund Husserl's phenomenological theory of language, as presented by Richard Harland in *Super Structuralism*. Husserl's human language posited an absolute distinction between human and natural signs. The German philosopher felt that true language had to be willfully intended by an utterer because relation to non-verbal phenomena making it incidental to linguistic signs could also form association.

That necessity that words mean only because someone means them to mean something naturally pushed Husserl's theory of language toward speech. (For example, what I meant was . . . what I was trying to say was . . .). Husserl was the promoter of pure phenomenology or a science of the essence of meaning.

Derrida totally reversed Husserl's argument by seeing written language as self- sufficient: "The structure, peculiar to language alone, allows it to function entirely by itself when its intention is cut off from intuition" (Harland 127). Again in *De grammatologie*, Derrida insisted that writing was language at its most self-sufficient because it was language at its most spatial. It did not exist briefly and transparently as sound waves but rather as solid, enduring marks on a page. There was no need for those marks to be propped up by their maker's presence. Actually, that person was always absent, maybe dead.

Writing releases thought from consciousness, functioning as an aide-memoire. Derrida said "writing, a *mnemotechnic* means, supplanting good . . . spontaneous memory, signifies forgetfulness . . . its violence befalls the soul as unconsciousness" (Harland 128).

The bottom line of Derrida's model was language-superseded speech. Phonetic languages fit the model, but in Chinese and Egyptian, which have hieroglyphic and ideogram scripts, the written sign does not need the spoken sign to signify. Historically, the development of those scripts preceded phonetic scripts. Derrida denied the logical assumption that the truest form is the original one. Therefore, even though speech precedes language in human development, there is no rational justification to assume rediscovering primitive communication will explain language. With this radical separation of historical and conceptual priority according to Spinoza, Derrida said the fact of writing followed from the fact of speech, but the idea of speech depended upon the idea of writing. Writing became the logically fundamental condition to which language aimed.

Derrida reversed Husserl's mental meaning behind verbal meaning as a means of controlling the verbal message. Instead, the writer only discovered the meaning in the act of writing. He said, "Before me, the signifier on its own says more than I believe that I meant to say and in relation to it, my meaning-to-say is submissive rather than active" (Harland 132). The writer just became another reader, which is exactly where this reader-researcher is leading with these details.

Derrida refused any conscious meaning in the sense of movement from marks on the page to mental concepts. When we could find only absence and emptiness for the elusive signified, Derrida told us that the signified was merely an illusion that we invented so as not to deal with the materialism of language. The signifiers are always signifying, pointing away from themselves to other signifiers, constantly in motion in a state of dissemination. That concept was different from *univocity*, which is 'the state of single meanings maintained by the signified in the reader's mind.'

Dissemination goes on in perpetuity as unfulfilled meaning in the absence of all signified. Language supplanted human control, revealing its own creativity to which writers and readers alike must succumb. There was no social or individual responsibility. In that endlessly unbalanced state, words no longer pushed against each other at the same time, they pushed successively, like falling dominoes of causal units.

The Saussurean *langue* that bounced from positive to negative now flowed from pole to pole in electrical terms. With that new model, Derrida brought a new dimension of study to structuralism, the dimension of time, which was excluded from the structuralism model. This is exactly the point of approaching the novels with a variety of critical processes. With *differance*, Derrida provided two meanings: difference as distinction, inequality or discernibility and the interposition of delay, the interval of a spacing and temporalizing, which allowed for the presently denied to be put off until later. Thus, the conception of time deferred meaning only for the present, and in time, the deferred meaning flowed over into it. An uttered word existed by its deferring of unuttered words. From Plato, in particular, to the Greek language in general, *parole* to *langue* was generated in that theory of language.

Another area of deconstruction of structuralism was opposing traditional philosophical dualism of mind/matter, soul/body, and spirit/natural world. Derrida saw a tremendous inequality in those oppositions. "In a classical philosophical opposition we are not dealing with the peaceful coexistence of a vis-a-vis, but rather with a violent hierarchy. One of the two terms governs the other . . . or has the upper-hand" (Harland 142). Rising up against this mind-soul-spirit concept was the unconscious mind in the form of writing, which Derrida called "arch-writing," a theory Harland contended he derived from Sigmund Freud, especially in his essay, "Note on the Mystic Writing Pad" (143).

He used Freud's mechanical model for perception and memory in the neurological system of the brain, where a force in the perceptual circuits opened up a pathway or trace of lowered electro-chemical resistance. That trace then remained as the physical form of an unconscious memory, a rut along which future forces could flow more easily and follow. Derrida connected that theory to the writing inscribed upon the waxed base of the "mystic writing pad," with the channel hollowed out by the stylus.

The important part was that Derrida combined the sign with causal force that had the effect of deconstructing the phenomenological concept of an absolute present moment, the idea of things themselves. The legibility of writing came not from the stylus pressing down, but the darkness of the base that showed up. "Writing . . . supplements perception before perception even appears to itself" (Harland 144). That was a valid advance to the philosophical idea of psychic vision as a movie theater, a non-stop picture show inside the head. Derrida's theory is particularly apt for an explanation of the creative process that is allegory. As the preceding outline of allegory's history revealed, it has been described as a trope, a metaphor, or discourse.

Derrida saw consciousness as an illusion that humans invented, fearing a purely materialist conception of the brain. Mind was a signified that we ascribe to the brain, divine spirit as a signified that we connect to the natural world, etc., etc. All of those impressions were, in Derridean terms, mere versions of *logos*, just a type of wishful thinking that his theory of writing as a theory of materialism deconstructed. That type of materialism provided for a path akin to meditation, a comparison made by Harland, as an expanding, unfolding general meaningfulness. Beyond the historical literary definition of allegory as trope, metaphor, or discourse, then this is meditation, or open reading.

In that way, linguistic claims of truth underwent a transformation, resulting in an opening up of literary language. By connecting its creative play with strategies of power, with real historical forces, writers could undercut authority, destabilize institutions, and realign social values and hierarchies by demystifying with revolutionary aims. That was the real paradox of literature already commented on by Sören Kierkegaard in *God Becoming Man in Christian Theology*, William von Schlegel, who linked it closer to poetry and irony in the human experience and Wordsworth in "Composed upon Westminster Bridge" (Princeton Encyclopedia 881).

The encyclopedic synopsis above takes us to a generalized idea of just how complicated it is to refer to an allegorical work. The implication is a criticism of the same systems that support the allegory itself, resulting in a struggle between the rejection of certain values while coordinating the same concepts being criticized: the paradox of postmodernism. One must relate to the surface story as well as the underlying allegory.

To look at allegory in Latin American postmodernist beginnings takes us back, as Fuentes announced, to the beginning of a new Latin American literary regionalism citing a "second conquest" other than the sixteenth-century Spanish one. He noted the symbolism of the conflict in the regionalist novel, *Doña Barbara* (1929,) by the later (1948) Venezuelan president, Rómulo Gallegos. There are two allegorical characters, Doña Barbara, who became the allegorical (Barbarity), the brutal cruelty of nature and the large landholders, against the character, Santos Luzardo (Civilization) represented by progress and laws. Eventually, this conflict lost its validity and was replaced by another more complicated polemic. Then, next to that mountain, the pampa, the mines and savage rivers of the Latin American novel, arises that other more-complicated archetype, the Dictator, as the new represents the immediacy of chronic dictatorial exploitation that resulted in a transformation of the author's romantic role as antagonist in conflict with the Common Man Protagonist.

If only for historical interest, it is still important to return to the Latin American "master narrative" to recognize *The Lost Steps* as part of the break from that romanticism. As Roberto González Echeverría has noted, the work is a synthesis of all Western discourse with high-culture references to Goethe, Shelley, Schiller, and Beethoven (15). Moreover, if we are searching for the beginnings of postmodernism, it serves to note the less than half a century of key works that have served as precursors. Although he references the Old World, he appears to be searching for the nature of being Latin American in the languages and traditions of the New World.

From the very first sentence, the unreliable narrator, who has confounded critics for decades, finds himself lost in time, a displaced signifier. The ambiguity of the subject hints at the multiplicity of topics to follow. His memories can be our memories or the memories of an entire civilization by intertextuality. The multiplicity of the narrator is a prototype for the Boom novels to follow. The narrative structure and the importance of place and space allow us to bounce from Carpentier's own intellectual and artistic musings to the allegorical story line that circles out from the "I" of the protagonist, perhaps reflecting Carpentier's own autobiography to Latin America to the world.

A reevaluation occurs in the sixties and seventies, both in literature and architecture. New social forces allowed for changes in literary theory by way of Russian formalists, French structuralists and German reception theorists who followed twentieth-century Latin American literature. Their writings referred to a new postmodern era as the end of the master narratives of truth, reason, and universal values in all areas of artistic endeavor, recognizing for the first time that space between the text and "I," the reader. While in the architectural world, Jean Gottman referred to a "ubiquitous placelessness" in the new "megapolis," of "polis" as a space where people congregate.

(Frampton 30). And now, the focus continues looking for living spaces, which allow for a return to walking, a natural human function.

Much has been written about the twentieth-century seminal work, *Los pasos perdidos,* due to the poetic language and the historical, literary, and musical allusions that give density to the novel. First, it is necessary to provide a very basic synopsis: *Los pasos perdidos* is a colorful allegoric tale in the form of an explorer's journal from inauthentic urban living to a past primitive life that is unattainable. A frustrated composer, fleeing an empty existence with his stage actress wife in New York City, accepts a commission to locate a primitive musical instrument he believes will explain the origins of musical instruments. He takes the first journey with his mistress to one of the few remaining areas of the world not yet touched by civilization—the upper reaches of a great South American river, presumably the Orinoco. The space/time journey takes the protagonist back through different epochs until he arrives at what he describes as "the first three chapters of Genesis" (229). *The Lost Steps* describes his search, his Ulysses-like adventures, return to civilization to complete his nature-inspired "real music" and then, back again to try to reach that secret village, Santa Mónica de los Venados, after failing to attain the cultured urban life he desired. He retraces his lost steps but high water keeps him out of that paradise where he sought to be master and live with the idyllic primitive woman of every man's dreams to serve him. Unfortunately for him, she has borne another man's child and she is now that man's "woman."

It is a trip to a tropical Venezuelan jungle, to what Carpentier called a *"real maravilloso"* culture. Carpentier is cited for having created this term as a precursor to other monikers for what is generally known today as Latin American Magic Realism. (Carpentier prologue). Some quarter of a century later, in a conference lecture, he expounded on the difference between his *real maravilloso* and surrealism. He described a trip to Haiti, where he found a magic syncretic world, where he said that all the surrealists had fabricated, mainly artificially, was real, apparent, and ready-made by nature (Carpentier in *Tientos* 265). *The Lost Steps* reflects this notion where his concrete jungle in the New York City of his real world does not match the fantasy or real lost civilization hidden by the real elements of nature that read larger than life in the South American jungle replete with its own myths and legends now so widely accepted as a Latin American Boom years style.

Readily apparent in a variety of authors in the sixties and seventies, Latin American Boom years, this mythic vision of a society still attached to its past and the great myths of indigenous civilizations was as yet still new as others proposed other terms leaving behind such terms as fantastic literature, mythic realism and the *real imaginario* in opposition to objective reality that could be magic, mythic-legendary, miracles or the fantastic. Mario Vargas Llosa defined Gabriel García Márquez' *One Hundred Years of Solitude* as magic realism, while Suzanne Jill Levine maintained that García Márquez gave life to what Carpentier merely defined" (Levine 563–576).

Miguel Ángel Asturias explained magic realism by telling the legend of the woman who falls in the abyss or the horseman who falls from his horse. The *indio* or *mestizo* may explain the circumstances by these legends: the god of the abyss attracted the woman to transform her into a serpent and it is not because of his drunkenness that the horse rider falls, but rather the river drowned him, it called to him. (Asturias 265). For some readers, *The Lost Steps* serves as an allegory for Latin American culture and identity, where nature and civilization alternate between the positive and negative. This is based on the idea that modernity in reality is a project without end. Literary metaphors are architectural throughout this work. Carpentier's architectural allegorical subtext creates the same illusion as every change in style in the architectural world has concerned human and societal needs.

The relationship will be presented by way of Frampton's article, "Towards a Critical Regionalism: Six Points for an Architecture of Resistance,"

> including the need to move beyond universalization to a regional criticism within the world culture considering culture and civilization, the rise and fall of the avant-garde, resistance of the place-form, culture versus nature in topography, context, climate, light and tectonic form, and the visual versus the tactile. (*Anti-Aesthetic* 16–30)

The "antithetical pairings," mentioned by Frances Wyers, are possible to identify in that same alternation from positive to negative, here (New World) and there (Europe) as mimesis in nature, as well as in culture. It will be used in considering the literary trope of allegory as a kind of architectural allegory revealed by way of pairs of delineated signs (Wyers 86). The very density of Carpentier's work with cultural fragments or grafts from here and there surely causes the commentary of Wyers that the allegorical subtext is not consistent.

González Echeverría, along with others, has noted the importance of the travel trope in this work by Alejo Carpentier: *The Pilgrim at Home* asks the question if Carpentier's *Los pasos perdidos* is "a travel journal in the process of becoming a novel or is it an unfinished novel that will imitate a travel journal?" (186).

There is a textural fracturing resulting from the impossibility of reconciling the faithful Christian with the creative writer. His entire trip to the interior is described in terms of European cultural history. There are so many allusions that at times there is an imitation of the sources themselves, such as when he imagines he is Humboldt. Primitive myths, operas, medieval legends, the long-ago chronicles of the first new continent explorers and travelers compete for space in the protagonist's diary.

There are overt traces of Ulysses, the same as an anthropological perspective of a trip to the origins of humankind: Yannes, the Greek miner, gifts him with a copy of the *Odyssey*, then, the narrator proposes to compose a "threnody," a funeral dirge based on the famous epic; he constantly refers to his own difficulties as epic tasks to be completed with the notion he will find a more genuine lifestyle to replace the modern existence he wants to escape (Carpentier 215). The indigenous myths can absorb some of the problems, but he does not find resurrection in the indigenous ruins because he sees the ruins of the city full of sick people and beggars in an abject view of society. The six chapters of this novel form the week of Genesis and González Echevarría announces a: "seventh chapter—day, that will be that fabulous Sunday of fiction" (53).

All of human culture and the civilization of another utopian world are reflected in Nature in terms of European human constructions or as copies of the animal world with "blocks of granite in the form of dinosaurs, tapirs, and other petrified animals" (199). "When an outcropping or granite roadblock prevents human navigation in the river, it began to produce literature around the grandiose spectacle" (198). Those "foaming pylons" of nature that kept out the first explorers would serve as a tourist attraction for Mouche, his mistress, who represents all the worst of the vanguard intellectual styles. The narrator speaks of the jungle "foyer" (198) in terms of a symbiotic metamorphosis that interchanges mimesis in nature, the world of art and human civilization that falsify, but not only do they falsify, but also negate the natural value. The narrator insists it is a "strange civilization that would have left the vestiges of an architecture created for ignored reasons" (199). The granite outcroppings in the river, the production of God and nature are compared to the most basic of human architecture always in terms of back there in Europe, the *menhires* appear to be the archaic "temple ruins of a lost necropolis" (199). González Echeverría identified the *monoliths* as the large man-made upright stones, typically dating from the European middle-Bronze Age. They can be found solely as monoliths, or as part of a group of similar stone. Broadly speaking, *menhirs* are single prehistoric standing stones. The word, *menhir,* is of Celtic origin *men,* "stone" and *hir,* "long." *Dolmens* are more complex structures, often, roofed passageways. The name is Celtic: from *dol,* "table" and *men,* "stone." Wyers also mentions the desire of the Spanish colonial culture to appropriate the same forms of the metropolis left behind that results in the architectonics of "that disperse capital city, without style, anarchic in its topography" (105).

The architectonic material in literature becomes the language and theory, imaginative, romantic, or baroque and requires no sweat on the part of the author to build his work (Vélez Catrain 4). The language material of this work is ironic and baroque that constructs a series of contradictions that result in an architectural allegory. This trope is introduced early on and is reinforced with a never-ending supply of detailed descriptions always couched in the builder's lexicon, as well as distinctive characterizations, motifs and plot structure.

Heidegger's notion of the privilege of technology cancelling human thought is present, as well as his definition of architecture in Greek terms: *arch*=the possibility to make visible to the world and *techne*=to produce. The context is important to create a building foundation since for the great philosopher: "space is not in the world, but rather the world exists in space" (98). Comparisons of ancient Greek buildings with indigenous living space refers to this idea of Heidegger's space as "dasein." They used "that fiber, that palm leaf, that clay or mud, they have set their standards, functional to resist the elements, as have all of the architectures of the world" (200). If poetry is the manifestation of truth in this world, then to build artistically returns man to his authentic existence. The Carpentierian narrator speaks of the "Helenism of that environment" (200) and compares the profiles of Yannes' three brothers to the "bas-relief of a triumphal arch" (200). This celebration of the domination of man is contrasted with the totalitarianism and violence of the megalopolis, New York City and the South American colonial city in the text. He says the Helenism has nothing to do with the hotel's labyrinth, that it could be the labyrinth of his existence (125). There is a constant description of construction material minutiae of the labyrinth including the ceiling, bronze figures, plaster, conventionalized representations of the acanthus leaf, that were used especially as a decoration for Corinthian column capitals, grey cement, etc. (200).

This description of the search for Mouche results in a hyperbolic labyrinth, borrowing Jacques Derrida's term (Leach 340) with "so many hallways . . . that house of confusion, with its dark cellars and countless rooms" (129). The dichotomy present within the narrator (body vs. spirit) is revealed when he says, "he and I, sustained by an occult architecture lived in one body, the libertine and the preacher, the first characters of all edifying allegories, of all exemplary morality" (87). According to González Echeverría, the narrator is referring to his penitence for having abandoned his studies, "seeing himself in the mirror, as one of those medieval representations of the struggle between soul and body" (88).

The act of constructing allows the space hidden in the jungle to provide a poetic home, that continues the parody or ironic mimicry of travel tales or lost world narratives, as other critics such as Lucy D. Harney have noted. She felt that the narrator-author (some have maintained the work is autobiographical) desires credibility and admiration from his reader and the irony comes from the unreliable narrator, who does not see what the reader does. "In this, Carpentier follows Lucian, Thomas More, and Swift. *Gulliver's Travels*, in its formal presentation, is a parody of travel literature of the day, especially with regard to its often perfervid, delusional or duplicitous narrators, and the preferred theme of lost worlds and civilizations" (Harney 50). She also mentions the work as an allegory of Latin American culture and identity and compares to the reference to the search for "El Dorado," so common in Latin American history and historiography.

In contrast to the Hellenic constructs, modern construction is so conditioned to technology that the possibility to create urban forms of any great significance has been enormously limited, perhaps going all the way back to the Enlightenment, the "*burolandschaft* city-scape of Hannah Arendt where . . . utility established as meaning generates meaninglessness" (*Anti-Aesthetic* 17). Frampton mentions more recent problems in the restrictions to distribution in city planning due to the commuter societies we live in so dependent on automobiles that has changed along with speculation by real estate developers. Architectural practice has been polarized between high-tech that depends only on a simulacrum or compensating façade to cover the hard realities of what is a universal set of systems. Frampton refers first to Paul Ricoeur with a quote from his *History and Truth* regarding this paradox of universalization as "an advancement of mankind, at the same time constitutes a sort of subtle destruction, not only of traditional cultures . . . the creative nucleus of great cultures, that nucleus on the basis of which we interpret life . . . the ethical and mythical nucleus of mankind," pointing out that mediocre civilization" is expressed throughout the world in "the same bad movie, the same slot machines, the same plastic or aluminum atrocities, the same twisting of language by propaganda, etc." He speaks to the special case of colonized underdeveloped countries who face this paradox: "how to become modern and to return to sources; how to revive an old dormant civilization and take part in universal civilization" (Ricoeur in *Anti-esthetic* 16).

Frampton comments on Clement Greenberg's essay on the "Avant-Garde and Kitsch," written earlier in 1939, in which he tasked the arts to resist their reduction to pure entertainment and maintains that retaining autonomy is the only way of resisting this commodification, a holding operation to protect culture, a quixotic by definition" in an interview with Thomas McQuillan about modern architecture. The rise and fall of the avant-garde is inseparable from the modernization of society and architecture, similar to the idea of "art for art's sake." Greenberg has concluded with a certain amount of ambiguity that we turn to socialism to preserve what has remained of living culture, but according to Frampton, the vanguard cannot sustain itself as a liberal movement "because its initial utopian promise has been overrun by the internal rationality of instrumental reason." It, too, feeds off capitalist commerce and utilitarianism and takes part in the "manipulative mass-culture politics." He mentions Charles Jenck's later classification of Post-Modern Architecture as pure technique or scenography in *The Language of Post-Modern Architecture* (1977). Then, he quotes the Marxist, Herbert Marcuse, on the failure of the avant-garde to produce on the utopian promise and when the universal form of production is purely technical, "it projects a historical totality—a world" (*Anti-Aesthetic*, 20).

It is interesting that Antonio Vélez Catrain refers to the entire period between the world wars as one long epic international style that initiated in the activities around the *Bauhaus* (construction house) movement that originated as a German school of arts in the early twentieth century. Walter Gropius founded it, and later, Ludwig Mies van der Rohe worked in this unique architecture and design for low-cost housing in Berlin, Frankfurt and Stuttgart that promised a better life for the common man (Catrain 51).

Carpentier may have had more architectural influence from the long career of the Swiss architect, Le Corbusier. The importance of architectural spaces to the author has been commented on by various suthors since he studied architecture at Havana University and his father was a Swiss-French architect; the young Carpentier spent many hours in his father's cultured European library on his own "bookish journeys," which is how *The Lost Steps* has often been described. He even wrote an article about the amazing Le Corbusier in 1953 and mentions in *The Lost Steps* how he viewed the buildings in the nameless Latin American capital city from the air as a work of an unimaginable civilization . . . During hundreds of years the city had fought against the roots that raised the floors and broke the walls; but when a rich owner went for some months to Paris, leaving his residence to the care of indolent servants, the roots took advantage of the lack of concern of songs and *siestas* to arch over the back everywhere, finishing in twenty days all the best functional intentions of Le Corbusier. (106)

In his first publications, Le Corbusier proposed a machine esthetic and the importance of work centered in the city in large urban developments and built many such groundbreaking buildings around the world. Villa Savoie (1929–30) in France showed a dramatic and complex organization of space with a certain ambiguity between interior and exterior spaces. During the fifties, Le Corbusier designed the capital city of Punjab, Chandigarh, as well as religious structures. His concrete structures revel in a manipulation of form and light for dramatic effect. He also created impressive works of art—with paintings, sculptures, drawings and collages, enamels and tapestries, as well as engravings.

There is an imitation of Le Corbusier's architectural organization of ambiguous space between interior and exterior spaces in the structural and symbolic places along the rather opaque and uncertain plurality of space/time continuum, along which the protagonist moves. The novel oscillates between an interior stream of consciousness by the protagonist's search for his own personal identity and Latin American identity. The tension between here and there is not between Europe and Latin America, but rather the allegorical primitively-cultural barbarity of the jungle versus the decadent, navel-gazing Western civilization mentioned earlier in reference to Sarmiento's famous work. These two allegorical journeys coincide, similar to the flow of a public or lobby-like exterior space into a more private space, such as an office or home.

Galen Brokaw has commented on the manipulation of the time perspective of the reader by the shifting of the narration that is mainly in the first person, past tense, focused on his own internal space. Normally, this kind of first-person narrator is revealing the experience as it happened, not what he learned later. However, several times in the novel, the past becomes the present tense:

At the beginning of the novel, the alienated, indecisive protagonist is in a museum, "I look at my watch to feign a pending reminder of an unavoidable appointment . . . But my watch, that I had not wound the night before–I realize now." When he asks the time, the curator tells him it does not matter (81).

Just before he meets with his friend-curator above, he slips into the present again and views the past retrospectively without the benefit of information gained later in the story. "The narrator remarks he cannot remember how much time has passed, he is speaking about time in the story, but his forgetfulness takes place outside on an exterior level of the story. This time of brief externalization contrasts and emphasizes the past tense, the internal focalization of the majority of the novel, interior monologue and stream of consciousness being the most pure examples." This complex narrative scheme moves into a single temporal frame with the future ad present becoming one. Therefore, the only possibility for survival is to go back in time toward a more cultured state (Brokaw 104).

Le Corbusier's concrete structures that manipulated form and light for dramatic effect are also apparent in the descriptions of light in nature in the primitive state. The darkness of a space without electrification is impressive, to which anyone who has observed the play of light on the water will relate. The protagonist describes the sensation of disorientation produced by a lack of distinction between reflection and what is being reflected as the "Adelantado" (an allegorical name for the guide since the definition is a military title given to conquistadors, allowing the bearer the right to become governor) shows him the way to the lost city. In Indiana Jones fashion, the guide finds a triple chevron on a tree "that multiplied as it reflected in the water" (222) and later, "it was no longer possible to say which was tree and which was reflection of tree. Was the light coming from above or below? Was the sky or earth water?" He is amazed by "the inexhaustible ability of virgin nature to imitate what he describes in architectural terms: open and closed angles, that he became to believe were illusions of hallways, exits, the edges or banks of the river" (223).

The Swiss architect, Mario Botta, refers to "constructing the site" that has various meanings since this represents the prehistory of place: the archaeological past, cultivation and transformation over time. These stages, without sentimentality, reflect idiosyncrasies of place. The case of climate and local light are actually part of topography. Frampton recommends natural light by way of skylights and speaks of the importance of how windows change according to the need for regional inflexions: ventilation and air conditioning, sometimes behind a brick façade or protected from the sun (Frampton 26).

Carpentier through his protagonist refers to windows throughout the work from the artificial window of his wife's mirror, the view from his wife's window of "a line of windows all the same, that I used to count on Sundays from my wife's bed," New York's windowless museums and his workspace in soundproofed musical studios. He notes a house on the streets of what could be Lima with "convoluted burglar bars on the windows, with old cats in every window, and balconies where dusty parrots napped (109), certainly noting a need for regional inflexion. Later, in Santa Mónica de los Venados, the city founded by *Adelantado*, that anticipates Macondo in *One Hundred Years of Solitude,* he comments on the barred ventilating windows of the bar, the gothic windows of the church, "windows of what appear to be deserted houses . . . " a view of the inside of one of those windows of "a parlor from another century where all had been prepared for a ball that no one had ever attended" (253), as well as comparing the number of windows in the funeral home as eight compared to only four in the Adelantado's big house in the valley. When he traveled to Italy with Mouche, his mistress, she expounds without any knowledge of the country about the "mysterious sensuality of the windows."

Artificial lights in art galleries reduce the art displayed to mere commodities and even I can see the difference in the natural daylight of the Museum of Fine Arts of Houston when I have been exposed to those galleries in the evening and at night. The Houston-based Costa Rican Rice University professor of architecture commented, in an interview with Kendall Schoemann for the school magazine, about the difference of light in the cloudy landscape of his native home and his fascination with the "purity of the blue skies of Houston. He painted his studio the same blue—one that could blend in and allow his work to create moments of pause and reflection of an experience of a space that disappears into the sky" (magazine.rice.edu 21–22).

Along the same lines as the windows, one of the most important principles of architectonic autonomy resides in the tectonics, even more than light and topography. Tectonics is the science or art of construction in relation to artistic design, raising the utilitarian construction to an art form. Especially in the discussion of columns and beams, they should not appear to hide or mask the structure. It is not purely technical; it is more than skeletal frame. Frampton quotes the architectural historian, Stanford Anderson: "The sense of bearing provided by the entasis of Greek columns became the touchstone of this concept of *Tektonik*" (*Anti-esthetic* 30).

The novel begins with the white Greek columns of the Civil War set of his wife's play after some 1500 performances, which he compares to the bars of her cell on Devil's Island. Then, again, they come up when he first rejects the commission to travel, as if they had invited him to throw filth on the white columns of the University that rose up with the majesty of a temple. Descriptions of all manner of classic columns are present, baroque and Renaissance styles, even when the revolution begins in the capital city, the soldiers advance through the columns.

The idea of a new utopian space—a lost city—is revealed by way of historical allegory both organizationally as above and conceptually. Francis Wyers sees two central motives: the opposition of culture versus nature and the mimetic revelations interchangeability of both spaces. This natural metamorphosis in a regressive human history that has been identified in this work as a return to the center, the mythical creation of the world, but she calls it the birth of civilization and the beginning of a familiar repressive kind of order to life (84).

This reflects Frampton's view that since the Enlightenment, civilization has been primarily concerned with instrumental reason, while culture has addressed itself to the specifics of expression. This is why he calls for a high-tech regional criticism without overreaction, but without returning to a preindustrial past. It is not populism, nor sentimental regionalism; it must follow local influences in site topography and structure. As in literature, he speaks of an architectural deconstruction of our inherited world culture and universal civilization. This requires leaving behind the exotic, borrowed eclecticism to revitalize a debilitated society. The skepticism and arrogance of the Western world that only identifies with our civilization, assuming anything outside of that world is a deviation, less advanced, primitive or only exotically interesting at a distance needs to continue to change.

The last category of resistance is the visual versus the tactile by way of critical regionalism that provides balance to image and the actual experience. This etymology of Heidegger's "loss of nearness" of perspective presupposes suppression of the other senses such as smell, sight and taste and a distancing of the direct experience of the environment so prevalent in this literary work. By the use of words, Carpentier awakens this desire to touch and feel the poetics of the constructions described. This perspective compares to the use of metamorphosis of natural and artificial forms that evoke works of art or fantastic creatures. There is a constant shifting back and forth of scenes of a mineral world, the granite stones, toward the animal, the architectural, references to the human race in metamorphosis, memories of the evils of European history compared to the artistic wonders of a natural world far from human experience even though he uses human experiences to make the comparisons. His paradigms include utopia, the same as apocalypse, the beginning and end of the world.

There will always be a type of modernity just dominated by different forms in both the architectural and literary worlds with a constant crisis of legitimacy. *The Lost Steps* represents this negativity, this paradox of representing the beginnings of the same modernism it criticizes with a desire to return to the indigenous as an authentic return to those traditions in a *mestizaje* with all that rational science and technological advances have to offer.

Note

1   All translations are mine.

Bibliography

Alonso, Carlos J. *The Spanish American Regional Novel: Modernity and Autochthony*. Cambridge University Press, 1990. Print.

American Society of Architectural Perspectivists. *Architecture in Perspective*. Boston: Draper Printing, 1990. Print.

Aristimuño, lgnacio. "Modernity and the Value of the Latin American Architectural Legacy." *Doshisha Studies in Language and Culture*, 10(4), 2008: pp. 707–731. Print.

Asturias, Miguel Ángel. *El Señor Presidente*. [1st American ed.] Atheneum, 1964. Print.

———. Interview with Gunter W. Lorenz, *Diálogo con Latinoamérica*, Barcelona: Ed. Pomaire, 1972, pp. 265–66. Print.

Benjamin, Walter, "The Work of Art in the Age of Mechanical Reproduction," *Illuminations*. Trans. Harry Zoh. New York: Schocken Books, 1969, pp. 217–251. Print.

Bhabha, Homi. "*The World and the Home.*" *Social Text* 31–32 (1992), pp. 141–153. Print.

Brokaw, Galen. "Oswald Spengler's *The Decline of the West* and Alejo Carpentier's *Los pasos perdidos.*" *Confluencia*. 15, pp. 100–110. Print.

Carpentier y Valmont, Alejo. *Los pasos perdidos*. Roberto González Echevarría, ed. Madrid: Cátedra, 1985. Print.

———. Prologue of *El Reino de este mundo*. México: Ediapsa, 1949. Print.

———. *The Pilgrim at Home*. Ithaca: Cornell UP, 1977. Print.

———. *Tientos y diferencias*. Montevideo: Ed. Arca, 1967. Print.

Eagleton, Terri. *The Illusions of Postmodernism*. Blackwell, 1997. Print.

Fletcher, Angus. *Allegory: The Theory of a Symbolic Mode*. Cornell UP, 1964. Print.

Fol, Jac y Christian Girard, eds. *L'architecture en theorie*. Paris: Jean Michel place, 1996. Print.

Foster, Hal. *The Anti-Aesthetic Essays on Postmodern Culture*. Seattle: Bay Press, 1995. Print.

Frampton, Kenneth. "Towards a Critical Regionalism: Six Points for an Architecture of Resistance." Hal Foster, ed. *The Anti-Aesthetic Essays on Postmodern Culture*. Seattle: Bay Press, 1995. Print.

——— *Modern Architecture: A Critical History*. London: Thames and Hudson, 1992. Print.

Frank, Ellen Eve. *Literary Architecture*. Los Angeles: University of California Press, 1979. Print.

Gallegos, Rómulo. *Dona Barbara*. Ediciones del Ministerio de Educación, Dirección de Cultura y Bellas Artes, Departmento de Publicaciones, 1964. Print.
González, Eduardo. 1986. "Framing Carpentier." *MLN*. (101): pp. 424–429. Print.
González Echeverría, Roberto. *Myth and Archive: A Theory of Latin American Narrative*. Durham: Duke University Press, 1998. Print.
Greenberg, C (1939). Avant-Garde and Kitsch. *Partisan Review* 6 (5): pp. 34–49. Print.
Habermas, Jürgen. "Modernity—an Incomplete Project." Hal Foster, ed. *The Anti-Aesthetic Essays on Postmodern Culture*. Seattle: Bay Press, 1995. Print.
Haddad, Elie. "Charles Jencks and the Historiography of Post-Modernism." *The Journal of Architecture*, 14: 4, pp. 493–510, DOI: 10.1080/13602360902867434. 2009. Print.
Harland, Richard. *Superstructuralism : The Philosophy of Structuralism and Post-Structuralism*. Routledge, 2003. Print.
Harney, Lucy D. *Los pasos perdidos* as Lost World Fiction. *Filología y Lingüística* 38 (1): pp. 47–62, 2012. Print.
Helmuth, Chalene. *The Postmodern Fuentes*. Bucknell University Press, 1997. Print.
Huxtable, Ada Louise. *The Unreal America: Architecture and Illusion*. New York: New Press, 1997, p. 181. Print.
Knapp, Bettina L. *Archetype, Architecture, and the Writer*. Bloomington: Indiana University Press, 1979. Print.
Krauss, Rosalind. "Sculpture in the Expanded Field." Hal Foster, ed. *The Anti-Aesthetic Essays on Postmodern Culture*. Seattle: Bay Press, 1995. Print.
Latin American Art and Architecture | Scholastic ART | Scholastic.com Web.
Latin American Art and Architecture from *The New Book of Knowledge®*
Leach, Neil, ed. *Rethinking Architecture*. New York: Routledge, 1997. Print.
Menton. Seymour. "Carlos Fuentes y Yo." *Mexican Studies/Estudios Mexicanos*, vol. 28, no. 2, 2012, pp. 225–241. *JSTOR*, www.jstor.org/stable/10.1525/msem.2012.28.2.225 Web.
New Princeton Encyclopedia of Poetry and Poetics. Ed. Alex Preminger and TV. F. Brogan. New York: Princeton Univ. Press, 1993. Print.
Tzonis, Alexander, et al. eds. *Tropical Architecture: Critical Regionalism in the Age of Globalization*. West Sussex: Wiley Academy, 2001. Print.
Vargas Llosa, Mario. *Historia de un deicidio*. Barcelona: Barral, 1971, pp. 528–538é. Print.
Vélez Catrain, Antonio. "Futuro, nostalgia y utopía en la arquitectura contemporánea." *Revista de occidente*. March 1970, no. 42. Print.
Wyers, Frances. "*Carpentier's Los pasos perdidos*: Heart of Lightness, Heart of Darkness." *Revista Hispánica Moderna*, vol. 45, no. 1, 1992, pp. 84–95. Print.

PART II

Social, Artistic, Religious & Political Crossroads

CHAPTER
5

Representation of the Absent Object: Pictorial Mysticism in El Greco and Pablo Picasso

Enrique Mallen

Mysticism

Mysticism commonly refers to a kind of altered state of consciousness (or ecstasy) which is given spiritual meaning. Through it, mystics often have access to a deeper truth, which they then attempt to reveal to others primarily through their writings. As a result of their strained efforts, the heightened consciousness attained by mystics is usually accompanied by an enhanced rhetorical expression. It is a recognized fact that, in their determination to communicate this deeper truth, Spanish mystics such as Santa Teresa de Ávila (1515–1582) and San Juan de la Cruz (1542–1591) strongly influenced the development of the Spanish language, ushering in what is commonly referred to as the Spanish Golden Age.

Many authors have claimed that the artist Doménikos Theotokópoulos (El Greco) (1541–1614) should be grouped among these Gold Age mystics, having also had deeper intuitions of a hidden truth, and having used comparable rhetorical methods as the two spiritual writers had, although applying them to visual language instead. I will focus primarily on two rhetorical techniques: (1) exaggerated gestures and deformation in the depiction of the human body and (2) the distribution of figures in specific compositional arrangements with respect to the viewer. I extend the classification of mystic artist to the Spaniard, Pablo Ruíz Picasso (1881–1973), basing it particularly on his work of the Blue, Rose and proto-Cubist periods, when he was, incidentally, also deeply influenced by the Greek master.

Other critics have already acknowledged this, although it has never been fully explored. As his biographer John Richardson states, "Picasso's roots in Spanish art and literature, mysticism and religion, go far deeper than anyone thought."[1]

Doménikos Theotokópoulos (El Greco)

El Greco produced his most characteristic paintings in Spain from 1578 until his death. While his roots were in Greek Orthodoxy, he cannot be characterized solely as a religious painter, since his *oeuvre* is varied and includes many secular themes as well. Although proof cannot be offered that El Greco read the writings of any specific philosopher, he was nevertheless an educated man, a true intellectual in possession of an extensive library, who would have certainly been aware of contemporary ideas in other parts of Europe, even in the relative isolation of sixteenth-century Spain.

As analyzed by Michael Baxandall, the work of Italian Renaissance artists was constrained by current ideas on the qualities of rule, order and measure that regulated ways of seeing the world, as witnessed by the culturally-relative "period eye" of the fifteenth century. These, of course, changed with the time and by the beginning of the next century, great artists like Leonardo da Vinci (1452–1519), Michelangelo Buonarroti (1475–1564) and Raphael Sanzio (1483–1520) were adding to those four qualities the intuitive and correcting judgement of the individual's eye, to create a *terza maniera*. This additional quality of visual judgement in naturalistic representation, not strictly based on mathematical principles, relieved the period of the "dryness" caused by the previous strict adherence to imposed regulations (derived from Vitruvius), especially with regard to the geometric construct of perspective, liberating artists of the former constraining rationalization of sight. It was during the development of such creative freedom in the arts that Mannerism flourished.

Jonathan Goldberg argues that the image represented in Mannerist art in the sixteenth century reflected Neoplatonic epistemological precepts in that the world it offered to viewers projected the activity of the mind and demanded a similar action as part of the viewing process. If Pietro Aretino (1492–1556) suggested in his *Lettere sull'arte* (published posthumously in 1557) that representation based on visual reality could be so strong as to be mistaken for reality, the Neoplatonic Marsilio Ficino (1433–1499) had argued that abstraction from matter (as in transcendental art) could be even stronger, since it reflected the activity of an intuitively-transformed reality. In transcendental paintings, illusion cannot be mistaken for reality itself, since reality is so imaginatively transformed into pictorial fact that it does not directly refer back to the world of nature, but rather evokes that of a Platonic higher order of subject and form, combined in an artistic alternative reality.

As David Davies demonstrates, El Greco fell under the influence of Renaissance Neoplatonism during his stay in Rome. In the Italian capital, he had been a member of the *Academia di San Luca* founded by Federico Zuccaro (1542–1609), president of this painter's guild at the time. Hence, he was most likely exposed to the latter's theories on art, especially his reinterpretation of the meaning of *disegno*. The Italian believed that the term originated from the phrase *segno di Dio in noi*, indicating that those skilled in drawing were divinely inspired. While in Spain, El Greco would continue to develop those Neoplatonic ideas he had absorbed during his Roman sojourn.

Even in his lifetime, his Spanish contemporaries looked upon El Greco as a philosophical artist who sought earnestly to find the inner meaning of life. In Toledo, the presence of both earthly splendor and ambition coexisting with mystical yearning offered him the ideal setting to resolve the tension created by these two tendencies.[2] In Spain, El Greco achieved a manner of painting in which physical reality was rendered only schematically or omitted completely, while the elongated figures in his compositions deviated greatly from anatomical correctness. The understanding of reality changed from what can be perceived in the physical world to what could be experienced in the mind and the spirit. Near the end of the sixteenth century, the painter turned his art into a mental construct through which to express his most obscure mystic experiences.

El Greco and Mysticism

As Shields notes, the juxtaposition of the paintings of El Greco with the writings of the mystics, San Juan de la Cruz and Santa Teresa, can help us gain a new perspective on the artist's works. His paintings seem to give visible expression to their written doctrine, while much that is implicit in his pictorial representations was made articulate in the writers' creed. However, El Greco's art is no a mere reflection of the Carmelite teaching but rather provides a new interpretive expression to that doctrine. As in the contemporary mystics, the soul in the Greek painter undergoes purification through the employment of successive stages of self-denudation, both active and passive until cleansed of any physical burden and emptied of self; it is drawn up in flame-like longing to participate in the intimacies of divine union.

In general terms, El Greco was influenced by the Plotinian dogma, which also predisposed the religious expression of various Renaissance artists. This doctrine asserts that human beings will truly find themselves when they are united with the Divine Mind and it is by means of ecstasy, that profound transfiguration of consciousness, that the spirit will achieve union with the One. As a projection of El Greco's own mystic self-discovery, his creatures are purified, delivered of their weight, filled with breath of divine omnipotence and drawn out of shape by an attraction they cannot resist. The elongation and attenuation we observe in these figures are expressions of a similar tension between the physical and the spiritual that we observe in mystic writers. Even before they leave the earthly domain they inhabit, they seem to have surrendered to a higher power, their bodies bathed in a kind of celestial light, their flesh spiritualized. The emaciated heads, their drawn and twisted limbs move irresistibly towards the magnet of the all-high force. In their dematerialized lightness and translucence, they seem to participate in life everlasting.[3]

Mystical discourse

Mysticism is commonly understood as becoming one with God or the Absolute, but may more generally also denote any kind of ecstasy or altered state of consciousness, which is given a spiritual significance, separate from any necessary religious connotation. In this wider reading, it may refer to the attainment of insight in an ultimate or hidden truth and to a mental transformation supported by various practices and experiences. In either interpretation, language plays a crucial, determining role.

Research into mystical mental states have relied primarily on retrospective self-accounts of these heightened perceptions. Readers of such reports often assume a direct correspondence between their narrative and the content of the experience. But, in fact, even those undergoing these states often express dissatisfaction with the capacity of language to convey the true nature of what they feel and the language they do choose to communicate it is typically vague and ambiguous.

According to Peter J. Adams, such vagueness is not an accidental feature of mystical discourse. Because of difficulties in direct expression, mystical authors rely on the active and imaginative participation of the listener/reader to complete the expression by filling intentional provocative "gaps." A gap is an open receptacle in linguistic space, providing a site within an utterance upon which receptive readers/viewers can insert content from their own experience. Gaps can be created by blatant omissions of content but are more likely to occur in subsidiary form by exploiting existing subtleties in grammar and meaning. This missing element is what I refer to as the "absent object."

Rhetoric and Mysticism

Grace Veach suggests that while language appears on the surface to be ill-suited to communicate mystic experiences, there are certain proclivities in language that actually provide the tools that ultimately qualify it as an ideal medium for mystic content. In particular, she proposes that we should explore the interconnection between the obscure expressions typical of mysticism and the language of rhetoric. In fact, according to the author, when Gregory Ulmer introduced divinization in his book, *Electronic Monuments*, he also reintroduced the idea of rhetoric as a link to that unknown and inexpressible "absent object" that mystics are usually at pains to communicate.

At the foundation of Ulmer's approach is the work of Kenneth Burke, as well as that of Ernesto Grassi. It is actually the combined work of these three theorists that laid out the possibility of creating a space in rhetoric where the mystical and the divinatory could be integrated. In their formulation, rhetoric can provide a link to the unknown precisely because it contains certain features that dwell outside of the *logos*. These features are what Ulmer groups under the term "*Chora*." More concretely, Ulmer and Burke both posit a domain of rhetoric that connects a logical, reasoned level of interactions (which they label "the city") with what they call "the abyss" (i.e., the realm into which the human can peer but not venture). In this intermediary space or *Chora*, reason mingles with mystery; events, images and encounters are random rather than causal, and it is up to the symbol-using human mind to make sense of such obscurity and unpredictability.

Hawhee attributes Burke's concept of the *Chora* to his embrace of the mystic P. D. Ouspensky's association of art and divination. According to the latter, "the artist must be a clairvoyant; he must see that which others do not see; he must be a magician; must possess the power to make others see that which they do not themselves see, but which he does see."[4] Although Ouspensky generalizes here about the artist, his description could as easily portray the mystics, who see and then seek to share their vision.

According to Ulmer, Plato had already used *Chora* "as a third metaphysical entity, namely as the space or region in which being and becoming interacted."[5] Ulmer's choice of the word *Chora* as the site of the mystical work of rhetoric intentionally places it outside the site of rhetorical invention (*"Topos"*), which emphasizes argumentation and logic. As opposed to *Topoi*, where the rhetorician purposefully seeks answers, the *Chora* is a domain of potentiality, where answers to a querent's dilemma may arise merely by chance. Thus, *Chora* names a place of action, of assigning potential meaning to a seemingly random occurrence. This is indicative of the importance of the performative in the rhetoric of mysticism. *Chora* gathers singular ephemeral sets of heterogeneous items based on associations of accidental details and establishes random metaphorical combinations among them.[6]

Burke identifies oxymoron as one of the characteristic rhetorical figures used in mystical narratives.[7] The space opened in the oxymoron's juxtaposition of heterogeneous and often contradictory elements is nothing else than the *Chora* being employed in discourse to extend meaning, i.e. to identify the "absent object" beyond the effable. The *Chora* involves an interaction with the abyss, what Jacques Lacan calls "the Real," to bring the absent object, the unknowable and ineffable, to the borders of the known, where, as Burke famously writes, humans "build their cultures by huddling together, nervously loquacious, at the edge of an abyss."[8]

Between the Symbolic and the Real

Lacan defines the Real as one of the three major structures that constitute the human psyche, roughly correlating with the three main stages of psychosexual development. The Real marks the state of nature in which there is nothing but "need" and from which humans are forever severed by the entrance into language. The Real continues, nonetheless, to exert its influence even after language starts to play a role since it is the rock against which linguistic structures must constantly prove themselves.

In contrast with the Real, a second order, the "Imaginary," identifies the movement of the subject from primal "need" to what Lacan terms "demand." Whereas "needs" can be fulfilled, "demands" are, by definition, unsatisfiable, the sort of lack that, for the psychologist, defines the human ego. Once the mind becomes aware of itself as an entity separate from its surroundings, it suffers anxiety caused by its lost integration, for which it tries to compensate by identifying with that external otherness.

While the Imaginary is all about equations and identifications, a third order, the "Symbolic," is directly linked with language and narrative. The acceptance of the rule of language is aligned with the Oedipus complex. Whereas the Real deals with "need" and the Imaginary concerns "demands," the Symbolic is all about "desire." As humans enter into language, their desire is forever afterwards bound up with the play of language. Nevertheless, the Real and the Imaginary would still continue to play a part in the evolution of human desire within the Symbolic order. The fact that fantasies always fail before the Real, for example, ensures that humans continue to desire; desire in the symbolic order could, in fact, be said to be the psyche's way of avoiding coming into full contact with the Real, so that desire is ultimately most interested not in obtaining the object of desire but rather in reproducing itself.

As stated earlier, in order to accommodate for the language of mysticism, authors like Ulmer have proposed an intermediary level known as *Chora*, located between the expressible (the Symbolic) and the inexpressible (the Real), and which cannot be equated with Lacan's Imaginary either. The *Chora* is the home of the sacred, as well as the metaphorical, the random, and many other communicative acts that employ indirectness rather than straight talk. "In the sacred place, human existence meets the figure of destiny fixed by the caprice of chance," in Bataille's words.[9] Ulmer's association of the rhetorical *Chora* with chance, mysticism, emblem, music and dance links its meaning with that type of suggestion which-is-not-quite-meaning, placed somehow both inside and outside of language.

If the abyss of the unknowable represents that space where foundations fail, the *Chora* stands for the expansive space between the expressible (the city) and the unspeakable (the abyss), a supplementary intermediary level between Lacan's Symbolic (language) and the Real (non-language). It is the *Chora* that rhetorical artists like El Greco resort to.

El Greco and Pictorial Rhetoric

The two assumptions that are central to the powerful claims made during the fifteenth and sixteenth centuries for the status of painting as rhetoric are (1) that the painter may be considered an "author" possessing "*ingenium*" and (2) that pictorial composition are structured analogously to literary works. With these two premises in mind, the viewer's involvement in the perception of pictorial representation was attained by applying the methods of rhetoric in visual compositions, relying primarily on (1) gestural expression and deformation in the depiction of the human figure, as well as, (2) the unexpected distribution of back-turned figures on the canvas.

With respect to the first, gesture, in painting as in oratory, was intended to provoke an emphatic response from the observer. The human "aspirants," whom El Greco portrays in ecstasy, lose themselves in mystical experience, as though merging with a divine vision. In his later representations, the functional or descriptive movement of the elongated raised hand, whether of an angelical or a human figure, conveys a super-ordinate symbolic meaning, the gesture becoming "the enthusiastic acknowledgement of divine revelation."[10] Viewers were expected to follow these gestures as links to a higher domain but tracking the gestures was precisely what put them in contact with an "absent object." And by doing so, they managed to enter a similar mystical experience. As for the second, the compositional artifice of depicting back-turned figures, it was used by El Greco to enhance the aesthetic experience, which the work strove to achieve. Ultimately, artifice served to stimulate the spectator's imagination induced by the absent object (the nonvisible frontal features), enabling him or her to approach the transcendental, and hence, to grasp higher truths. In both instances, figural deformations and oddly-positioned characters, it was the expressed interconnections of semantically unrelated elements in the composition, the *Chora* in Ulmer's terminology, which was at the core of El Greco's mysticism.

Pablo Picasso and El Greco

Many modern artists, among them Pablo Ruíz Picasso, have acknowledged that El Greco changed the communicative function of painting from commenting on reality to constituting a reality. Formally, the Greek master's late paintings were mental constructs, representing only a schematic version of reality. While he learned his craft by copying works by Italian Renaissance masters, no artist would be able to learn to draw in a traditional naturalistic way by copying his later paintings. On the other hand, young twentieth-century artists, in a quest for a new approach to art, could find in El Greco's unprecedented manner of figural expression, a source of inspiration for an extreme degree of anti-naturalism and compositional abstraction.

Richardson dates Picasso's passion for El Greco back to 1897, his sixteenth year, when he had gone to study at the *Real Academia de San Fernando* in Madrid:

Picasso produced very little work during his nine months in Madrid, but he painted at least one copy of El Greco: a portrait . . . The fact that El Greco was still perceived by most of the art establishment in Spain as a freak or madman only increased young Pablo's enthusiasm for the artist. In this spirit, he went to Toledo to copy the *Burial of the Count Orgaz*[11] but contempt for his teachers prevailed over admiration for the master. After first identifying the old master with his father, Picasso evidently came to identify El Greco with himself. No wonder his work of 1899 . . . includes so many pastiches of El Greco's portraits.[12]

Proof of Richardson's explanation is a burial scene of his friend, Carles Casagemas, by the youthful Picasso in which he emulated El Greco's painting with its fabulous funereal symphony, its serene clarity arranged on a bright, sad palette of blacks, whites, and gold: *Evocation (L'enterrement de Carles Casagemas).*[13]

Picasso's canvas, currently at the *Musée d'Art Moderne de la Ville de Paris*, is divided into two parts—earth and heaven. Paradise is populated with earthly, weeping figures in long dark cloaks with large, heavy legs that surround the body of Casagemas. One of them is helping the deceased mount a white horse. The other dominant motif is that of maternity, which is represented by a woman preceded by two little angels, symbols of life and renewal. The influence of El Greco is not limited to the clear two-tier organization of the canvas. It is also manifest in the expressionistic manner in which the work is painted with blue-green tones applied in rough strokes, emphasized by areas of white and cream thick impasto.

Picasso returned to El Greco in another canvas painted in Barcelona in 1903, *Le vieux guitariste aveugle*,[14] at *The Art Institute of Chicago*. The image flattens and the figure is distorted and elongated for emotional expression. Picasso wrenches the player's shoulder blade almost out of its socket so we feel the pain, using the body as a metaphor for an out-of-body, spiritual or metaphysical experience. The distorted style is again reminiscent of the drama found in the Greek master's religious painting, particularly his elongated, spiritual figures, although the melancholy and pathos of Picasso's work specifically continued to reflect his sadness at the suicide of his young friend, Casagemas.

As described by O'Brian,

> the body of the guitarist's tall, gaunt figure is cramped into the rectangle of the frame and whose raised left hand, stopping the strings at the top of the diagonal formed by foot, knee, the guitar, and the

guitar's long neck, suddenly arrests the line with four pale transversal bars across the darkness, forming a point of tension that counterbalances the sharply-bowed blind head.[15]

The painful distortions of the body make the viewer respond empathetically. Draped in blue rags, the emaciated old guitarist sits cross-legged, strumming his guitar in a desolate setting. Like the blind prophet, Tiresias, in the Greek tragedies, he has seen all and knows the tragic destination of human strivings: the loneliness of death. Picasso here plays on the theme of the blind mystic, hinting at the special insight that comes only from closing one's eyes. The mood is one of mystery. Everything points inward instead of outward, an allegory of the human soul in search of the unknowable rather than of clear answers.

The predominantly blue palette is not descriptive, intended instead to merely set the mood. As an otherworldly color, blue retreats with a haunting, enigmatic sense of mystery that is unfathomable, an image of inner-vision, pointing toward psychological depths rather than surface appearances. No longer interested in deep perspective, depth is denoted by mood more than by space. Inspiration for this work might have come from El Greco's *The Trinity*[16] at the *Museo del Prado* in Madrid. God the Father, with an Eastern Miter on his head, holds the body of Christ in his lap. The dove of the Holy Spirit appears over his head, while six young angels surround the scene. Several cherubs heads appear at Jesus feet and under God's robes. The zigzagging legs of the crucified figure clearly echo the rhetorical arrangement of the guitar player's legs.

Two years later, Picasso executed his masterpiece at the *National Gallery of Art*, Washington, D.C., *La famille de saltimbanques (Les bateleurs)*,[17] which describes a troupe of *saltimbanques*/acrobats as a metaphor for the rootlessness of the modern artist no longer under the patronage of a powerful patron and modernity as a state of alienation. That empty space registers an absence that continues the themes of the Blue Period: loss, longing, loneliness and alienation in the void. The unity of the composition lies in the emotional content more than in the legible details. The over-all sense of restraint is accentuated by the fact that the two figures closest to the viewer are seen from the back. The colors, which range from terracotta pink and ocher to gray and bright blue, typical of the Rose Period, suggest the same inhibition, their effects subdued and reduced to a discreet, unobtrusive harmony. The drawing and the tonality endow this painting with a quiet, oddly-elegiac charm. A certain tenderness is clearly conveyed, precisely because the colors are tempered by the subtle linear arrangements, so very different from the harsh, thicker outlines of the preceding period.

The positioning and enclosing framework of the figures bring to mind El Greco's painting, *The Martyrdom of Saint Maurice*,[18] in the *Monasterio de San Lorenzo, El Escorial*. As an allegory of the Holy League, the subject expresses conviction of faith, the militant spirit of the crusades itself. The physical side of the martyrdom is not emphasized, but rather merely alluded to by the small group on the left comprised of the one martyred figure, the character (in the pose of his Christ of the Baptism) awaiting martyrdom and the large back-view of an executioner. The latter echoes the equally back-turned figure to its right wearing a blue Roman armor. Both characters help bring the viewers into the depicted scene, only to be confronted by the smaller soldier in the center of the composition. This male figure is particularly relevant, because his body is defined externally by the outlines of the characters that surround him. The impression of the ranks of the Saint's army adopts a rhetorical configuration that we find in the crowds of some of his Adoration paintings, declaring in both instances the devotional fervor of the participants, as well as that of the artist and the viewers themselves.

The following year, Picasso painted *Composition: Les paysans*[19] in *The Barnes Foundation*. The expressive distortion of anatomy and the swirling dynamic composition shows a new interest in the tumultuous ebb and flow of form and space. As Gray indicates, "it was not yet form for form's sake, not yet form as a return to a more concrete realism that interested Picasso; it was rather form used to heighten expression."[20] The work shows a clear correlation with El Greco's *St Joseph and the Christ Child*[21] in the *Museo de Santa Cruz* in Toledo. The saint is shown as a figure of trust and protection to the child, who indicates the way. The colors and rhythms of the tower-like figure of Saint Joseph express perfectly the meaning of the painting. There is no Mannerist ambiguity at this point in El Greco's life in the relationship of figure to setting.

At the midpoint of his career in 1907, Picasso once again turned to his Greek predecessor for inspiration on his revolutionary masterpiece in the permanent collection of *The Museum of Modern Art* in New York, *Les demoiselles d'Avignon*.[22] The affinities between *The opening of the Fifth Seal of the Apocalypse*[23] in the nearby *Metropolitan Museum of Art* and Picasso's canvas are so striking, not only in the multiplicity of visual levels, but also in its spiritual and psychological content, that it is hard not to believe that the artist had begun its actual execution under its direct stimulus.[24] Picasso had known and consulted El Greco's work for some time in the past and he had almost certainly often seen this particular work, which belonged to the Spanish painter, Ignacio Zuloaga (1870–1945), then resident in Paris. Richardson even suggests that compositional artifice in El Greco may be considered the true father of Picasso's full-fledged Cubism from 1908 onwards.[25]

In the foreground of El Greco's work, we find the incredibly elongated, ecstatic figure of Saint John, his head turned towards heaven, his arms raised imploringly. Behind him are two groups of figures. The three on the right, seen against a green drapery, are male and reach upwards for white garments distributed by a flying cherub. The four on the left are shown in front of a dark-yellow cloth. Two are male, two female, and they seem to be covering (or uncovering) themselves with the yellow drapery. It was Cossio who, in 1908, first proposed that these features suggested a visualization of the Book of Revelation, when Saint John the Evangelist witnesses the breaking of the Fifth Seal by the Lamb of God:

> When he opened the fifth seal, I saw under the altar the souls of those who had been slain because of the word of God and the testimony they had maintained. They called out in a loud voice, 'How long, Sovereign Lord, holy and true, until you judge the inhabitants of the earth and avenge our blood?' Then each of them was given a white robe, and they were told to wait a little longer, until the full number of their fellow servants, their brothers and sisters, were killed, just as they had been. (Rev. 6: 9–11)

The towering figure in the foreground shifts the emphasis from an illustration of an incident to Saint John and his mystic vision.

The structure that Picasso builds into the composition is primarily based on triangular forms, which the arms of the central figures already emphasize, and is further accentuated by the shape of the table in the foreground of the painting. The numerous open-bottom triangles are evenly distributed around the vertical axis, the two top ones (the raised arms of the central figure) splitting equally and the bottom one (the table) having its apex coincide exactly with the vertical axis. They are countered by a series of inverted (v-shaped) triangles. The result is an overall emphasis on the diagonal axes, which increase the dynamic force of the figures in response to their potentially static tripartite distribution about the vertical axis. The diagonal lines indicate the direction of penetration into the scene represented on the canvas (from the pushing aside of the curtain in the foreground to the opening of the one in the background). They also bring forth the relevance of the seated woman in the dynamics of the painting. The importance of this figure is clear when we observe its relation with the others. It shares frontality in its gaze with the two central women and simultaneously adopts the profile pose as the two entering figures.[26]

In Picasso's canvas, as in many of El Greco's paintings, we witness the visual experience of two different beholders: (1) the virtual back-turned personality in the painting and (2) the beholder in real space. The back-turned figure serves as an internal beholder, a nodal figure in the composition, who experiences a mystical vision as the main theme presented in the painting, while the beholder in real space perceives the back-turned figure, his vision and the total composition. Picasso adds to this effect the use of the inward-oriented diagonal. Thus, these back-turned figures serve to lead the viewer into the composition, as the narrator would in a novel. Kendall Walton has explored the question whether there is ever anything comparable to narrators in depictive representation and explains: "When we look at a picture, it does not seem that there is a (fictional) personality mediating our access to the fictional world, not that we are presented with someone's conception of it; we 'see for ourselves' what goes on in the picture-world."[27] However, as he postulates, there might be an "apparent artist" who serves some of the functions of a narrator. That is, "in certain special cases there are in depictions fictional characters which are closely analogous to narrators."[28]

But more importantly, back-turned figures (due to the failure of facial recognition) share something in common with figure deformation: both introduce an absence of figuration as the figure subserves the background in both cases. In other words, neither the figure's deformations or gestures nor the odd distribution of those figures is conditioned by features inherent in the figures themselves, their only purpose is to bring attention to the very act of viewing. The viewer searches for any possible figuration in the scene depicted (the absent object) only to find that the composition itself is the content of the representation. In more abstract terms, we would say that both (1) deformations/gestures and (2) back-turned figures function as a "displacement into the pictorial [which] signifies for the beholder ... one step closer to the heavenly," to quote Schwartz.[29] Through these rhetorical mechanisms, viewers are brought into contact with the "absent object," sharing in the mystical ecstasy experienced by both artists.

Notes

1 Richardson 1987, 40.
2 Shields 1952, 313–314.

3 Shields 1952, 315.
4 Hawhee 2009, 37.
5 Ulmer 2005, 6.
6 Ulmer 2005, 120.
7 Burke 1950, 331.
8 Burke 1935, 272.
9 Ulmer 2005, 125.
10 Wittkower 1977, 53.
11 Doménikos Theotokópoulos (El Greco). *The Burial of the Count of Orgaz*. 1586–1588. Oil on canvas. 480 x 360 cm. Santo Tomé, Toledo.
12 Richardson 1987, 42.
13 Pablo Ruiz Picasso. *Evocation (L'enterrement de Carles Casagemas)*. Paris, September–October/1901. Oil on canvas. 150 x 90 cm. Musée d'Art Moderne de la Ville de Paris. (Inv AMVP 1133). OPP.01:046
14 Pablo Ruiz Picasso. *Le vieux guitariste aveugle*. Barcelona, Fall/1903. Oil on panel. 122,9 x 82,6 cm. The Art Institute of Chicago. (Inv 1926.253). OPP.03:022
15 O'Brian 1994, 117.
16 Doménikos Theotokópoulos (El Greco). *The Trinity*. 1577. Oil on canvas. 300 x 179 cm. Museo del Prado, Madrid.
17 Pablo Ruiz Picasso. *La famille de saltimbanques (Les bateleurs)*. Paris, [Fall]/1905. Oil on canvas. 212,8 x 229,6 cm. National Gallery of Art, Washington, DC. (Inv 1963.10.190). OPP.05:002
18 Doménikos Theotokópoulos (El Greco). *The Martyrdom of Saint Maurice*. 1580–1581. Oil on canvas. 448 x 301 cm. Chapter House, Monasterio de San Lorenzo, El Escorial.
19 Pablo Ruiz Picasso. *Composition: Les paysans*. Gósol–Paris, Late-August/1906. Oil on canvas. 221 x 131,4 cm. The Barnes Foundation, Merion, PA. (Inv BF.140). OPP.06:014
20 Gray 1953, 21–40.
21 Doménikos Theotokópoulos (El Greco). *Saint Joseph and the Christ Child*. 1600. Oil on canvas. 109 x 56 cm. Museo de Santa Cruz, Toledo.
22 Pablo Ruiz Picasso. *Les demoiselles d'Avignon*. Paris, June–July/1907. Oil on canvas. 243,9 x 233,7 cm. The Museum of Modern Art, NYC. (Inv 333.1939). OPP.07:001
23 Doménikos Theotokópoulos (El Greco). *The opening of the Fifth Seal of the Apocalypse*. 1608–1614. Oil on canvas. 224,5 x 192,8 cm. The Metropolitan Museum of Art, NYC.
24 Golding 2001, 19–20.
25 Richardson 1987, 46.
26 Mallen 2003, 8.
27 Walton 1976, 50.
28 Walton 1976, 61.
29 Schwartz 1995, 234.

Bibliography

Adams, Peter James. *A Rhetoric of Mysticism*. PhD Thesis – University of Auckland, 1991. Print.
Aretino, Pietro. *Lettere sull'arte*. Ed. by F. Pertile and E. Camesasca. Milan: Edizione del Milione, 1557. Print.
Baxandall, Michael. *Painting and Experience in Fifteenth-Century Italy*. London, Oxford, New York: Oxford University Press, 1972. Print.
Bowie, Malcolm. *Lacan*. Cambridge, MA: Harvard University Press, 1991. Print.
Burke, Kenneth. *Permanence and Change: An Anatomy of Purpose*. New York: New Republic, 1935. Print.
——. *A Grammar of Motives*. Berkeley: University of California Press, 1945. Print.
——. *A Rhetoric of Motives*. Berkeley: University of California Press, 1950. Print.
Davies, David. "The influence of Christian Neoplatonism on the Art of El Greco". *El Greco of Crete: Exhibition on the Occasion of the 450th Anniversary of his Birth*, 21–55. Nicos Hadjinicolaou, ed. Iraklion: Municipality of Iraklion, 1990. Print.
Evans, Dylan. *An Introductory Dictionary of Lacanian Psychoanalysis*. New York: Routledge, 1996. Print.
Goldberg, Jonathan. "Quatrrocento Dematerialization: Some Paradoxes in a Conceptual Art". *Journal of Aesthetics and Art Criticism* 35 (2, Winter 1976), 153–168. Print.
Golding, John. "Les Demoiselles d'Avignon and the Exhibition of 1988." *Picasso's Les Demoiselles d'Avignon*, 15–30. Christopher Green, ed. Cambridge: University Press, 2001. Print.
Gray, Christopher. *Cubist Aesthetic Theories*. Baltimore: The Johns Hopkins Press, 1953. Print.
Hawhee, Debra. *Moving Bodies: Kenneth Burke at the Edges of Language*. Columbia: University of South Carolina Press, 2009. Print.
Laessoe, Rolf. "A Source in El Greco for Picasso's *Les Demoiselles d'Avignon*". *Gazette des Beaux-Arts* 110 (October 1982), 131–136. Print.
Mallén, Enrique. 2003. "A Minimalist Approach to Picasso's Visual Grammar: *Les demoiselles d'Avignon*." *Interdisciplinary Journal for Germanic Linguistics & Semiotic Analysis*. Vol. 8.1, 2003, 1–21. Print.
——. *Online Picasso Project*. http://picasso.shsu.edu. Sam Houston State University, 2018.
Maré, Estelle Alma. "The Being and Movement of the Angel in the Burial of the Count of Orgaz by El Greco." *South African Journal of Art History* 14, 1999, 41–47, 1999. Print.
——. "El Greco's Representation of Mystical Ecstasy." *Acta Theologica Supplementum* 11, 2008, 108–127. Print.
——. "Greco, A Mediator of Modern Painting." *South African Journal of Art History*. Vol. 25, No. 1, 2010, 133–153. Print.
——. "The Mystical Visions of El Greco's Back-turned Figures." *South African Journal of Art History*. Vol. 26, No. 3, 2011, 127–141. Print.

O'Brian, Patrick. *Pablo Picasso. A Biography*. New York: W.W. Norton & Company, 1994. Print.
Richardson, John. "Picasso's Apocalyptic Whorehouse," *The New York Review of Books* (23 April 1987), 40–47. Print.
Shields, Daniel. 1952. "Three Mystics: El Greco, St. John of the Cross, St. Teresa." *The Irish Monthly*, Vol. 80, No. 950 (August, September, October 1952), 311–315. Print.
Schmidt, Leigh Eric. "The Making of Modern 'Mysticism.'" *Journal of the American Academy of Religion,* June 2003, Vol. 71, No. 2, 273–302. Print.
Schwartz, Michael. 1995. "Beholding and its Displacement in Renaissance Painting". *Place and Displacement in the Renaissance. Medieval & Renaissance Texts & Studies 12*, 1995, 231–254. Alvin Vos, ed. New York: Centre for Medieval and Early Renaissance Studies, State University of New York at Binghamton, 1995. Print.
Ulmer, Gregory. *Electronic Monuments*. Minneapolis: University of Minnesota Press, 2005. Print.
Veach, Grace. "Divination and Mysticism as Rhetoric in the Choral Space." *The Journal of the Kenneth Burke Society*. Vol. 8, I. 1, Spring Special Issue 2012. Print.
Walton, Kendall L. "Points of View in Narrative and Descriptive Representation." *Noûs* 10 (March 1976), 49–61. Print.
Wittkower, Rudolf. "El Greco's Language of Gestures." *Art News* 56 (March 1957), 45–55. Print.
Zuccaro, Federico. *L'idea de'pittori, scultori et architetti*. Turin: Disserolio, 1607. Print.

CHAPTER

6

Transmogrifying Traditions: *el guadalupanismo*. The History of *Sociedades Guadalupanas* and Other Hispanic Organizations in Texas, Especially in Houston

DEBRA D. ANDRIST

This essay traces the demographics of Mexican American population growth over the last two centuries into the 21st century and highlights the development of two Hispanic, specifically Mexican-American/Chicano/[ethnically-limited Latino(x)], organizations. One concerns religious practice and the other addresses education in East Texas, specifically in Houston, during the 20th century, against some formidable odds, especially including the geography—and still-extant prejudice. The presence of Mexicans in general, as in indigenous peoples in the area which is today Texas, dates from time immemorial, and of those known as Mexican Hispanics/mestizos from shortly after the Conquest of the early 16th century. In fact, as political history documents, the area which is now the state of Texas was part of the country of Mexico until the Mexican Cession of 1848 when the Treaty of Guadalupe was signed.

In spite of the fact that Galveston, just a few dozen miles south of Houston, on the Gulf, was named for the Spanish officer, governor of Louisiana and later hero of the Revolutionary War due to thwarting the British, Bernardo Gálvez, East Texas and the city of Houston were not ever heavily-populated by Mexicans of either type until much later.

Guadalupanismo refers to a religious devotion to the cult of Our Lady of Guadalupe, the patron saint of Mexico.

Any U.S. map indicates why south and central Texas, being physically closer to Mexico, had much larger Mexican populations and immigration, just due to convenience of access.

Numerous historical sources tell us that around 1836, some Mexican prisoners of war did clear and drain swampland so the city now Houston could be settled by *anglos*[1] (the Allen Brothers specifically are credited with initial efforts to found the city). The map shows the city's geographic proximity to Louisiana and the topographical similarities between the areas; these are also factors in the low initial numbers of Mexicans. Yet, while some parcels of land were given to 100 of the prisoners, they, strangely enough according to history, then became household servants. So, throughout most of the 19th century, most Mexican immigrants traveled to the Río Grande Valley, El Paso, and San Antonio and did not go to East Texas cities like Houston.

Further, the *angelos* (non-Hispanic, English-speaking *whites*) in East Texas had a Deep South culture more akin to Louisiana and preferred sharecroppers who were African American and Anglo. Robert R. Treviño, author of *The Church in the Barrio: Mexican American Ethno-Catholicism in Houston*, points out that the Anglos "made it clear that Mexicans were not welcome." At various points between 1850 and 1880, six to eighteen Mexicans lived in Houston. Treviño recognizes that "Mexicans were almost invisible in Houston during most of the nineteenth century." Nestor Rodríguez, author of *Hispanic and Asian Immigration Waves in Houston*, wrote that the 1880 U.S. Census showed a "handful" of Mexicans in Houston.

However, Mexican migration into Houston increased with two factors, the expansion of the railroad system and the installation of Porfirio Díaz as the President of Mexico. Mexicans dissatisfied with Díaz used the railroads to travel to Texas. In the late 1800s and early 1900s, Mexican Americans and immigrants from Mexico began to stay in Houston permanently. Many worked in unskilled labor and as food vendors. About 500 people of Mexican origin lived in Houston by the year 1900. In 1907, a *junta patriótica* (cultural committee) opened Mexican Independence Day festivities. In 1908, at least one Mexican American mutual aid society had formed. This increased to 2,000 by 1910 and Treviño notes that "the haphazard trickle had become a steady influx."

In the early 20th century, the population further increased due to several factors. The 1910 Mexican Revolution drove many Mexicans to Houston. Employers recruited Mexican Americans and made them into *enganchadores* (labor agents) so they could recruit more workers; the *enganchadores* recruited Tejanos and immigrants. In addition, many Mexican Americans in rural areas faced unemployment as commercial agriculture increased and they traveled to Houston since Houston's economy was increasing. The labor shortage during World War I encouraged Mexicans to work in Houston.

The immigration restrictions put in place in the 1920s did not affect Mexicans, so Mexicans continued to come to Houston. The increased work demands came from the building of the Houston Ship Channel and railroad construction in addition to the agricultural work in areas around Houston. Rodríguez wrote that "The labor-hungry Houston economy probably had as much influence" as the Mexican Revolution did." In 1920, Houston had 6,000 residents of Mexican origin. In 1930, about 15,000 residents were of Mexican origin. Originally, Mexicans settled the Second Ward.[2] Jesús Jesse Esparza of *Houston History* magazine said that the Second Ward "quickly became the unofficial hub of their cultural and social life." Magnolia Park began to attract Mexican immigrants in the 1920s. As time passed, Mexicans began moving to other neighborhoods, such as the First Ward, the Sixth Ward, the Northside (then a part of the Fifth Ward), and Magnolia Park. A group of about 100 Mexican families also settled the Houston Heights.

By 1930, Houston had about 15,000 Mexicans. This was almost twice as many as the 8,339 first and second-generation Eastern and Southern European immigrants in Houston. Treviño said that the Mexican American community "took root in a society that had been historically black and white but one that increasingly became tri-ethnic—black, white, *and* brown." He added, "In a city that considered them nonwhite, Mexicans stood out even though their numbers were smaller than those in such places as San Antonio and Los Angeles."

José F. Aranda, Jr. of Rice University, who reviewed the book, *The Church in the Barrio: Mexican American Ethno-Catholicism in Houston*, wrote that, historically, Mexican immigrants "found the racial landscape particularly unwelcoming" because Houston was not in proximity to the, at the time, larger Mexican American communities in Texas.

Scholars of Mexican-American studies say that, in regards to Houston's Mexican-American population, the "immigrant era" ended in the 1930s. As the Great Depression affected Houston, City of Houston officials accused Mexican Americans of being economically harmful and launched raids into their communities. Local and federal interests, which included American-born ethnic Mexicans, had feared that the Mexican population would try to escape the economic problems by attempting to obtain public relief, so they pressured

Mexican immigrants to leave Houston. Many Mexican-Americans did not receive federal benefits meant to alleviate the effects of the Great Depression. At that time, the immigration wave ended and about 2,000 Mexicans left Houston during the Depression era. Several Mexican-American organizations, such as the Our Lady of Guadalupe Church and the *Sociedad Mutualista Obrera Mexicana*, provided relief services to the community during that era.

However, in terms of religion, many Mexican immigrants to Houston came from areas where folk religion was common (think Day of the Dead),[3] with aspects of indigenous religions as well as Roman Catholic traditions; this conflicted with the practices of existing U.S. American Roman Catholicism. In 1910, there were no Mexican Catholic churches in Houston. Some Mexicans were excluded from attending Anglo Catholic churches. Mexicans who did attend found themselves discriminated against. In 1911, the Roman Catholic Diocese of Galveston brought the Oblates of Mary Immaculate, one order of a series of priests intended to minister to the Mexican population of Houston. In 1912, Our Lady of Guadalupe Catholic Church, the first Mexican Catholic church, opened. Due to an increase in demand in Catholic services, Oblates established missions in various Mexican-American neighborhoods. The Roman Catholic Church established Our Lady of Guadalupe so that *white* people accustomed to segregation of races did not find offense with the presence of Mexican people in their churches. The second Mexican Catholic church, Immaculate Heart of Mary Catholic Church, opened in the 1920s. It originated as an Oblate mission in Magnolia Park, on the second floor of the residence of Emilio Aranda. A permanent two-story building, funded by the community, opened in 1926.

About this time, *guadalupanismo* among Mexican Americans in Texas came to be ubiquitous, culminating to some degree in the early 20th Century *Sociedades Guadalupanas*. According to the Texas State Historical Association website,

> These organizations are religious associations organized by Mexican-American Catholic *women* [italics mine] to provide leadership in social concerns and perform works of charity. The organization's name derives from *Nuestra Señora de Guadalupe*, Patroness of the Americas. *Sociedades Guadalupanas* have helped to foster female development and leadership.

Though there are societies throughout the U.S., Houston, Texas was one of the most active sites for not only the *Guadalupanas* but

also for other religious, political and social organizations associated with Hispanic populations, women, men and mixed groups, which fostered cultural pride, among other benefits and advantages of organized activities. According to the *Guadalupana Papers*,
In terms of how these independent parish "chapters" come about,

> women may establish *sociedades* in a parish by gaining the approval of the priest of a parish, and they often recruit members on an informal basis. However, individuals may also join by approaching the group to ask for admission. Still others become members due to a familial devotion to *Nuestra Señora de Guadalupe*, including a tradition of familial involvement in a *sociedad* that has been passed from one generation to the next. Working-class and poor women have often made up the bulk of membership in *Sociedades Guadalupanas*; recently, however, younger and more educated members have joined. Despite the preponderance of women in the *sociedades*, a number of men, teenagers, a few Anglos, and entire families also belong. Indeed, a male parishioner, José Navarro, was the first president of the first known sociedad in San Antonio, which was started around 1912 by Fr. Juan Maizteguí, the first chaplain at Our Lady of Guadalupe Chapel, which later became Our Lady of Guadalupe Church.

Though no precise date for the founding of Guadalupe Societies in the state is known, the devotion of Mexicans to *Nuestra Señora de Guadalupe* dates to her reported apparition in Mexico in the sixteenth century. The cult (or devotion) of *guadalupanismo* soon arose in response to this event and likely evolved into the sociedades. In San Antonio, the *sociedades* were formed in direct response to the need to build a school for the parishioners at Our Lady of Guadalupe Chapel, which served the poor Mexicans of the archdiocese. As the groups developed, they focused more attention on both the secular and religious educational needs of the people by teaching their members English, reading, and writing and by providing religious education to children in the parish. The *guadalupanas* in San Antonio helped develop and maintain Hispanic membership in the Roman Catholic Church. Fr. Virgilio Elizondo, rector of San Fernando Cathedral, claimed, "Had it not been for the *guadalupanas*, Hispanics would not be Catholic today." In establishing a base for Mexican Americans in the Church, the women also learned and applied new leadership and organizational skills; many participated in the grassroots group Communities Organized for Public Service. In time, the *sociedades'* overwhelmingly large female membership evolved into a support system for Mexican-American women, who value gathering with other women to pray, to converse and to provide one another emotional support during illnesses or other difficulties. Many women also consider the growth in their own spirituality directly related to their participation in a *sociedad*. In particular, they believe that miracles are wrought in their lives by *Nuestra Señora de Guadalupe* as a result of their faith, which has been deepened through the affiliation.

Requirements for participation vary from one *sociedad* to another. In some cases, members must be at least sixteen years old. In addition, if they are married, they must have been married in the church; if they are single, they must have received the sacraments of initiation (baptism and confirmation). Other *sociedades* permit much younger individuals to enter, considering their devotion to the Virgin as the most important attribute for membership. Overall, *sociedades* accept women of good standing within the community. Entering a *sociedad* also entails attending a few preliminary meetings of the group and going through a formal ceremony performed by the priest during Mass. At one time, this ceremony, known as *recibiéndose* (being received into the *sociedad*), was an elaborate ritual during which specific prayers were recited.

The Roman Catholic Church has been an integral part of Texas history ever since the Europeans first set foot on the land. Over the three centuries leading up to 1821, during the Spanish-Texas period, Hispanic Roman Catholicism had religious and civil ownership that went nearly unchallenged among the European-origin settlers in what is now Texas. This allowed the Hispanic Roman Catholics to gain total control over Christianization efforts among the Native Americans. Events after Mexican independence in 1821 soon left Catholics in a minority status in the land. But even then, they always remained one of the largest single religious bodies in Texas, and Hispanics continued to be one of the largest ethnic groups among Texas Roman Catholics.

Renewed population growth in Texas after World War II resulted in a near doubling in the number of dioceses over the next 20 years. The diocese of Austin was just one of the newly created branches, established in 1947. The display of Catholic presidential candidate, John F. Kennedy, in front of the Ministerial Association of Protestant leaders in Houston in 1960 marked a threshold in Catholic prestige in the United States. The Kennedy assassination in Dallas in 1963 marked the onset of the decline of postwar American self-confidence. The complicated and dissenting times of the next 20 years in both the nation and the Catholic Church—sorting out civil rights, the Vietnam War, and the church's Vatican Council II—were indicated by the numerical leveling off or even decrease in the church's accustomed ministerial personnel.

Due to the considerable sociocultural and ministerial shifts, new backdrops of church life and outreach started to develop. Among the outreach efforts were las *Sociedades Guadalupanas*, which are organizations made up of mainly women that demonstrate leadership in social concerns and carry out acts of charity among the church and surrounding communities. Although the first *Sociedad en Texas* was created in 1912 by Fr. Juan Maiztegui in San Antonio, the *Sociedades* began to take off more rapidly after the societal and religious displacements. In San Antonio, the *sociedades* were formed in direct response to the need to build a school for the parishioners at Our Lady of Guadalupe Chapel, which served the poor Mexicans of the archdiocese. As the groups developed, they focused more attention on both the secular and religious educational needs of the people by teaching their members English, reading, and writing and by providing religious education to children in the parish. The *guadalupanas* in San Antonio have helped develop and maintain Hispanic membership in the Catholic Church. The name of the organization is derived from the Patroness of the Americas, *Nuestra Señora de Guadalupe*. *Sociedades Guadalupanas* have cultivated female advancement and leadership in the Catholic Church. *Sociedades* are established in a parish by authorization of the pastor and women frequently initiate members on an informal basis. Despite the dominance of women in the *Sociedades*, a small number of men, teenagers, a few Anglos and entire families also belong.

Just ten years after the Diocese of Austin was established, a woman named Nellie Pérez Téllez and her husband, Sipriano, petitioned for a church to be built near her home in the Govalle neighborhood of East Austin. In January of 1957, construction began for a church structure, a parish hall, a school building and a rectory on a three-acre site of land on the corner of Tillery Street and Lyons Road. The dedication mass that took place on November 24, 1957 marked the creation of a strong community bond, an alliance between the members of the church and the surrounding neighborhood that has been strengthened through the years and is still as strong as ever. This *guadalupana*, lauded by her peers, exemplifies what *guadalupanismo* and the *guadalupanas* mean to Texas:

> If there is one woman who epitomizes the role of a *guadalupana* it is Nellie. Since the founding of the church, Nellie and her family have been integrally involved in the establishment of several of the various organizations that are offered to members of the parish community at Sta. Julia's Church, Nellie served as president of the *Sociedad Guadalupana* (known at the time as Our Lady of Guadalupe Women's

society) for some time [iv]. Some of the activities the *Guadalupanas* partake in include visiting the sick, doing rosaries of the Virgen and giving back to the church and community in any way possible. Nellie did not only possess agency within her church community, but she had much influence in the political realm of her district as well.

Alongside other members of the Sta. Julia community, Nellie was involved in organizing a strike against Economy Furniture Co., the struggle to rid Boggy Creek of flooding, the formation and organization of Concerned Parents for Education, founding the first advisory board at Zaragosa Park, lobbying to get the Oak Springs Library built, establishing the Conley-Guerrero Senior Activity Center and more. Nellie has earned the reputation of a committed volunteer and community activist and has earned various awards including but not limited to the Outstanding Woman of the Year from the Mexican American Business and Professional Women's Association, a Lifetime Achievement Award from Conley-Guerrero Guild, Inc., and has even received recognition from U.S. Representative for Texas's 25th congressional district's Lloyd Doggett.

Not only has she set an example for her community and church comrades, but she has guided and raised a philanthropic and charitable family. Her husband, Sipriano, also has had a great impact on the Sta. Julia community through the Men's Club, which was key in the foundation and construction of the Parish community. Her oldest son, Arthur, was a leader in another church organization that sought to develop leadership, civic-conscious community pride, and parochial services for boys aged thirteen to eighteen, which was called the Columbian Squires. He had even been awarded Squire of the Year by the J. F. Kennedy Council 5505 Knights of Columbus [ix]. One of Nellie's other sons, Gilbert, was also an active member in a church organization called the Altar Boys Society [x]. All of these entities within the Sta. Julia church community have aided *tejanos* in their own uplifting and exhilaration and has given them power in operation in a land that they have been a part of from the beginning. As a *guadalupana*, as an active member of her church, her neighborhood, her community, as a mother and wife, and as an outstanding leader, Nellie Téllez is one *tejana* that is worthy of some long-due recognition and reverence. Nellie is only one person, but the contributions she has made along with many other *tejana/os* will no longer go unrecognized.

Today, although simplified, the event has retained elements that are common to all groups. For example, individuals publicly acknowledge their commitment to Our Lady of Guadalupe, and they are presented with the Guadalupe Medal, which is adorned with the image of the Virgin on the front and other religious emblems on the back. Later, the member also receives the *sociedad*'s official rose-colored *capa* (cape), which is used on special occasions. Once in the organization, a member is known as a *socia* (associate) and maintains her religious participation in a variety of ways. Attendance at regular monthly meetings, praying the Rosary, involvement in the *sociedad*'s monthly Holy Communion, and other acts of religious devotion are normal requirements. As part of their Rosary recitations, some *sociedades* acquire an image of *Nuestra Señora de Guadalupe*, known in this context as the *Virgen Peregrina* (Pilgrim Virgin), and set it up at a member's home for the gathering. After the event, the image is taken to another member's house for a similar religious ritual; her journey from one member's house to another's suggesting that her pilgrimage through the neighborhood lends protection to its residents. A special book of prayers accompanies the image for use in the Rosary. Many members also maintain home altars dedicated to *Nuestra Señora de Guadalupe*. For many members, participation in *Sociedades Guadalupanas* ends only at death. To acknowledge a deceased member's longtime devotion to the group, her *sociedad* attends a special Mass and recitation of the rosary, as well as the singing of hymns, for the repose of her soul.

Just as important as their spiritual practices are the society's works of charity, which further demonstrate the members' devotion to the Virgin, who represents all-encompassing love. *Guadalupanas* have set up diabetes-detection campaigns, volunteered at battered-women's shelters and nursing homes, ministered to prisoners, organized social activities for church youth, and served on parish councils. One of the most significant events that they sponsor is the annual celebration of the memorial of Our Lady of Guadalupe on December 12. In cities with a strong *Guadalupana* tradition such as San Antonio, this event, often referred to as *La Serenata a la Virgen Morena* (the Serenade to the Brown Virgin), is a major citywide celebration. Besides the traditional Mass in honor of Our Lady of Guadalupe, other Mexican-American cultural expressions-mariachi music and *matachines*[v], for instance-are also part of the commemoration.

Although *Sociedades Guadalupanas* can be found throughout the state, no statewide organization exists; however, the Federation of *Guadalupanas* was organized in the archdiocese of San Antonio in 1981 with the endorsement of Archbishop Patricio Flores to give Hispanic women in the archdiocese their own base. Previously, no similar organization that took in such a large geographic area existed for Hispanic Catholics in Texas. Since its founding, the federation has established guidelines for society activities in the region, and it has also carried out state-level activities that have benefited groups outside the area. The presidents of the region's *sociedades* make up the federation, with officers selected from among the members. Margaret Nieto, who headed the group at Our Lady of Guadalupe Church in Seguin, was the first federation president. The group held the first of its regular archdiocesan conferences in August 1981 and has since sponsored state conventions, at which more than 1,000 delegates representing societies in various regions of the state have participated. Besides spiritual topics, the conferences have also addressed social and economic problems of Mexican Americans.

In 1972, the Catholic church leaders and lay Hispanics in Houston participated in the *Encuentro Hispano de Pastoral* ("Pastoral Congress for the Spanish-speaking"). Treviño, the aforementioned author of *The Church in the Barrio: Mexican American Ethno-Catholicism in Houston*, said that the event "stands as a watershed in the religious history of Mexican American Catholics in Houston." Treviño also said that Mexican-American Catholics "competed for cultural space not only with the Anglo majority, which included various groups of *white* Catholics, but also with a large black population and a Mexican protestant presence as well." As time passed, additional churches established by Mexicans opened, and as some neighborhoods became majority Mexican, the churches became Mexican churches.

Before either Texas or Houston existed, Our Lady of Guadalupe was fervently celebrated by Mexican-Americans living in this area. And as new generations of immigrants bring Mexican customs and culture across the border, the celebration has continued to grow. In their homes, they celebrate *Las Mañanitas*, the traditional serenade of the Virgin, and share *pan dulce* (sweet bread), chocolate and *tamales*. But it wasn't until 1973 that Houston began official celebrations of the Virgin of Guadalupe. Then-Bishop John Markovsky recognized the need to serve the diocese's growing Hispanic community.

The first procession and Mass took place that year, 1973, in Our Lady of Guadalupe Church in Houston's East End. "The crowd was too big and the church too small, so the mass was moved to outside the church, and later to the market across the street," says Elenita Ruíz, a historian for the *Guadalupana* Association. She is one of the last living organizers of the early celebrations.

A feature story in the *Houston Chronicle* (the only daily newspaper left) in 2016 traced this procession and explained *guadalupanismo* to those not conversant in the tradition. Interestingly enough, everyone quoted in that story is male, as is the current president of the

Guadalupanas of Houston, Pablo Guzmán. The article by Olivia P. Tallet explained that

> the Guadalupe is the Virgin Mary of Mexico, but more and more, she is now known as the Virgin of Houston, as well. Dec. 12 is the last day of the novena in celebration of Our Lady of Guadalupe, the Virgin who appeared to Juan Diego, an indigenous peasant, on that date in 1531. It was at the top of the Tepeyac Hill, north of what is now Mexico City. "Spaniards had already conquered Mexico, but there was a lot of tension and animosity between the native people and the Europeans," explains Fr. Michael Buentello, director of Campus Ministry at the University of St. Thomas in Houston. So it was significant, Buentello says, that Diego saw this "blessed mother appearing as an Aztec woman, with very native, indigenous features, and she is pregnant, telling Juan Diego in his own native language that she wanted a chapel built in her honor." It's said that the area's bishop did not believe the indigenous man until he saw a miracle for himself. As proof, Juan Diego brought the prelate a bouquet of roses that the Virgin had given him. He wrapped the roses in his *tilma*,[4] an Aztec cloak. When he opened the *tilma*, the image of Our Lady of Guadalupe was printed in the fabric.
>
> Buentello says the Basilica of the Virgin of Guadalupe, in Mexico, where the image is enshrined, has become the second most visited site in the Catholic world, second only to the Vatican. Since Pope Leo XIII granted permission for her coronation in 1895, she has been proclaimed as the Patroness of the Americas.
>
> Houston's icons: According to the Archdiocese, until recently, the 6-feet-by-4-feet Our Lady of Guadalupe icon carried in Houston processions was brought from Mexico, where it had made contact with St. Juan Diego's *tilma*. That 6x4 icon was used in the procession until last year. "It was very heavy to carry and difficult to move," says Guzmán. It was also logistically difficult to work with, since it was used not only for the procession but also for many other activities around the city. In 2015, the association introduced a Houston image of the virgin to the celebrations. This icon is 4-feet-by-3-feet, smaller and lighter than the first. Amada Támez, a devotee of Our Lady of Guadalupe, bought it at the *Cristo Rey* shop in the East End. "In looking for a theological meaning, our lighter Virgin can be carried by just two persons, like the two disciples of Jesus Christ," says Guzmán. In the Gospel of Luke, Jesus sent his disciples on missions in pairs, two by two. Guzmán calls the newer, smaller icon "La Peregrina" (The Pilgrim) because she spends each month in a different family home. Her hosts are members of the Guadalupana Association,

whose members belong to almost 50 churches in the archdiocese. Before this year's procession, *La Peregrina* stayed in the home of Roberto Chávez.

"We have hosted the Virgin several times," Chávez says, "and when she is in our house, we pray to her every day and celebrate rosaries at least once a week." For those rosaries, Chávez invites all the members of his family—the daughter with her husband and kids, the mother, brothers and everyone who wants to join. "We all pray and then we share food together," he says. "It does not matter what we eat as long as it's homemade: *tortillas with huevos rancheros, pan dulce, tamales* and then our son and the younger children can bring something else if they want, like *barbacoa*." Their celebration is more than a family moment. "Having the Virgin of Guadalupe visiting our home, to me, is an opportunity to show our gratitude because she is the one to whom we go in our difficult times," says Roberto's wife, Nelly Chávez. "She gives us strength for not having fear. She assures us that she is there; that she is our protecting mother."

The Guadalupe has been adopted by Hispanic groups other than Mexicans. Her celebration is a "very important feast for all Catholics, and I am not aware of any other Virgin Mary that is more celebrated than Our Lady of Guadalupe in Houston," says Buentello. "Whether we are Hispanic or non-Hispanic, we certainly know and have an understanding of the significance of her apparition in Mexico and what it means for all of us Catholics."

The Virgin, who appeared to native people as a native herself represents, according to Buentello, "hope for those who may not have been seen important in the eyes of the world. Hope, as the blessed mother is telling that God cares about all and especially those (who are) economically disadvantaged, those who are rejected, who are not part of the inner club. She reaffirmed that there is dignity to all people." To the hill. Guzmán says that many call the new icon "Lady of the Immigrants." He likes to see her as the Patroness of Houston, a diverse city where the majority of people come from some other country or state. "Our Lady of Guadalupe meets people where they are. It does not matter where we are—Houston, Latin America or anywhere in the world. When you find yourself wrapped in your mother's gaze, you are home," says Sergio Castillo, Director of the Archdiocesan Office of Hispanic Ministry.

Fr. Buentello says that in a diverse city like Houston, most people understand "what it is like to be displaced." If you think about it, he says, "shortly after the birth of Jesus, Joseph takes Mary and Jesus to Egypt. They were fleeing the oppression of King Herod, who was trying to kill them. People come [to Houston] not only fleeing oppression but also for a better life. They leave behind everything, and they come with not much."

With the older and newer icons both now in service, Houston has now a unique Lady of Guadalupe tradition. In the procession, the newer, lighter *La Peregrina*, Our Lady of the Immigrants, Patroness of Houston, is carried to an altar at the Convention Center, where the older, larger icon waits. "Maybe we could say that the George R. Brown [Convention Center] is the *Tepeyac* (hill)," says Guzmán. "We go with the pilgrim in the procession, but the old one that was touched by the *tilma*[6] is waiting at the top, and we go through the streets like going to meet the lady. She is always in spirit with us, but physically, she is waiting for us at the top of our hill in Houston."

In terms of education, in the 20th century, when schools were legally segregated by race (the Jim Crow era), there were some ethnic Mexican-majority elementary schools in Houston; Mexican students attended schools classified as being for "white" students. At some schools, such as Rusk Elementary School near the Second Ward, school administrators established de facto segregation by assigning Mexican students to separate classes. At the time, no ethnic Mexican-majority high schools yet existed. The first school with a majority ethnic Mexican student body was Lorenzo de Zavala Elementary School in Magnolia Park, built in 1920 because school district administrators established De Zavala elementary to alleviate fears from Anglo "white" parents who noticed an increase in Mexican students in the area's so-called "white" schools. An increase in the Hispanic presence of public schools in Houston began in 1937. After the 1960s, many of the secondary schools began to change from being mostly Anglo to mostly Hispanic.

In the late 1970s and early 1980s, tens of thousands of Mexicans arrived in Houston due to increased economic opportunities from an increase in the oil business. In the 1970s, 63,000 Mexicans arrived in the Houston metropolitan area. In the more recent immigrant wave, the Mexicans tended to work in informal labor markets. Most Mexicans in the immigrant wave in the 1970s and 1980s originated from Coahuila, Nuevo León, and Tamaulipas, states along the U.S.–Mexico border. In 1980, according to the U.S. census, 93,718 Mexicans were born outside of the United States; 68% of the Mexicans in that figure had immigrated since 1970. In the early 1980s, there was an estimation of 80,000 illegal immigrants from Mexico, along with 300,000 native Hispanics.

Mexican immigration in Houston fluctuated due to the 1980s oil bust. The oil bust resulted in hardships and job losses for area

Mexicans. Because many Mexicans sought to find work in other U.S. cities, Houston-area transportation businesses started by Mexicans sought to flourish. In 1986, a federal law was passed that prohibited hiring of illegal immigrants, reducing possibilities of work for Mexican illegal immigrants. Despite this fluctuation, in the 1980s, 89,000 Mexicans arrived in Harris County. After 1987, when the oil bust ended, the wages stagnated and the number of jobs had a slow growth. The Immigration Reform and Control Act (IRCA) offered amnesty and legalization for illegal immigrants who arrived before 1982. The same law fined employers hiring illegal immigrants.[13]

In concern for the growing Houston Hispanic population with low educational percentages associated with that population, plus concern for the enormous number of dropouts for economic reasons, and general lack of knowledge about higher education opportunities among that population, Houston Hispanic Forum was established in1986 by Dr. Dorothy Farrington de Caram and others, mostly also Mexican Americans. From their website, the Houston Hispanic Forum is a 501 (c) (3) non-profit organization focused on empowering and inspiring the success of the large and fast-growing Hispanic community in the greater Houston area, thereby strengthening the entire community.

Vision
All Hispanics in the Greater Houston area will possess the knowledge and tools to be successful.

Mission
Empower and inspire the success of the large and fast-growing Hispanic community in the Greater Houston area, thereby strengthening the entire community.

Values
- Giving back to the community
- Organizational integrity and transparency
- Collaboration with organizations with strong reputations
- Education is the most important vehicle for self-improvement
- Education is an individual right
- Equality of opportunity
- Appreciation of Hispanic heritage as part of the organization

Goals
1. To serve as an organized, non-partisan group of concerned individuals who provide leadership, vitality and unity among Hispanics.

2. To enhance, strengthen and recognize the image of Hispanics.
3. To act as a liaison for Hispanic interests with constituent individuals and groups in the city, state, and nation.
4. To assist Hispanic youth develop their talents and abilities and help them achieve their professional and personal goals.
5. To provide a means for educational growth and help to the community at large.

The main project of HHF is the annual Career & Education Day, attended by up to 20,000 Houston area students, and their families, teachers, counselors, etc., open to all. The event is divided between an exhibition area of entities offering higher education and professional options and an area of professionals giving panels about what it's like to practice any number of professions and how to get there, including financial and scholarship advice and more.

A sidelight, previous to Houston Hispanic Forum, the organization of HATFL, Houston Area Teachers of Foreign Language, was established in the 1950s by the activist public school teacher, Curtis Farrington, married to a Mexican national and father of the aforementioned Dorothy!

In 1990, there were 132,596 Mexican immigrants in Houston, making up 69% of the 192,220 foreign-born Hispanic residents of Houston. That year, 46% of all immigrants to Houston were Mexican. In 1990, in Harris County, and the median household income of ethnic Mexicans was $22,447 and 6% of its ethnic Mexican population had a bachelor's degree or higher education. Nestor Rodríguez wrote that the percentage of those with a bachelor's degree or higher illustrates "a major educational disadvantage" and "partly explained the low median household income."

From 1990 to 1997, the number of Mexican immigrants in Houston increased by over 110,000. In the 1990s, the burgeoning economy, a decline in the Mexican economy, and thousands of legalized immigrants filing family reunification petitions encouraged additional Mexican immigration. The decade saw an increase in anti-immigrant sentiments, the anti-hiring illegal immigrant laws and a new law passed in 1996 that restricted immigration had, in the words of Nestor Rodríguez, "lessened the explosive energy that characterized Mexican undocumented immigration in the 1970s and 1980s."

In the book, *Ethnicity in the Sunbelt: A History of Mexican Americans in Houston*, author Arnoldo De León, described the relationship between Houston Mexican-Americans and newly arrived immigrants from Mexico. De León imparts that the traditional residents disliked how they believed that the new immigrants were giving the Mexican-American community in Houston a bad reputation but added that, at the same time, the new immigrants kept the city's Mexican-American community in touch with the home country. As of 2007, most of the Hispanic and Latino(x) political power in Houston consists of Mexican Americans. In 2010, many residents of Monterrey, Mexico moved to Houston to escape drug cartel violence. By June 2012, the *Yo Soy 132* movement in Mexico spread to Houston, using the hashtag #YoSoy132-Houston.

From such a history as I shared earlier, in the 21st century, according to a *Houston Chronicle* feature story, Houston has become not only the fourth largest city in the U.S. but the most diverse in terms of ethnicity and languages spoken! The Houston region is now the most ethnically-diverse large metropolitan area in the country, surpassing New York City. Two suburbs, Missouri City and Pearland, have become even more diverse than the city of Houston. Other suburbs are not far behind. These findings are from a report released Monday by Rice University researchers, based on an analysis of census data from 1990, 2000 and 2010.

"We are a little United Nations," Pearland Mayor Tom Reid said. "You go to one of our neighborhoods, and there will be a person from Nigeria living next to somebody from India, living next to somebody from Mexico and somebody from Louisiana." The report covered a five-county area—Harris, Fort Bend, Montgomery, Brazoria and Galveston—and was produced by the Kinder Institute and Rice's Hobby Center for the Study of Texas, which says,

> Meanwhile, the percentage of Latinos has increased from one fifth of metropolitan residents (20.8 percent) in 1990 to more than one third (35.3 percent) in 2010, only slightly smaller than the Anglo population. At current rates of population change, Latinos are poised to become the Houston region's largest racial/ethnic group sometime within the next few years.

While Mexican Americans arguably remain the largest (Chicano)/Latino(x)/Hispanic group, so many Central Americans have immigrated for various reasons that, for example, there are now more *salvadoreños* in Houston than in the capital of El Salvador, San Salvador, not to mention the *guatemaltecos* and so many other Latino(x)/Hispanics!

While it may seem like common knowledge that Houston is an incredibly diverse city, the results of another new study indicate that, indeed, the Bayou City deserves such recognition. WalletHub's 2015 Most Diverse Cities in America study ranks Houston as one of the top 10 most diverse cities in America, coming in at #7 overall. Houston is the only city ranked in the top 10 that is not located in California or Washington. To identify the most diverse cities in America, the personal financial site analyzed 230 cities across four major categories: economic class diversity, ethno-racial and linguistic diversity, economic diversity and household diversity. (In the rankings of each category, 1 is considered most diverse and 115 average diversity.) It found that Houston ranked #16 for ethno-racial and linguistic diversity, #20 for economic diversity, #67 for economic class diversity and #81 for household diversity. Other categories measured other qualifiers for Houston, such as educational diversity (Houston ranked #6 in the nation), industry diversity (#27), racial and ethnic diversity (#37) and language diversity (#49). When all these factors were averaged in and compared with the other cities, Houston ties with Kent, Washington for the #7 spot. All of the top five ranked cities are located in California, including Los Angeles (#1), Long Beach (#2), San Diego (#3), Anaheim (also tied for #3) and Sacramento (#5). Other Texas cities that ranked highly on the list for overall diversity included Fort Worth at #12, Arlington at #14, Dallas at #16 and Austin at #20.

And, the number of organizations of all sorts, not just religious or educational but business, medical, etc., etc., etc., continue to grow and serve those populations!

Notes

1 *Anglo*, the abbreviated form in both Spanish and English of "Anglo-Saxon," traditionally refers mostly to those European immigrants and their descendants who were/are dominant in English. However, it is used today as an ethnic term more than a linguistic one—and may be used for immigrants and their descendants not originally from English-speaking countries, i.e., the "other," as opposed to those dominant in Spanish or who identify culturally and/or ethnically with the so-called Hispanic countries. "White" is sometimes (incorrectly) used as a synonym.
2 *Wikipedia* notes that "When the city of Houston was founded in 1836 and incorporated in 1837, its founders—John Kirby Allen and Augustus Chapman Allen—divided it into political geographic districts called "wards." The ward system, a precursor to today's City Council districts, was a common political tool of the early 19th century, and is still used in some American cities. When the system was at its peak [Houston] had six wards, from the first to the sixth."
3 The Day of the Dead (El Día de los Muertos), Nov. 2, is an amalgamation of indigenous and Roman Catholic practices, now mostly in rural Mexico, when ancestors are honored on that date with home altars, picnics at gravesites and more.

4   *Tilma* is the indigenous word for a cactus-fiber cape. An indigenous man, Juan Diego Cuauhtlatoatzín, carried roses, given to him out-of-season on the hill of Tepeyac, near today's Mexico, D.F., by an indigenous-appearing Our Lady of Guadalupe, as evidence of her appearance to him on her fourth appearance to him, in 1531, in order to convince church officials that the original *Basílica de Guadalupe* should be built as per her request.

Works Cited

Capps, Randy, Michael Fix and Chiamaka Nwosu. *A Profile of Immigrants in Houston, the Nation's Most Diverse Metropolitan Area.* Washington, D.C.: Immigration Policy Institute, March 2015. file://winfshd3/ users$/dda003/Downloads/HoustonProfile.pdf Web.

Caram, Dorothy E. Farrington. *Hispanics in Houston and Harris County 1519–1986.* Houston: Houston Hispanic Forum, 1986. Print.

Esparza, Jesús Jesse. "*La colonia mexicana*: A History of Mexican Americans in Houston." (Archive) *Houston History,* Vol. 9, no. 1, pp. 2–8. Center for Public History, University of Houston. Web.

Garza, Natalie. "The "Mother Church" of Mexican Catholicism in Houston." (Archive) *Houston History.* Vol. 9, I. 1, 14–19. Center for Public History, University of Houston. Web.

Guadalupana Papers, Today's Catholic, May 22, 1981, Mar. 3, 1988. San Antonio: Catholic Chancery Archives. "Houston, Texas." Web.

History of Texas. https://www.history.com/topics/us-states/texas Web.

Houston Hispanic Forum. https://hispanic-forum.org/ Web.

Klineberg, Stephen L, Jie Wu, Kiara Douds and Diane Ramírez. *Shared Prospects: Hispanics & the Future of Houston. Findings from the Houston Surveys 1994–2014.* Houston, TX: Kinder Institute for Urban Research at Rice University, Nov. 2014. https://kinder.rice.edu/sites/g/files/bxs1676/f/documents/LatinoReport FINAL.pdf Web.

Humanities Texas. "Stephen Klineberg on Houston's Immigrant Advantage" Apr./May 2013. https://www.humanitiestexas.org/news/articles/stephen-klineberg-houstons-immigrant-advantage Web.

Palomo Acosta, Teresa. "Sociedades Guadalupanas." Texas State Historical Association. https://tshaonline.org/handbook/online/articles/ics10 Web.

Rodríguez, Nestor. "Hispanic and Asian Immigration Waves in Houston." *Religion and the New Immigrants: Continuities and Adaptations in Immigrant Congregations.* Chafetz, Janet, Salzman and Helen Rose Ebaugh, eds. AltaMira Press, Oct. 18, 2000. Print.

Sociedades Guadalupanas. https://tshaonline.org/handbook/online/articles/ics10 Web.

Tallet, Olivia P. "Our own hill to Our Lady of Guadalupe" *The Guadalupe of Houston.* Dec. 11,2016. Updated: Dec. 12, 2016. https://www.houstonchronicle.com/lifestyle/calle-houston/article/The-Lady-of-Houston-10786790.php Web.

Texas State Historical Association.
 https://tshaonline.org/handbook/online/articles/hdh03 Web.
Treviño, Robert R. *The Church in the Barrio: Mexican American Ethno-Catholicism in Houston.* Chapel Hill: The University of North Carolina Press, 2006. Print.

CHAPTER

7

Mestizaje as Lateral Universality: Moving In-Between Elitist Cosmopolitanism and Populist Tribalism

JOHN FRANCIS BURKE

Populism has been spreading across Europe, the United States, and other parts of the globe in recent years. This populist wave has had a destabilizing effect both on internal politics of liberal democratic countries, as well as on the international world order established after World War II. The onset of populism, as well as its elitist counterpart, cosmopolitanism, is connected to the transition from an industrial economy to a technological global economy, as well as to the migration of peoples from lands mired in political and/or economic turmoil to countries seen as offering better prospects. Both cosmopolitan elitism and nativist populism are threatening to erode the conception of liberal democratic citizenry essential to 1) fostering an inclusive pluralism in an intercultural age and 2) deepening the commitment to a "win-win" collaborative set of international relations established post World War II.

Liberal democracy seeks to establish majority rule that respects individual and minority liberties and rights. Although each citizen has the choice to participate or not in the body politic, liberal democracy stresses the importance of expanding the right to participate in political deliberations as broadly as possible and that the vitality of democracy depends upon people exercising their right to participate on a frequent basis. In addition, a liberal democracy also stresses that, at times, the democratic state, through taxing and spending policy, has to redistribute social and economic resources to ensuring genuine equality of opportunity, without guaranteeing equality of result.

This vision of democracy, as William Galston points out, is being challenged from two directions. In light of the complexities of the global economy, he contends that elitists argue, "they best understand the means to the public's ends" and therefore, should proceed without much concern for "popular consent" (Galston 2018, 4). As a result, elitists use administrative, judicial, and international institutions, which are not directly accountable to the people, to make and enforce public policy. Conversely, populists, he argues, in reaction to such elites, stress majority rule at the expense of "individual rights and the limits on public power at the heart of liberal democracy" (Galston 2018, 4). Populists invoke an undifferentiated will of the people and paint the above elites as enemies to democracy in their distant disdain for the people (Galston 2018, 4–5).

Clearly, those of us committed to liberal democracy need to examine how to revitalize it to encourage contributions from diverse members of the body politic and conversely to ensure that democratic public policy not culminate in abstract rules and regulations which give enormous say to judicial and administrative elites in the running of democratic countries. Toward this end, we need to examine how to promote and practice a dynamic pluralism that counters 1) the ability of enabled elites to direct public policy under the guise of democracy and 2) the capacity of mobs under the name of majority rule not only to counter such elitism, but to erode civil liberties and rights.

Although there are a number of intellectual heritages that could be drawn up to project this dynamic pluralism, I will explore how the notion and practice of *mestizaje* suggests a democratic ethos that steers between cosmopolitan elitism, my term for Galston's concept of elitism and nativist populism. Both cosmopolitanism and populism end up imposing one way of doing things, whether it is the former's detached public policy or the latter's undifferentiated majority will. *Mestizaje*, understood as a democratic ethos, instead, I will argue, is attentive to the rich cultural heritages that inform any body politic and that elites too easily dismiss. In turn, a *mestizo* democracy projects that such heritages can lead to integrations that are genuinely inclusive of these heritages and counters the populist notion of an amalgamated will of the people. *Mestizaje* understood as a democratic ethos is particularly critical to an age in which more and more diverse peoples and cultures are intersecting.

My essay has five sections. The first section will explore the characteristics of the cosmopolitan elites of the global economy. The second section will review the essential characteristics of nativist populism. In the third section, I will review past historical renderings of *mestizaje* that lend themselves respectively to either elitist notions of cultural purification or conversely, a tribalism that rejects what they see as hegemonic political, socio-economic systems. The fourth section will then explore the possibility of a lateral *mestizaje* that shifts the dynamic from the oppressor-oppressor dynamic to the diverse interaction of peoples and cultures and equals. This lateral vision of *mestizaje* is especially crucial to providing an alternative to the elitist temperament of cosmopolitans and the nativist identity politics of populists. The concluding synthesis will then suggest the import of a lateral *mestizaje* for a dynamic liberal democratic pluralism. In my arguments, I will be drawing amply from the work of Ian Bremmer (2018), William Galston 2018), David Goodhart (2017a & 2017b), Anthony Heywood (2017), John Judis (2016), Jan-Werner Muller (2016), as well as my own past writings on *mestizaje* (Burke 2002, 2008, & 2016).

Cosmopolitan Elitism

Central to the populist critique of contemporary liberal democracy, be it in the United Kingdom, France, Eastern Europe, the United States or Brazil, among other countries, is that the leaders of these so-called democracies are out-of-touch with the lives of either the traditional working class or people who adhere to traditional moral systems. Well then, who are these elites?

David Goodhart specifically refers to cosmopolitans as the "anywheres." In his analysis, they are well-educated and occupy middle-class or upper-class professional positions, especially in the domains of health, education, media, finance, business, and law (Goodhart 2017b, 23–24). Essentially, they are "anywhere" because their education and access to wealth could lead to jobs not just in their own country, but in any developed countries across the globe. In a sense, if they are Parisian bankers, e.g., they have more in common with similar professionals in London, New York or Tokyo than they do with the person in the street in their country.

Philosophically speaking, cosmopolitans stress personal autonomy and self-reliance rather than community stability and tradition (Goodhart 2017b, 3–5). Consequently, cosmopolitans put the priority on the creativity and independence of liberal values such as liberty of thought and expression and protection from persecution rather than the democratic emphasis on majority rule. Cosmopolitans place a lot of emphasis on dreaming new lives unfettered by a specific thick cultural tradition and on the capacity to navigate the dynamics of the global economy across cultural boundaries.

Politically speaking, especially from the standpoint of the populists, these cosmopolitans are overrepresented in moderate-left and moderate-right parties that have dominated both US and Western European politics since World War II. Such centrist dynamics between two parties would include the Democratic and Republican parties in the United States, the Labour and Conservative parties in the United Kingdom, and the Social Democrats and Christian Democrats in Germany.

Economically speaking, these educated and professional elites benefit immensely from a global society. Both in terms of a global economics and open-ended liberal values, cosmopolitans embrace the inclusion of migrants and refugees in their society and have little to lose with the arrival of these populations, except perhaps political support from the sectors of society supporting populism.

In the 2016 Brexit vote, in which the UK narrowly approved leaving the European Union, those voting to stay in the EU were younger, well-educated voters, especially in London, who have the educational and technical skills to compete effectively in the global economy (Goodhart 2017b, 19. 26). Indeed, many students in Northern Ireland, as a consequence of the Brexit vote, are seeking passports from the Republic of Ireland so that they can still in the future pursue educational and economic opportunities across the EU.

In many respects what I am terming cosmopolitanism elitism, ultimately, is very much a 21st-century version of the call of liberal nationalism in the late 18th and early 19th centuries. Inspired by the visions of personal liberty, equality, and self-rule put forward by the American and French Revolutions, liberal nationalists sought in the 19th century to create liberal democratic societies across Europe and eventually, across the globe, that would demolish monarchies and aristocracies that argued that there were inherent differences between human beings that justified political, social, and economic inequality (Heywood 2017, 164–65, 177). Cosmopolitan elites in the 21st century now move beyond the nation-state to envision transnational communities that practice liberal democratic political, social, and economic arrangements.

Nativist Populism

In contrast to the global vision of cosmopolitan elites, populists represent a perspective that is much more rooted to specific places and is leery of, and certainly does not benefit from, the fast-paced disruptions of a global technological economy. As opposed to the "anywhere" disposition of cosmopolitans, populists are from particular "somewheres" (Goodhart 2017b, 3).

To be fair, populisms come in both left-wing and right-wing varieties. Left-wing populism pits the so-called "people" against a shrinking small percentage of a country that increasingly controls the vast majority of wealth in a country (Judis 2016, 15). Historically, Huey Long's "share the wealth" initiative comes to mind. Hugo Chavez' movement against the Venezuelan well-to-do would be a left-wing populism or more recent vintage. The Wall Street Occupy Movement and then Bernie Sanders' attack on the privileged one percent in the 2016 Presidential election would be other examples.

Looking ahead to the 2020 Presidential election, certainly many of the candidates on the Democratic side are moving the party to the left with policies such as Sanders' call for "Medicare for all." A vital question will be whether they will prove any more open to the call for pluralism or tolerance, classic liberal values, than their right-wing counterparts.

Right-wing nativist populists, on other hand, not only pit the people versus a detached elite, but also claim that this elite focuses their policies too much on the needs of immigrants and/or cultural minorities (Judis 2016, 15). These "somewheres," as presented by Goodhart, tend to be less-educated, from rural areas, and from working class livelihoods (2017a, 24–26). They need not be from all three demographic categories, but essentially are people both rooted in specific places and all-too-often have been left behnd in the transition from an industrial to a technological economy and society.

Whereas a half century ago, it was still possible in the United Kingdom and the United States to get a well-paying working-class job without having a college degree, the transition away from an industrial economy has eliminated these positions and the middle-class lifestyle that came with it. In rural areas, increasing numbers of small farms have been taken over by mega-agribusinesses.

Especially since the mid-1970s, at the very moment these jobs in steel mills, auto plants, coal mines, and other staple industries were disappearing, especially in the United States, affirmative action initiatives were being undertaken to enable historically-discriminated against populations to get access to economic opportunities they had previously been denied or only allowed access to in a subordinate status. Dwindling well-paid working-class jobs, combined with an expanding pool of workers, was a powder keg just waiting to explode.

Socially speaking, nativists populists place importance on security, family, group attachments, and being rooted in a specific place. These values are the antithesis of the cosmopolitan emphasis on personal self-definition, pluralism, tolerance, and the exploration of multiple cultures. Indeed, right-wing populists are suspicious of moral relativism and "'anything goes' attitudes" (Goodhart 2017a, 24).

In political terms, therefore, nativist populists place more emphasis on democratic majority rule than the liberal emphasis on different lifestyles and the protection of individual liberties and rights. They are particularly leery of political practices that threaten to take away their long-standing "way of life." Internally, the more open-ended definition of marital and sexual relationships to right-wing populists threatens the moral fabric of the family and in turn, society (Goodhart 2017a, 24). Externally, immigrants and asylum seekers both become competitors for their jobs and threaten the cultural values that right-wing populists see as vital to sustaining their communities. Consequently, "aliens" from within (moral relativists and minorities) and from without (immigrants) are targeted for derision and exclusion.

Populist leaders, like Donald Trump, Le Pen in France, and their executive counterparts in Brazil, Hungary, the Philippines, Poland, and Turkey, among other countries, know very well how to stir up and play to these sentiments in propagating politics of fear. These leaders emphasize that the people in rooted communities that have been left behind in the post-industrial economic order are the undifferentiated "real people" that are being ignored and getting the shaft from elites controlling the liberal democratic legislative institutions. Consequently, the leaders put themselves forward as the ones who can speak for the "real people" and cut through all the emphasis on checks, balances, and due process in a democratic system (Muller 2016, 1–7, 101–3). Of course, the more populist leaders are successful in achieving this end around the liberal democratic framework, the more they are instituting an authoritarian system in its place.

Whereas cosmopolitanism can be traced back to 19th century liberal nationalism, right-wing populism can be traced back to 19th century conservative nationalism. In the 19th century, in reaction to the rise of liberal calls for self-determination and pluralism, conservative nationalist leaders such as Bismarck countered with the call for political systems that sustained a sense of national customs and traditions. Conservative nationalists, more so than liberal nationalists, put forth a more emotive, organic sense of what it is be British or French or Spanish, etc. In the 20th century, Charles de Gaulle and Margaret Thatcher come to mind (Heywood 2017, 180–82). Liberal nationalism articulates a cerebral vision of democracy that embraces new beginnings and pluralism; conservative nationalism celebrates a heartfelt devotion to the country that is leery of values or cultures that threaten this heritage.

Of course, conservative nationalism, if taken to an extreme, becomes a form of expansionist nationalism that found its embodiment in Hitler's Nazi regime and also the pan-Slavism articulated by Russian nationalists in the late 19th and early 20th centuries. For expansionist nationalists, it is not enough just to sustain the culture of a particular people or place, but it is necessary to extend the presumed superiority of this culture over presumed inferior cultures (Heywood 2017, 182–83). In the 21st century, Vladimir Putin's quest for a greater Russia, especially through extending Russia's presence into the Crimea and Ukraine, manifests this orientation. In addition, Putin has effectively used the liberal character of internet communication to spread fake news and conspiracy theories that play to the fears of nativist populists and therefore, further erode the viability of liberal democratic institutions.

To summarize, the conception of cultural identity on the one hand is very different between cosmopolitan elitists and nativist populists. Cosmopolitan identity envisions a person who is not rooted in a particular place and who pursues a wide array of lifestyle choices. Populist identity by contrast sees people as rooted in a particular geographic or emphasizes sustaining these longstanding identities, not the pursuit of personal choices.

At the same time, common to both camps is the inclination to separate "us" from "them" (Bremmer 2018). Cosmopolitan elitists distance themselves, either intentionally or unintentionally, from the rabble. Nativist populists, on the other hand, do target cosmopolitan elitists as being out of touch with the displacement of so-called real people in the global economy. To a certain degree, both sides of the dyad distinguish themselves from what they are not. Neither approach envisions a concept of cultural dynamism where one can sustain a cultural identity yet have it remain open to constructive transitions and new outlooks. Such an ethos is critical for revitalizing a liberal democratic pluralism that recognizes the legacies of longstanding perspectives, but also realizes that the strength of community life is enriched rather than threatened by the contributions from diverse cultures and groups.

Mestizaje both North and South of the Border

Many different traditions could be drawn upon to try to move inbetween the thin individualist articulation of culture by the cosmopolitan elitists and the thick-rooted articulation of culture by the nativist populists. For instance, Philip Gorski (2017) draws upon the heritage of civil republicanism to articulate a civil religion that seeks to balance individual choice and community norms. His argument is very indebted to the previous civic republican scholarship of Robert Bellah (1986, 1992) and Robert Putnam (2001, 2010).

Instead, given the growing Latinxization[1] of the United States, I suggest we readjust our compass and consider the heritage of mixing cultures—*mestizaje*—in the Latinx world as another possible resource for revitalizing the ethos of liberal democracy. Moreover, the lived experiences, positive and negative, of the peoples of the US Southwest offer a concrete, rather than an abstract, engagement of navigating difference without sacrificing a substantive sense of community in the process.

The original *mestizaje* refers to the mixing of the European conquerors and the natives of what we now refer to as Latin America. This biological and culture mixing, largely due to conquest and rape, nevertheless created hybrid peoples, especially in Mexico and Central America. The African heritage was also in the mix due to the importation of slaves into the New World by both the Spanish and Portuguese.

Within Latinx studies, some scholars contend a new *mestizaje* is emerging in the mixing of Anglo (European-American) and Latinx populations especially in those parts of the US Southwest that were part of Mexico prior to the 1846–48 war between Mexico and the United States (Anzaldúa 2012, Elizondo 2000). In turn, African-American, Asian-Americans and other cultural Americans also are increasing contributors to this mix. As opposed to assimilation in which diverse entities are mixed together to form an undifferentiated whole, or separatism in which diverse cultures are kept utterly distinct from each other, in *mestizaje,* a new identity emerges through the intersection of the contributing identities. At the same time, one can still discern in this new *mezcla* the contributions of the specific cultures—a unity-in-diversity.

In all frankness, when one examines the history of *mestizaje*, the normative articulation and actual practices of such hybrid mixing have hardly been exemplary when it comes to facilitating a lateral mixing in which the intersecting cultures are on equal terms. In Latin America, the articulation of *mestizaje* has stressed the European over the African and indigenous perspectives. In particular, Latin American *mestizaje* has had a sense of the European heritage uplifting or purifying the indigenous and African cultures (Burke 2008 & 2016; Miller 2004). Mexico, in particular, is notorious for a racial classification grid that ranks different mixtures of the African, European, and indigenous heritages. The more pure European one was, the higher was one's classification in the hierarchy. The more African or indigenous one was, the lower one's status in the classification scheme. This privileging of those European or of lighter skin still remains evident in beauty contests, where the light skin, blue eyes, and blond hair, are preferred.

Even José Vasconcelos (1997), in his seminal work published in 1925, *The Cosmic Race*, ends up privileging the European heritage. Vasconcelos waxes romantically about how in Latin America, racial mixing has been embraced as opposed to the assimilation and positivist approached of both the United States and Northern Europe. He, in particular, was reacting against the notions of manifest destiny in the United States and the master race in Nazi century (Burke 2002, 53–55). Yet, as much as Vasconcelos, in a Hegelian fashion, discusses different stages of history that will culminate in *la raza cósmica*, he ultimately argues how the European heritage will uplift and purify the African or the Indian (Burke 2003, 55–57).

This uplifting or purifying rendering of *mestizaje* thus is a subtle form of assimilation. Admittedly, it does not talk about an undifferentiated whole as in the melting pot, but in the end does suggest that a particular culture should be a privileged one in the mixing. This rendering of *mestizaje* is a precursor, in a sense, to the transnational norms and haughty disposition of cosmopolitan elitism.

Conversely, in US Latinx studies, the articulation of *mestizaje* is the opposite of that of the above Latin American renderings. If in Latin America, the European heritage is privileged in *mestizaje*, in Latinx studies, the inclination is to identify Latinxes with the Indian heritage of being a subjugated people.

Especially in Chicanx studies, much stress is put on the double conquest—first by the Spanish over the Indian—and then of the European-American over the Latinx (and especially Mexicans). In this sense, the Latinx are a conquered people much in the manner of the indigenous tribes that once roamed what is now the continental United States. As a result, this *mestizaje* articulates a resistance toward the European heritage, be it the European-American in the United States or the Spanish/Portuguese heritages in Latin America (Burke 2016, 209–13; Pérez-Torres 2006).

The articulation of a mythical *Aztlán* in the U.S. Southwest in Chicanx studies projects an aesthetic homeland that is a bulwark for Latinx cultural norms against the hegemonic European oppressor. To its credit, this resistance rending of *mestizaje* rightfully focuses on the social, economic, and political oppression endured by US Latinx.

Unfortunately, this same insistence on resisting the oppressor does not lend itself to a lateral mixing between cultures as equals.

The figure who is most widely well-known for her articulation of what it is like to be caught between cultures as a Latina is Gloria Anzaldúa. Her legacy is well-known, not only in Latinx studies, but also in feminist and gay/lesbian studies. In a very passionate way, she speaks out against having to apologize to purists on either side of the US-Mexican border for her type of English, Spanish, and cultural practices. Her narrative is also particularly good for trying, almost in an archeological sense, to uncover an indigenous spiritual heritage from the recastings done by both the Spanish and then Anglo conquerors. Her articulation of the Coatlicue state is both passionate and moving (Anzaldúa 2012).

As much as Anzaldúa's narrative is both congenial to the resistance narrative found in Chicanx studies, it remains unclear how much her articulation of crossing borders provides a basis for an egalitarian mixing of cultures. Without a doubt, Anzaldúa evokes a borderlands between Mexico and the United States that stresses plurality, ambiguity and new cultural combinations. Certainly, her general disposition is congenial to crossing figurative borders such as gay/straight, female/male, and Mexican/US American. Yet, there remains in her narrative a privileging of her own stance vis-à-vis her deconstruction of the prevailing cultural hegemonies both north and south of the US–Mexican border.

Reifying the oppressor does not take us any further toward realizing an equal mixing of cultures any more than the uplifting/purification perspective did. In so doing, the privileged heritage in the mixing has simply been reversed. In addition, rendering the reviled dominant culture (European-American in the US case) in a unidimensional way too easily gives fodder to nativist critics like Victor Davis Hansen (2007) when they excoriate Chicanx and Latinx studies programs for being too therapeutic and not very rigorous in character.

As much as the resistance rendering of *mestizaje* is very critical of the historic domination of the Latinx by European Americans and therefore, is distinct from the rejection of aliens and minorities by nativist populists, in another way, this resistance framework has a connection to such populism. The rejection of universals beyond particular places and the leeriness of discussions of unity in the resistance approach ironically and unintentionally lends justification to the nativist populists' resistance to the cosmopolitan norms of the global economy.

Indeed, the recognition that "Latinx lives matter" is crucial, but the resistance articulation of *mestizaje* can be too easily co-opted ironically by White nationalists who sees themselves marginalized by changes in the economy and by public policies toward minorities which in their eyes amounts to reverse racism. The reduction of cultural intersections to the priority of particular places and perspectives too easily begets a vision of cultural intersections that stresses clashes between civilizations (Huntington 1996). The challenge in moving beyond the cosmopolitan-populist and uplifting-resistance binaries narratives remains 1) to evoke a narrative that moves beyond sheer division to evokoing a unity that is not just a uniformity and 2) to cultivate a sense of plurality that does not reduce cultural intersections to "tribes" in agonal conflict.

Seeking a Lateral *Mestizaje*

What we need to seek is a perspective that moves beyond these poles of universalism and particularism. In contemporary phenomenology, this quest has been characterized as a lateral universality. Rather than seeing universality as transcendent and all-encompassing, truth is found in diverse cultures. In other words, the diverse expressions of experiences point toward a reality also being pursued in other cultures. The disclosure of truth is lateral, not top-down.

Calvin Shrag (2002), Fred Dallmayr (2002), and Hwa Yol Jung (2002) have been among the thinkers who have been articulating a transversal philosophy. This transversal perspective is mutually critical of universal perspectives that project "one size fits all" at the expense of diversity and postmodern perspectives that stress particular experiences and resistance to metanarratives, but have a difficult time articulating any sense of substantive unity.

Situating this philosophical debate in the context of the culture wars between cosmopolitans and populists, I contend that Latinx heritage of *mestizaje* can be recast in way that envisions and pursues a lateral universality. In previous publications, I have articulated how the work of Virgil Elizondo (1997 & 2000), Jacques Audinet (2004) and Jorge Gracia (2000) in Latinx studies puts forth a *mestizaje* that moves beyond the uplifting-resistance binary (Burke 2008). I have also suggested previously how their work fits into how transversal philosophy's quest to move beyond the universal-particular binary (Burke 2016). My aim in this essay instead is to reflect upon the embedded norms of a lateral *mestizaje* and how they suggest a political philosophical perspective that bridges the divide between cosmopolitan elitists and nativist populists.

First, a lateral *mestizaje* suggests a unity that does not suffocate diverse cultures, but rather encourages a much richer sense of community by embracing the contributions of diverse cultures. Conversely, this perspective is critical of perspectives of diversity, which suggest that the differences between cultural groups are so wide that no pursuit of unity is possible without leading to one group dominating or marginalizing the other. Unity without diversity leads to uniformity—the critique populists make of the cosmopolitans. Diversity without unity leads to parochialism, intolerance, and conflict—the critique cosmopolitans make of populists.

Indeed, a lateral *mestizaje* envisions a cultural mixing that moves beyond binary thinking. The cosmopolitan-populist split embodies such a binary. One is either in a noble culture that eschews primitive or parochial places or conversely, one is grounded in a particular locale and is leery of political social-economic connections that link diverse places. A lateral *mestizaje* puts forth *and-both* thinking. The key is to foster a space that recognizes the legacy of a particular place yet is open to the dynamic that alternative perspectives not only broaden one's horizon but bring into sharper focus the positive aspects of one's own culture. Instead of *either-or*, we need to grasp that much of our personal and community identities are formed by *and-both* thinking.

Second, a lateral *mestizaje* does not privilege any heritage and welcomes new possibilities of cultures. Elizondo (2000) articulates how his own formation in San Antonio led him to an articulation of *mestizaje* that is neither a glorification of the European heritage nor sheer resistance to it, but is an intriguing combination of both the European-American and Mexican heritages. Especially when one compares his rendering of *mestizaje* to that of Anzaldúa, although he criticizes European-American culture in terms of the discrimination he endured from European-American instructors, he articulates a *mestizaje* in which both the European and indigenous heritages make integral contributions.

Specifically, his rendering of Our Lady of Guadalupe is both Spanish and indigenous in character (1997); in turn, his rendering of Jesus is both Jewish and Gentile in character (2000, 67–86). Admittedly, in both instances, he stresses the connection of these pivotal figures to those on the margins of society, but in his rejection of political socio-economic domination, neither does he privilege the resistor. In a lateral *mestizaje*, moving beyond privileging a particular cultural heritage enables new combinations of cultures to unfold.

Third, a lateral *mestizaje* stresses that unity and diversity are integral, not antithetical, to each other. As we have seen in previous renderings of *mestizaje*, the tendency is either to project an uplifting of one culture by another or conversely, the rejection of a subjugated culture of its oppressor. In terms of cosmopolitanism and populists, the cosmopolitan, in rendering particular cultural practices as too parochial too easily overlooks the importance of deep connections between people in particular places. On the other hand, the populists, by staying within a rigid safety zone, too easily shut themselves out from the growth that can ensue by engaging outside perspectives.

Fourth, rather that identifying one's cultural identity by what I am not—the us vs. them binary—we have to grasp that cultures are transformed in relationship to each other. At some point in the past, Angles and Saxons became Anglo-Saxons. Nor is such mixing necessarily an ordered process. Gracia, in particular, discusses the "promiscuity" that emerges in *mestizaje* (2001, 121). The relationships diverse people make with each other call into question the settled values of the original cultures from which they come. Lateral mestizos break down the walls of our comfort zones and suggest there is a vitality in making new combinations. Such subversion is not stuck in permanent resistance, but seeks new ways of being that in turn may be called into question by subsequent promiscuity. One should beware of reification, be it the snobbery of the cosmopolitan or the fortified boundaries of the populist.

Fifth, a lateral *mestizaje* moves beyond its moorings in the Latin American tradition and seeks to envision and embrace new combinations of cultures between the many regions of the globe. Due to the dislocations wrought by the global economy within countries and vast number of migrants crossing national boundaries due to international economic and political conflicts, such as the displacement of Syrian refugees to Europe, peoples are encountering each other in ways that challenge the traditional practices and mores of particular locales. If one can grasp that the plight felt by the refugee is in many ways that which was felt by the exodus of one's own ancestors from one place to another, a connection can be established that furthers constructive interaction between the so-called native and the so-called pilgrim.

The other vital dimension to grasping the contemporary dynamics of migration is to study how, for instance, the United States, through political initiatives, entrepreneurial activities, and at times, military intervention, for the past two centuries has been intimately involved in the political struggles and economic divide that is vivid in most Latin American countries. Seen against this backdrop, US citizens have a moral responsibility to welcome rather than reject migrants from these regions.

Sixth, a lateral *mestizaje* counters the commodification of human relationships. One of the troubling aspects of the reform of immigration practices in the United States is the suggestion that only those immigrants would be allowed in who have extensive education and credential skills that meet the needs of the economy. This public policy proposed would dehumanize those rejected. The talents and gifts of human beings end up being treated as objects; the dignity of these human beings ends up being defiled.

Quite frankly, displaced longstanding workers, workers from minority groups that have been historically discriminated against, and more recent migrants fleeing political and economic persecution each suffer humiliation. The worker who counted on his industry giving him good wages and a decent pension sees his factory close without ever receiving retraining for jobs in the technological service economy. The minority worker who had been denied equal employment opportunity prior to the last half-century now finds that although *de jure* discrimination has been eliminated, his entry into the competitive job market comes at a time of growing inequality between the haves and the have nots (Hudson 2017, 277–79). More recent migrants to the US and Europe who likewise are seeking better educational and employment opportunities only add to the complexity of people competing for jobs. The sad thing is that these three groups of workers start blaming each other when, in fact, they have much in common. The challenge, in terms of a lateral *mestizaje*, is to seek a globalization from below that gives everyone a chance in the global economy, and not just the cosmopolitan elites.

Seventh, a lateral *mestizaje* suggests that a pluralistic liberal democracy in which there is dialogue between diverse peoples and cultures is something we are working toward, not something we have achieved. The challenge is to foster terms of engagement in which people feel they are honestly being heard and at the same time, develop deep listening skills that enable them to consider alternative points of view. Instead of seeking to coerce others to our ways of thinking or to disparage quickly the views of others, a lateral *mestizaje* offers an ethos of openness and persuasion. How often do each of us too easily dismiss the outlooks of others because our predispositions prevent us from grasping the gems of wisdom from the so-called *loco*?

An unwillingness to at least try to think from the standpoint of the other thus ends up petrifying the perspectives of both cosmopolitans and populists. To the one camp, the perspectives of the other are that of primitive thinkers. To the other camp, the perspectives of the first camp are seen as that of elitist snobs. In a sense, a lateral *mestizaje* continually beckons us to figure out how we can even begin to have an *equal* dialogue that facilitates intercultural mixing.

Eighth, a lateral *mestizaje* grasps that facilitating discourse between polarized groups at times will involve consensus and at other times, conflict. The historical heritage of *mestizaje* is very vital in this regard. Certainly, much of the initial *mestizaje* in Latin America ensued through conquest and rape. The subsequent *mestizaje* in the US Southwest again emerged frequently through the taking of land by conquest. The vilification of the indigenous person was integral to the double conquest of the US Southwest, first by European colonization and then by US American expansion linked to manifest destiny. Yet, despite this agonal legacy, a mixing does ensue between African, European, and indigenous peoples that entails cultural cross-fertilization. From this experiential legacy of an integral mixing in the cauldron of conflict, a lateral *mestizaje* cautions the cosmopolitans not to manifest the bogus superiority of the European conquerors and the populists not to embrace an exclusive ethnic identity that rejects the miscegenation of peoples, cultures, and economies.

Ninth, a lateral *mestizaje* shifts the local of the discourse from the places that separate us to the spaces over which we can build bridges that foster constructive mixing. Certainly specific places and their heritages are important. The cosmopolitan perspective too easily looks down at the mores of "fly-over country," the US heartland. The populist perspective too easily tries to petrify the legacy of a region into "it is, was, and always shall be." Conversely, transgressing the spaces that lie between places links an activity happening in one space with that of another. Too-scripted a sense of place denies people the opportunity to learn other ways of being. The reverence we have for one place can be a medium through which we can be open to the beauty of another place. If cosmopolitans are too unrooted, populists are too rooted.

Tenth and finally, a lateral *mestizaje* neither places the privileged on a pedestal nor remains content to do just resistance on behalf of the subjugated. The difficulty with the Latin American *mestizaje* was the presumption that the European elites were superior and therefore, have a responsibility to uplift the African and the Indian. A softer version of such condescension ensues among cosmopolitans too easily dismisses the deleterious impact the global economy has had on long-standing ways of life. Conversely, the populists get mired in mythic "good old days" which never were as blessed as imagined and indeed did entail repressions on the basis of race, ethnicity, sex, gender, among other categories, that had to be overcome to sustain a viable liberal democracy.

The shifts begat by the 21st century global economy, be they in terms of labor, investment or resources, are going to transform communities. Taking a cue from E.F. Schumacher's ethos of using intermediate technology in developing world economies, a lateral *mestizaje* seeks to foster economies such as microfinancing that enable all persons to make transitions to the dynamic global economy without sacrificing their vital cultural heritages in the process (Schumacher 1975, Yunus 2003).

Synthesis

In the end, a lateral *mestizaje* has much to offer for revitalizing a substantive pluralism essential to a liberal democracy. As Jan-Werner Muller suggests, even if the solutions populists frequently advocate . . . support for a demagogue who supposedly speaks on behalf of the "real people" and the notion of a people, a place, or a nation as a homogenous undifferentiated whole—are misbegotten, the intense political disaffection populists have manifested point to legitimate problems within liberal democracy. Currently, the deck is stacked toward participation by the wealthy and the educated. Especially in the United States, the impact of wealth in political campaigns limits who can run and succeed at obtaining public office and essentially corrupts democratic political practices. In turn, institutional political practices such as gerrymandering of electoral districts, as well as linkages between specific congressional committees, bureaucratic agencies and interest groups around a common policy interest, enable a myriad of well-financed sectors to maximize their well-being at the expense of the common good as a whole.

But it is not just the institutions of democratic pluralism that need to be changed but their ethos. In *Mestizo Democracy*, I projected how to envision a transnational democratic government in which Madisonian pluralism gets recast through the Mesoamerican sensibility of *mestizaje* (Burke 2003, 254–59). But keeping the frame of reference to the United States, too many engagements of difference, which either in a conservative fashion reject diversity out-of-hand or in a radical fashion conclude longstanding hegemonies of race, gender and other categories, are too inscribed in our political practices to enable a genuine mutual interchange. Consequently, the challenge in reforming liberal democracy so as to respond to the disparate critiques by cosmopolitan elitists and nativist populists becomes to envision and practice "a thick and respectful pluralism" that enables discourse "across difference" (Brooks 2019). A lateral *mestizaje* fosters discourse that explores commonalities and differences between groups, rather than the exchange of invectives and calumny that all too often characterizes cable news networks and social networking platforms.

Indeed, a *mestizo* democracy pursues a "unity-in-diversity." As opposed to the universal-particular binary, a lateral *mestizaje* stresses that each of us is a mixture of backgrounds and the focus on some pure truth on the one hand or on truths that are specific to particular places are misbegotten. As opposed to the cosmopolitan-populist binary, a lateral *mestizaje* seeks to open the eyes of the former to the unhealthy detachment from the specific impact policies have on particular places. In turn, it seeks to open the eyes of the populists that there is much to gain from experiencing alternative cultures and places. Finally and fundamentally, contrary to the homogenous community vs. anarchic diversity binary, a lateral *mestizaje* stresses that the personal and community well-being is best advanced by enabling the respective gifts of personas and particular cultures to be brought forward to spice up the community as a whole.

At the same time, to praise how the virtues of a lateral *mestizaje* constructively responds to the challenges cosmopolitans and populists pose to contemporary liberal democracy is just to wax romantically if we do not recommit ourselves to reforming the social, economic and political processes that all too often thwart the capacity of diverse persons and groups to enrich our polity with their specific contributions. Toward this end, we need to rededicate ourselves to addressing the dislocations wrought by the global economy by providing the educational opportunities and economic livelihoods that enable all persons to be liberal democratic citizens that build bridges that integrate diverse communities rather than walls that separate them.

Note

1 Latinxization is a derivative of the current social movement to use "Latinx," rather than "Latino," especially among under-thirty Latinx, to avoid what they interpret as the gender discrimination of using the standard Spanish "Latino" as generic for both sexes.

Works Cited

Anzaldúa, Gloria. *Borderlands La Frontera: The New Mestiza* (4th Edition). San Francisco, Aunt Lute Books, 2012. Print.

Audinet, Jacques. *The Human Face of Globalization: From Multiculturalism to Mestizaje*, Frances Dal Chele, Trans. Lanham MD: Rowman & Littlefield Publishers, 2004. Print.

Bellah, Robert N. et al. *Habits of the Heart: Individualism and Commitment in American Life*. New York: Harper & Row, 1986. Print.

——. *The Good Society*. New York: Vintage Books, 1992. Print.

Brooks, David. "The Coming G.O.P. Apocalypse: Stumbling Blind Into the Age of Diversity. *The New York Times*. June 3, 2019. https://www.nytimes.com/2019/06/03/opinion/republicans-generation-gap.html Web.

Burke, John Francis. *Mestizo Democracy: The Politics of Crossing Borders*. College Station, TX: University of Texas A&M Press, 2002. Print.

———. "The Three Paradigms of Mestizaje: Realizing Democracy in a Transnational World of Crossing Borders." *Portularia: Revista De Trabajo Social*, 8 (2), 2008. Pp. 19–22 (Spanish) & pp. 34–37 (English). Print.

———. "Transversality and Mestizaje: Moving Beyond the Purification-Resistance Impasse." In *Political Phenomenology: Essays in Memory of Petee Jung*, Hwa Yol Jung and Lester Embree, Eds. Springer, 2016, pp. 305–21. Print.

Bremmer, Ian. *Us v. Them: The Failure of Globalism*. New Delhi: Portfolio Penguin, 2018. Print.

Dallmayr, Fred. "Polis and Cosmpolis." In *Comparative Political Culture in an Age of Globalization*, Hwa Yol Jung, Ed. New York: Lexington Books, 2002, pp. 419–32. Print.

Elizondo, Virgilio, *Guadalupe: Mother of the New Creation*. Maryknoll, NY: Orbis Press, 1997. Print.

———, *The Future is Mestizo: Life Where Cultures Meet* (Revised Edition). Boulder, CO: University Press of Colorado, 2002. Print.

Galston, William A. *Anti-Pluralism: The Populist Threat to Liberal Democracy*. New Haven: Yale University Press, 2018. Print.

Gorski, Philip. *American Covenant: A History of Civil Religion From the Puritans to the Present*. 2007. Print.

Goodhart, David. *The Road to Somewhere: The New Tribes Shaping British Politics*. Penguin Random House UK, 2017. Print.

———. *The Road to Somewhere: The Populist Revolt and the Future of Politics*. London: Hurst & Company, 20018. Print.

Gracia, Jorge J. E. *Hispanic/Latino Identity: A Philosophical Perspective*. Malden, MA: Blackwell Publishers, 2000. Print.

Hansen, Victor Davis. *Mexifornia: A State of Becoming* (2nd Edition). New York: Encounter Books, 2007. Print.

Heywood, Andrés. *Political Ideologies: An Introduction* (6th Edition). Palgrave Macmillan, 2017. Print.

Hudson, William. *American Democracy in Peril: Eight Challenges to America's Future* (8th Edition). Thousand Oaks, California: CQ Press, 2017. Print.

Huntington, Samuel P. *The Clash of Civilizations and the Remaking of World Order*. New York: Touchstone, 1996. Print.

Judis, John B. *The Populist Explosion: How the Great Recession Transformed American and European Politics*. New York: Columbia Global Reports, 2016. Print.

Jung, Hwa Yol. "Introduction." In *Comparative Political Culture in an Age*

of Globalization, Hwa Yol Jung, Ed. New York: Lexington Books, 2002, pp. 1–22. Print.
Miller, Marilyn Grace. *Rise and Fall of the Cosmic Race: The Cult of Mestizaje in Latin America*. Austin: University of Texas Press, 2004. Print.
Muller, Jan-Werner. *What is Populism?* Philadelphia: University of Pennsylvania Press, 2016. Print.
Pérez-Torres, Rafael. *Mestizaje: Critical Uses of Race in Chicano Culture.* Minneapolis: University of Minnesota Press, 2006. Print.
Putnam, Robert D. *Bowling Alone: The Collapse and Revival of American Community*. New York: Touchstone, 2001. Print.
Putnam, Robert D. and David E. Campbell. *American Grace: How Religion Divides and Unites Us*. New York: Simon & Schuster, 2010. Print.
Schrag, Calvin O. "Hermeneutical Circles, Rhetorical Triangles, and Transversal Diagonals." In *Comparative Political Culture in an Age of Globalization*, Hwa Yol Jung, ed. New York: Lexington Books, 2002, pp. 381–95. Print.
Schumacher, E.F. *Small is Beautiful: Economics as if People Mattered*. New York: Perennial Library, 1975. Print.
Vasconcelos, José. *The Cosmic Race: A Bilingual Edition*. Didier T. Jaén, Trans. Baltimore: Johns Hopkins Press, 1997. Print.
Yunus, Muhammad. *Banker to the Poor: Micro-lending and the Battle Against World Poverty*. New York: Public Affairs, 2003. Print.

Part III

Crossroads of Social & Literary Time & Space, Not to Mention Tradition & Modernity, in Spain

CHAPTER 8

Pablo Picasso's Semantically-Complex Visual Poetry Through Modern Technology

Enrique Mallén and Luis Meneses

Pablo Picasso dedicated a considerable amount of his time to writing starting around 1935. He wrote primarily poetry in Spanish and French, at times mixing the two languages. In this essay, we explore the essential characteristics of his writings in comparison to his plastic works and the question of whether there was any correlation between these two aspects of his career.

First, Picasso's poetry is extremely visual to the point that his manuscripts could almost be taken to be independent works of art. Second, the method Picasso used in his writings is essentially combinatorial in nature, with words co-occurring often in unexpected ways. We propose to explore the possibility that the transition into poetry that we observe in Picasso is simply one more manifestation of his pursuit of alternative approaches to language as a means of representation. With that in mind, we first analyze the concepts Picasso used independently of any specific language. Second, we group those concepts into larger semantic categories. Furthermore, we plan to explore how those semantic categories might cluster into even larger semantic domains. Our analysis will allow us to more precisely delimit the lexical manifestation of certain concepts in the two languages, enabling us to see interrelations between words and particular topics. Ultimately, our analysis will allow us to identify and classify representative themes and correlations in the two different languages that Picasso used. Furthermore, we will examine how semantic categories and semantic domains interact within what is possibly a very complex semantic network. The final goal of our research is to establish the network of semantic distinctions that Picasso worked with in his writings, as it would provide a window into the mind of the artist, which we may then be able to link to the themes he dealt with in his artworks.

Picasso the Writer

The reasons for Picasso's new emphasis in his artistic career are open to debate. Many have cited, among possible causes, the Spanish artist's emotional crisis, the political turmoil in Europe in the period between the two world wars, or the menace of a fratricidal confrontation in Spain. All of these views assume an irreducible conflict between visual expression and his new verbal compositions. However, we cannot forget that Picasso's interest in verbal communication had already started during his cubist period. To quote Marie-Laure Bernadac:

> Picasso always played with the ambivalence of words ... The *papiers collés* [may be thought of] as 'proverbs;' that is, as things that take the place of the verb 'to paint' ... The battle between word and image, between art and reality, between different systems of signs ... but one must never forget that Picasso's cubism is two things at once; it's painting and it's language ... His whole life he was obsessed with the relationship between painting and writing ... the battle between word and image.[1]

The connection between his writings and his plastic works has been explored by Baldassari (2005):

> In the decade between 1925 and 1935 ... the scrolling lines, bursting constellations, curving grids, and broad strokes that cross the surface of his pictorial work then found a new dimension in his poetic writing. Breton fully sensed its importance ... 'This poetry is unfailingly visual in the same way that the painting is poetic.'[2]

Earlier, Daix (1993) had pointed out that "the graphism of his letters and the way they were placed on a page were also a deliberate, visual creation."[3] However, although his hand-written poems at times remind us of medieval illustrated manuscripts, one cannot deny that Picasso's poetry is essentially verbal and not conditioned exclusively by plastic principles.

Combinatorial Poetry

The method he used in his poems and the manner in which he combines its constituents could very well derive from the lessons learned during his involvement with the cubist *collage*. Phrases link to each other in fluctuant attachments, intentionally left tentative and ambiguous, open to potential deletions and additional insertions, just as pieces of paper were precariously pinned to the support in the cubist *collage*. Moreover, as was the case with *papier collés*, words do not lose their physical presence as they enter the realm of signification; they are equally valid as material elements, providing tonality and rhythm to the lines of the poem, as the color and texture of the pasted papers did in the cubist composition. His poems are open to a flux of changes, additions, and erasures. Very few of his poems remain in their pristine state. To Louis Parrot he had declared:

> When I began to write [poems] I wanted to prepare myself a palette of words, as if I were dealing with colors. All these words were weighed, filtered and appraised. I don't put much stock in spontaneous expressions of the unconscious and it would be stupid to think that one can provoke them at will.[4]

There is no question that Picasso was trying to express deeply-guarded ideas and feelings, many of which he had not yet fully come to terms with, but it is also true that the poems he composed were thoroughly thought out and were far from random.

The type of verbal expression he employed is probably also intentional. Evading a hierarchical clausal structure, his paratactic writing proceeds nomadically by conflictive relations between words on a "plane of consistency" that produce concatenations held together (and simultaneously separated) either by pure spatial metonymical juxtapositions or by the play of connectors. These concatenations result in the postponement of semantic completion. The implicit desire of an attainable reference remains unfulfilled. As in Lacanian psychology, we are not dealing with desire for some concrete referential object (which would be defined as need) or desire for the reader's recognition of what the writer has to say (which would be interpreted as demand), but desire itself at the pulling center of the communicative system, the core of the Symbolic, the governing principle of language itself. This is what Pablo Picasso tries to express by his combinatorial method of assembling poetic texts and pictorial compositions.

As a good example of Picasso's technique, we may examine a poem written in Spanish on August 7, 1935, entitled *Recogiendo limosnas*.[5]

*recogiendo limosnas en su plato de oro — vestido de jardín —
aquí está ya el torero — sangrando su alegría entre los pliegues de la
capa — y recortando estrellas con tijeras de rosas — sacudiendo su
cuerpo la arena del reloj — en el cuadrado que descarga en la plaza
el arco iris — que abanica la tarde del parto — sin dolor nace el
toro — que es al alfiletero de los gritos — que silban la rapidez
de la carrera — los aplausos en su tinta ardiendo en la
cazuela — las manos removiendo el aire de cristal en fusión
— la corona de bocas — y los ojos oiseaux du paradis
— que las banderas de la mano despiden — al borde del
tejado — baja por la escalera suspendida al cielo — envuelto
en su deseo — el amor — y se moja los pies en la barrera
— y nada campeón en las gradas*

Another good example of Picasso's technique is provided by the poem entitled *Lengua de fuego abanica*, also written in Spanish on November 28, 1935.[6]

*lengua de fuego — [abanica] su cara — en la flauta —
— la copa — que cantándole — roe — la puñalada
del azul — tan gracioso — que sentado
en el ojo del toro — inscrito en su cabeza — adornada
con jazmines — [espera] que hinche la vela — el trozo de cristal
— que el viento — envuelto en el embozo del mandoble
— chorreando caricias — reparte el pan — al ciego
y a la paloma — color de lilas — y aprieta —
de toda su maldad — contra los labios
— del limón [ardiendo] — el cuerno retorcido — que
espanta — con sus gestos de adiós — la catedral —
que se desmaya — en sus brazos — sin un olé —
[estallando en su mirada] la radio amanecida — [que] fotografiando
— en el beso
— una [chinche] de sol — se come el aroma
de la hora — que cae — y atraviesa la página
que vuela — deshace el ramillete — que se
lleva metido entre el ala que suspira y el miedo
que sonríe — el cuchillo que salta de contento —
dejá[ndole] aun hoy — flotando como quiere y de cualquier
manera — al momento preciso y necesario —
en lo alto del pozo — el grito — del rosa
— que la mano — le tira — como una
limosnita*

A third example is the French poem entitled *Le radeau de la méduse*, written on February 29, 1936.[7]

le radeau de la méduse se détache
de la mer pour prendre dans ses bras
le sillage de la glace de poche de l' oiseau
si le radeau de la méduse enfin détaché
de ses chaînes vole dans le noir son
front accroche le sillage de la glace
de poche
si le radeau de la méduse déshabille
son corps de ses chaînes et laisse
flotter [accroché] par les bouts des doigts des lambeaux
de vagues son front moud sa
caresse sur la pierre du sillage de
l' aile détachée de la glace de
poche
si mon radeau de la méduse déshabille son
corps de ses chaînes et ne laisse flotter
accroché par les bouts des doigts que
des lambeaux de vagues
son front moud sa caresse sur la
pierre du sillage creusé par l'aile
détachée du [tendre] oiseau [blessé] [qui chante posé] sur
la pointe de la corne du grand buffle
amoureux.[8]

The unpunctuated prose blocks in these three poems—coming at the time they do—identify Picasso's peculiar style and bring with them a number of other techniques, exploring the varied possibilities of what Bernadac calls

> this new 'plastic material' [of language] . . . chipping, pulverizing, modeling this 'verbal clay,' varying combinations of phrases, combining words, either by phonic opposition, repetition, or by an audacious metaphorical system, the seeming absurdity of which corresponds in fact to an internal and personal logic . . . Lawless writing, disregardful of syntax or rationality, but which follows the incessant string of images and sensations that passed through his head.[9]

Let us analyze one of these linguistic features in detail. The first thing one notices as one skims across the lines of the poems is the persistence of connectors such as *de*, *y* and *que* (in Spanish); or *de*, *si* (in French).

> . . . *en su plato de oro* . . . *vestido de jardín* . . . *entre los pliegues de la capa* . . . *y recortando estrellas con tijeras de rosas* . . . *la arena del reloj* . . . *el cuadrado que descarga* . . . *que abanica la tarde del parto* . . . *el toro que es el alfiletero de los gritos* . . . *que silban la rapidez de la carrera* . . . *el aire de cristal* . . . *la corona de bocas* . . . *y los ojos oiseaux du paradis* . . . *que las banderas de la mano despiden* . . . *al borde del tejado* . . . *y se moja los pies en la barrera* . . . *y nada campeón en las gradas*
> *lengua de fuego* . . . *que cantándole* . . . *la puñalada del azul* . . . *que sentado en el ojo del toro* . . . *que hinche la vela* . . . *el trozo de cristal* . . . *que el viento* . . . *el embozo del mandoble* . . . *color de lilas* . . . *y* . . . *de toda su maldad* . . . *del limón* . . . *que espanta* . . . *sus gestos de adiós* . . . *que se desmaya* . . . *que* . . . *una chinche de sol* . . . *el aroma de la hora* . . . *que cae* . . . *y* . . . *la página que vuela* . . . *que se lleva metido* . . . *entre el ala que suspira y el miedo que sonríe* . . . *el cuchillo que salta de contento* . . . *flotando como quiere y de cualquier manera* . . . *al momento preciso y necesario* . . . *en lo alto del pozo* . . . *del rosa* . . . *que la mano*
> *le radeau de la méduse se détache de la mer pour prendre dans ses bras le sillage de la glace de poche de l'oiseau* . . . *si le radeau de la méduse enfin détaché de ses chaînes vole dans le noir son front accroche le sillage de la glace de poche* . . . *si le radeau de la méduse déshabille son corps de ses chaînes et laisse flotter accroché par les bouts des doigts des lambeaux de vagues son front moud sa caresse sur la pierre du sillage de l'aile détachée de la glace de poche* . . . *si mon radeau de la méduse déshabille son corps de ses chaînes et ne laisse flotter accroché par les bouts des doigts que des lambeaux de vagues son front moud sa caresse sur la pierre du sillage creusé par l'aile détachée du tendre oiseau blessé qui chante posé sur la pointe de la corne du grand buffle amoureux.*

De may at first appear to be different from the other connectors (*y*, *que*, *si*), as grammatically it is categorized as a preposition. However, when arranged in multiple concatenations, these prepositions display a clear rhizomatic quality, "linking wildly heterogeneous series of terms," subverting any of their single or double genitive functions, and "forcing the reader to eventually abandon causal/grammatical readings," in Rothenberg and Joris's description. This relinquishing of the desire to locate the specific semantic unit from which a given term is supposed to be derived leads the reader to experience an endless chain of derivations as an ongoing forward drive or as what has been termed a "*dérive*," as Joris (2003) notes.[10]

The conjunctions lose the causal or subordinating effects they have in conventional syntactical constructions to be transformed by Picasso into accelerators, thus allowing readers to connect one object to the next, in multiple ramifications. Their accentuated frequency immediately overcomes their common occurrence when used singly, in which case they function as dividers, creators of dialectical and ontological differentiations between two terms, or originators of all sorts of dualism. In contrast, these multiple connectors function vectorally, pointing to nomadic spaces outside and beyond the words they relate, rather than setting up one-to-one relations between them. As Deleuze writes: "And is not even a specific relation or conjunction, it is that which subtends all relations, the path of all relations, which makes relations shoot outside their terms and outside the set of their terms, and outside everything which could be determined as Being."[11]

Ramifications also affect the writing process itself. Poems are revisited in different supports, changing from one state to another at various moments of their genesis. Thus, the second and third poem are presented simultaneously in several versions.

> *lengua de fuego su cara en la flauta vs. lengua de fuego [abanica] su cara en la flauta; cabeza adornada con jazmines que hinche la vela vs. cabeza adornada con jazmines [espera] que hinche la vela; los labios del limón vs. los labios del limón [ardiendo]; sin un olé vs. sin un olé [estallando en su mirada]; or cabeza adornada con jazmines que hinche la vela vs. cabeza adornada con jazmines [espera] que hinche la vela; los labios del limón vs. los labios del limón ardiendo; se desmaya en sus brazos sin un olé vs. se desmaya en sus brazos sin un olé estallando en su mirada; la radio amanecida fotografiando en el beso vs. la radio amanecida que fotografiando en el beso; una de sol se come el aroma vs. una chinche de sol se come el aroma; le radeau de la méduse déshabille son corps de ses chaînes et laisse flotter vs. le radeau de la méduse déshabille son corps de ses chaînes et laisse flotter accroché; sillage creusé par l'aile détachée du oiseau vs. sillage creusé par l'aile détachée du tendre oiseau vs. sillage creusé par l'aile détachée du tendre oiseau blessé vs. sillage creusé par l'aile détachée du tendre oiseau blessé qui chante posé.*

Each layer with new additions and deletions is carefully dated by the author. Unfortunately, the "final" copy we often read in printed versions is artificial in that the editor has subjected it to reductive transformation. It essentially consists in transcribing the polydirectional space of the manuscript, which offers a multi-centered spatial visual reading, into a monodirectional linear space, providing a restrictive and unidirectional reading. However even such frozen linearized transcriptions (often carried out by Picasso's secretary, Jaime Sabartés) fail to conceal the ambiguity of the text and its appositive syntactic structures.

Adjunctive Poetry

Another clear link between Picasso's visual works and his poetry is the presence of graphic elements in his writings. Cowling (2002) refers to both his poems and his artworks as executed in a "spider's web" style:

> A glance at the manuscripts reveals that he was attentive to the look and lay-out of the pages, relishing the dramatic impact of such things as variations in the size and style of the script, changes in the flow of ink or the thickness of the nib (and the color when he used crayons), contrasts between letters, numbers, dividing lines and the special punctuation marks he favored, different systems for crossing-out and large blots of ink. The calligraphy varies a good deal and is sometimes ornate and the effect handsome and arresting.[12]

These graphic elements could be quite decorative, giving the manuscript the appearance of an artwork.

In these poems, we significantly notice the presence of hyphens. Upon close examination, we discover that the syntactic constituents contained within hyphens are, for the most part, adjunct phrases:*

> [VP recogiendo$_1$ limosnas en su plato de oro] — [AP vestido$_1$ de jardín] — [IP aquí está ya el torero$_1$] — [VP sangrando$_1$ su alegría entre los pliegues de la capa$_2$] — y [VP recortando$_{1/2}$ estrellas con tijeras de rosas] — [VP sacudiendo$_{1/3}$ su cuerpo$_3$ la arena del reloj$_3$] — [PP en$_{1/3}$ el cuadrado que descarga en la plaza el arco iris$_4$] — [CP que$_{1/4}$ abanica la tarde del parto$_5$] — [PP sin$_5$ dolor nace el toro$_6$] — [CP que$_{1/6}$ es el alfiletero de los gritos$_7$] — [CP que$_7$ silban la rapidez de la carrera$_8$] — [VP los aplausos$_8$ en su tinta ardiendo en la cazuela$_{10}$] — [VP las manos$_9$ removiendo el aire de cristal en fusión] — [NP la corona de bocas$_9$] — y [NP los ojos oiseaux du paradis$_9$] — [CP que$_9$ las banderas$_{10}$ de la mano despiden] — [PP al borde del tejado$_{10}$] — [VP baja$_{11}$ por la escalera suspendida al cielo] — [AP envuelto$_{11}$ en su deseo] — [NP el amor$_{11}$] — y [VP se moja$_{11}$ los pies en la barrera] — y [VP nada$_{11}$ campeón en las gradas]

[NP *lengua de fuego₁*] — [VP *abanica₁/₂*] [NP *su cara₂*] — [PP *en la flauta*] — [NP *la copa₃*] — [CP₃ *que cantándole*] — [VP *roe₃/₈*] —[NP8 *la puñalada del* [NP4 *azul*]] — [AP4 *tan gracioso*] — [CP4 *que sentado en* [NP11 *el ojo del toro*]] — [AP4/11 *inscrito en su cabeza₅*] — [AP5/8 *adornada con jazmines*] — [VP *espera₄*] [CP *que hinche₆ la vela*] — [NP6 *el trozo de cristal*] — [CP *que el viento₇*] — [AP7 *envuelto en el embozo del mandoble*] — [VP7 *chorreando caricias*] — [VP *reparte₆ el pan*] — [PP *al ciego y a la paloma*] — [AP *color de lilas*] — *y* [VP *aprieta₆*] — [PP *de toda su maldad*] — [PP *contra los labios*] — [PP *del limón* [VP *ardiendo*]] — [NP *el cuerno retorcido*] — [CP7 *que espanta*] — [PP *con sus gestos de adiós*] — [NP8 *la catedral*] — [CP8*que se desmaya*] — [PP *en sus brazos*] — [PP *sin un ole*] — [VP8 *estallando en su mirada*] [NP9 *la radio amanecida*] — [CP9 *que*] [VP9*fotografiando*] — [PP *en el beso*] — [NP 10 *una* [NP *chinche*] *de sol*] — [VP *se come₈/₉/10* [NP12 *el aroma de la hora*]] — [CP12 *que cae*] — *y* [VP *atraviesa₈/₉/10/12 la página que vuela₁₃*] — [VP *deshace₁₃* [NP14 *el ramillete₁₄*] — [CP14 *que se lleva metido*] — [PP *entre el ala que suspira y el miedo que sonríe*] — [NP *el cuchillo₁₅ que salta de contento*] — [VP₁₅ *dejá[ndole] aun hoy*] — [VP16 *flotando como quiere y de cualquier manera*] — [PP *al momento preciso y necesario*] — [PP *en lo alto del pozo*] — [NP17 *el grito*] — [PP *del rosa₈*] — [CP18 *que* [NP19 *la mano*] — [VP *le tira₁₉*] — [PP *como una limosnita*]

The third poem lacks hyphenations; however, here the inserted elements again are systematically-adjunctive phrases:

> *si le radeau de la méduse déshabille son corps de ses chaînes et laisse flotter* [AP *accroché*] *par les bouts des doigts des lambeaux de vagues son front moud sa caresse sur la pierre du sillage de l'aile détachée de la glace de poche . . . si mon radeau de la méduse déshabille son corps de ses chaînes et ne laisse flotter accroché par les bouts des doigts que des lambeaux de vagues son front moud sa caresse sur la pierre du sillage creusé par l'aile détachée du* [AP *tendre*] *oiseau* [AP *blessé*] [CP*qui chante posé*] *sur la pointe de la corne du grand buffle amoureux*

Indeed, the first poem, in its totality, consists of a compound sentence, with two adjoined main clauses: *"aquí está ya el torero"* and

---

The abbreviations CP, NP, VP, AP, PP stand for Complementizer Phrase, Noun Phrase, Verb Phrase, Adjective Phrase and Preposition Phrase, respectively. Brackets are used to separate different phrasal constituents.

"*baja por la escalera suspendida al cielo el amor.*" Adjunct phrases, such as "*recogiendo limosnas en su plato de oro,*" "*vestido de jardín,*" "*sangrando su alegría entre los pliegues de la capa,*" "*recortando estrellas con tijeras de rosas,*" "*sacudiendo su cuerpo la arena del reloj,*" "*en el cuadrado que descarga en la plaza el arco iris,*" etc., modify the main subject, "*el torero.*" Other adjuncts serve the same purpose, also modifying noun phrases such as "*el toro*": "*que es el alfiletero de los gritos;*" "*los gritos;*" "*que silban la rapidez de la carrera;*" "*los aplausos;*" "*en su tinta ardiendo en la cazuela,*" etc.

The second poem also involves a compound sentence, with one main clause, "*lengua de fuego abanica su cara en la flauta,*" amended by a series of adjoined phrases. The first one is appositive, "*la copa que cantándole roe la puñalada del azul tan gracioso*" and is followed by several subordinate relative clauses introduced by the conjunction "*que*": "*que sentado en el ojo del toro inscrito en su cabeza adornada con jazmines espera que hinche la vela el trozo de cristal,*" "*que el viento envuelto en el embozo del mandoble chorreando caricias reparte el pan al ciego y a la paloma color de lilas y aprieta de toda su maldad contra los labios del limón ardiendo el cuerno retorcido,*" "*que espanta con sus gestos de adiós la catedral,*" "*que se desmaya en sus brazos sin un ole estallando en su mirada la radio amanecida,*" "*que fotografiando en el beso una chinche de sol se come el aroma de la hora,*" "*que cae y atraviesa la página,*" "*que vuela deshace el ramillete,*" "*que se lleva metido entre el ala que suspira y el miedo que sonríe el cuchillo,*" "*que salta de contento dejándole aun hoy flotando como quiere y de cualquier manera al momento preciso y necesario en lo alto del pozo el grito del rosa,*" "*que la mano le tira como una limosnita.*"

The third poem contains one declarative sentence, which is followed by three sentences with conditional clauses introduced by the conjunction "*si*" and which provide variants of the first sentence. The reflexive "*se détache*" in the declarative sentence is changed to the adjective "*détaché*" in the first conditional clause, which is now headed by the verb "*vole*". The main clause of this second sentence has as its subject "*son front,*" "*accroche*" as its verb and "*le sillage de la glace de poche*" as its complement. The latter is a repetition of the complement of the main clause minus "*de l'oiseau.*" The main clause of the third-sentence sentence repeats the same subject "*son front*" which is now combined with the reflexive verb "*sa caresse*" and the former complement is expanded with two modifiers and itself becomes a modifier to "*pierre:*" "*du sillage de l'aile détachée de la glace de poche.*" The latter is further expanded in the last sentence with one of its prepositional modifiers changed by the insertion of an additional adjectival phrase: "*du sillage creusé par l'aile détachée.*" In this last sentence, the noun phrase *"la glace de poche de l'oiseau"* of the first sentence has been metaphorically extended to *"l'aile détachée du tendre oiseau blessé qui chante posé sur la pointe de la corne du grand buffle amoureux."*

In current syntactic theory, adjuncts are modifiers which freely attach at a hierarchically-higher level in a phrase and provide circumstantial information pertaining to its nucleus and the latter's relation to both complement and specifier. In contrast to these two, adjuncts are constituents which may be found in iteration, and their relation to the nucleus is that of a modifier, often left ambiguous. In Picasso's case, we see that the different adjunct modifiers interact with other constituents in the poem in strings of metaphoric confrontations shown by coindexation. Adjuncts are also the ones that are purposely left differentiated (often placed at a different level, or in the margins, etc.), as if they were footnoted "afterthoughts" to the already-validated text when revisions occur. In fact, it is sometimes quite a task for the editor of these poems to decide exactly where the added text must be incorporated, as the writer intentionally leaves this detail ambiguous. The reader is left to choose whether to follow the suggested insertions in one direction or another or to even continue with the original text, ignoring the later additions.

Let us use the second poem as illustration of the modifying function of adjuncts. The series of adjoined phrases can be correlated with different thematic roles. Thus, in *lengua de fuego abanica su cara en la flauta*, the [NP *lengua de fuego*] could be taken as the agent or patient, depending on how [NP *su cara*] is interpreted. The two noun phrases may exchange roles. This is due to the possibility of having topicalized patients in Spanish. The same applies to the sentence *la copa que cantándole roe la puñalada del azul tan gracioso*, where the noun phrase [NP *la copa*] may swap roles with [NP *la puñalada del azul*]. Often adjectival modifiers and relative clauses are left ambiguous. Thus, in the sentence *(azul) que sentado en el ojo del toro inscrito en su cabeza adornada con jazmines espera que hinche la vela el trozo de cristal*, the adjectival phrase [AP *inscrito en su cabeza*] may be predicated of [NP *azul*] or [NP *el ojo del toro*]; and [AP *adornada con jazmines*] may modify [NP *su cabeza*] or [NP *la flauta*]. This is also applicable to noun phrases that are interpreted as being in apposition, such as [NP *el trozo de cristal*], which may then be read as a metaphor of [NP *la vela*].

We find many cases where one sentence links to the next by having one phrase serve a double function. Thus, the prepositional phrase [PP *en la flauta*] in *(en la flauta) la copa que cantándole roe la puñalada del azul tan gracioso* can be taken to modify the following sentence whose subject is [NP *la copa*]. Also the noun phrase [NP *el trozo de cristal*] is not only an appositive modifier of the previous sentence, but also the agent of the next one, (*el trozo de cristal*) *que el viento envuelto en el embozo del mandoble chorreando caricias reparte el pan al ciego y a la paloma color de lilas*; and through the conjunction, also of the following third sentence: *y* (*el trozo de cristal*) *aprieta de toda su maldad contra los labios del limón ardiendo el cuerno retorcido*. And the noun phrase [NP *el cuerno retorcido*] is not only the patient of this sentence, but also the head of the subsequent relative clause (*el cuerno retorcido*) *que espanta con sus gestos de adiós la catedral*. This is also the case in the three following sentences:

> (*la catedral*) *que se desmaya en sus brazos sin un ole estallando en su mirada la radio amanecida que fotografiando en el beso una chinche de sol se come el aroma de la hora*; *el aroma de la hora que cae atraviesa la página que vuela deshace el ramillete*; and (*el ramillete*) *que se lleva metido entre el ala que suspira y el miedo que sonríe*.

We must also mention here the frequent use of gerunds, which are open to be interpreted as modifying an immediately preceding noun phrase or a more distant one. Thus [VP *estallando en su mirada*] could coindexed with [NP *un ole*], but also with [NP *la catedral*].

The last two complex phrases in the poem under discussion may be interpreted as two additional asyndetic coordinations: [NP *el cuchillo que salta de contento dejándole aun hoy flotando como quiere y de cualquier manera al momento preciso y necesario en lo alto del pozo*] and [NP *el grito del rosa que la mano le tira como una limosnita*].

Graphic Poetry

The paratactic interpretations and the simultaneous presence of verbal and graphic elements that we observe in Picasso's writing bring back to mind the different "planes of consistency" of his Cubist *collage*s, which can, in fact, simultaneously exist at many different levels, as Golding (1968) has argued: as representation of real objects; as independent pictorial symbols; and as solid, tactile pieces with their own material existence. Thus, in the first *collage*, *Nature morte à la chaise cannée*, the letters JOU, excised from *Jour* or *Journal*, glide above and below a geometrically-complex composition, associated and dissociated at once with it, "the O being mixed with color, the U brightly-impaled by a ray of light which is itself the extension of a linear definition," so they serve as pictorial symbols but can also be read as verbal signs referring to the newspaper they are intended to stand for.[13] The chair caning, moreover, "counters all the painterly areas—both by its insistent rhythmic pattern, and as an unexpected incorporation of unreconstructed object." Its materiality also makes its tactile presence obvious. Thus, it may be interpreted as a table surface, but not entirely, because it also contains lateral and cross strokes that reasserts the plastic form over the referential object.[14] Thus, as in his poems, Picasso combines reality with representation and also introduces different types of signs co-occurring in the same composition.[15]

A technical variant of the *collage* is the *papier collé*, though the two methods are different in practice. *Collage* involves the incorporation of various object material in a painting, while *papier collé* implies the manipulation of printed papers, newsprint clips—themselves illusory, manufactured images or patterns. The separate strips of paper neither refer to subject nor assume dimension as object. Important modifications may also take place through the fusion of the drawing with the bits of paper. These may serve as background or foreground of the composition. Each of the added elements modifies the others, although both physically and conceptually, they only meet as independent entities which scarcely intersect.

Papiers collés ultimately served as seeing-machines, forming the testing ground for the dialogue between material and sign for Picasso. It is at this point that he makes several attempts at totally abstract expression with only a semiotic link with external reality. As Golding (1968) shows, figuration is accomplished by laying next to each other a series of stylized forms that represent its component parts. Works are now built up of abstract shapes given a representational role only by the symbolic way in which they are assembled to depict a particular subject. Shapes that bear very little resemblance to the original parts of the body are used as conventional symbols for them. Such constructions account for the simplifications and distortions that begin to appear in Picasso's paintings towards the end of 1913. Deviations of this type enhance the metaphoric correlations that had begun to appear in Picasso's work during the previous year and which are now fully accomplished.

Complex Poetry

Throughout his writing career, Picasso uses the process of addition and accumulation. His creations are elaborated through rewritings and repetitions. This process may actually be linked to his conception of creativity in general, which is for him forever evolving, forever transforming itself. As in his plastic works, Picasso, the writer, was constantly searching, attempting to uncover through the medium of language that which cannot otherwise be revealed. It may be argued that discontinuity and rupture are the features that most characterize his works, both in the area of the visual arts (as during the different phases of Cubism) and in literature. Michaël (2000) defines Picasso's poetry as a space of "labyrinthine writing." Words proliferate, attract others, breaking the syntagmatic line of language and freeing words from grammatical constraints. The poem is made up of an overflowing sentence, a kind of "hypersentence," which, in its expanding, continually folds and unfolds in a non-linear, undulatory parataxis.

In Most's (2006) description of Picasso's poetry,

> a language-chain is created that tangles and untangles itself effortlessly and repeatedly. It is not as simple as a paradox, controlled chaos, nor as complex as a sleight of hand, a language game for the sake of a language game. The connecting words allow you to hear life multiplying life, multiplicity in everyday things.

As Michel Leiris points out, Picasso is "an insatiable player with words ... [who, like] James Joyce ... in his *Finnegan's Wake* ... displayed an equal capacity to promote language as a real thing (one might say) ... and to use it with as much dazzling liberty."[16]

Each reading falls back on its initial steps and each time we are brought back to a beginning. The poem is, therefore, endless. Never static, it opens onto an infinite time, because it is possible to go on reading it circularly. We could say that Picasso's writing is perpetually in the making, constantly evolving. The text unfurls and transforms itself. It can be read in the continuity of its states like a unique, metamorphosing text. However, its different moments can also be read separately. As mentioned earlier, the many revisions and alterations Picasso makes to the poems are often introduced in the form of adjuncts. Hence, we are faced here with a "multiple text," which offers several conflicting readings through its successive "rewritings."

As in his *collage*s, Picasso's poems are a not a conscious search for a form to express a specific idea, so much as a radical exploration of the linguistic forms that themselves project ideas. Representation of reality is the final objective rather than the starting point. While Analytical Cubism worked from a specific motif towards its reconstitution in terms of painting, Picasso's *collage*s and his surrealist writings start with the basic categories of painting and language—and from them, compose images which we could justly claim are more real, since they are in no sense distorted or imitative of something else.[17] With *papier collé* and his complex poetry, Picasso manages to create reverberations in the beholder's mind and eye: graphic and verbal components make their effect simultaneously, though they have nothing to do with one another. The various realities echo to-and-fro in the reader's perception, heightening one another and unsettling all preconceived notions of the truth.[18]

This last point brings us to the reason behind Picasso's emphasis on indeterminacy in his compositions. In their inconclusiveness, the poems are intended to set in motion variable fluctuant representations. The more complex and undefined his artistic output becomes, the richer the delineation of reality Picasso achieves, including his own persona. It is the search that matters, rather than any possible object that may be found. According to the German philosopher Johann Gottlieb Fichte, if the subject is to posit itself at all, it must simply discover itself to be limited, a discovery that Fichte describes as a "check" or *Anstoß* to the free, practical activity of the subject. It provides the essential occasion or impetus that first sets in motion the entire complex train of activities that finally result in conscious experience both of the empirical self and of the world of spatio-temporal material objects. *Anstoß* does not come from outside, it is strictly speaking "ex-timate," a non-assimilable "desire" at the very core of the subject. What "desire" desires is not a determinate object but the unconditional assertion of "desiring" itself.[19] *Anstoß* in German has two primary meanings: "check, obstacle, hindrance;" but also "impetus, stimulus." Fichte himself defines *Anstoß* as the foreign body that causes the subject division into the empty absolute subject and the finite determinate subject, limited by the non-I. *Anstoß* is thus closer to Jacques Lacan's *objet petit a*, to the primordial foreign body that "sticks in the throat" of the subject, to the object-cause of desire that splits it up.[20] Fichte made clear the subject's dependence on a cause which is de-centered with regard to the subject. In this sense, he was the first philosopher to focus on the uncanny contingency in the very heart of subjectivity: the Fichtean subject is caught, in a contingent situation forever-eluding mastery. It is this contingency and the impossibility of mastering an inexpugnable interpretation that governs Picasso's poetry.

Contingent simultaneity[21] is an essential component of Picasso's combinatorial work as a whole. The left-to-right, top-to-bottom arrangement of the text and linear configurations is nothing else but the disguise of an internal, multi-directional search. The multiple ramifications of his verses and linear traces constantly branch off and cross each other. The semantic and syntactic space of the representations that Picasso constructs is one in which the perspective perpetually conceals itself. Its vanishing point is forever displaced. It is a way for Picasso to provide multiple points of view and to cancel the perspective, as he did during the period of Cubism.

In his role as poet and artist, Picasso becomes a blind "seer" (blind to actual reality, but sensitive to the virtual dimension of things), to use Gilles Deleuze's metaphor. Like a spider deprived of eyes and ears, he becomes infinitely sensitive to whatever resonates through the virtual web he has tangled in his poems. Actual or constituted forms slip through the web and make no impression, for the web is designed to vibrate only on contact with virtual forms. The more fleeting the movement, the more intense its resonance through the web. The web only responds to the movements of a pure multiplicity before it has adopted any definite shape.

A Digital Humanities Approach

Picasso's poetry demanded a different type of analysis because of its features and characteristics. In order to better ascertain the semantic characteristics of Picasso's writings, we analyzed the lexicon he used with the computational tools made available in the Digital Humanities.

We start our analysis by providing an overview of how our document collection is stored. The repository of poems and the concepts were stored using MySQL: an open source relational database. In this sense, the relational aspect of a database allowed us to break up the different components of his writings into increasingly-larger parts (lines, pages, poems) and assign them to separate tables. The original poems were later reconstructed at runtime using Standard Query Language (SQL) join operations—allowing the terms and lines to be retrieved along with additional metadata such as title (for poems), section (for pages), and number (for lines). Additionally, the poems were divided by the language they were written in, which can be either Spanish or French. The use of a database for our type of analysis is expected within the context of the Digital Humanities. However, the way we applied the affordances of relational and non-relational databases towards the analysis of the corpus of poems makes our approach different.

Words and Concepts

First, we retrieved each of the words Picasso used in his poems in both languages separately, indicating its category and its exact location in each poem. Next, each of the words was identified morphologically by such features as gender, number, etc. (in the case of nouns), and tense, aspect, mood, etc. (in the case of verbs), etc. Third, each word was linked to a set of possible meanings (using English as the translation). The reason for using one single language for the concepts was to allow for a study of possible semantic overlaps and contrasts French and Spanish. With the identified meanings (concepts), we created a set of database tables that allowed us to map each concept to related terms in Picasso's poetry, regardless of the original language. In other words, we were able to temporarily overpass the language barrier in our semantic classification of concepts. Being aware that some fine-tuning would be required in the future to account for obvious dissimilarities between the two languages, we created Web interfaces to define and view semantic relationships between the concepts, which in turn could still be linked to the concordance of terms, if needed.

The outcome of this approach was (1) a bilingual concordance of all of the words Picasso used in his poems and plays, identifying every word by language, as well as its morphological features and its meaning; and (2) a comprehensive dictionary of the concepts that Picasso worked with independently of the language he used.

After carrying out this portion of our analysis, we felt that some semantic aspects of Picasso's poetry required further exploration. One thing that remained to be determined was how concrete concepts in both languages cluster into representative larger units (semantic categories) and how these categories interact with each other in global conceptual networks.

Semantic Categories

Thus, the next step was to attempt to group concepts into larger semantic categories. At first, we decided to approach this problem from a purely computational perspective and expanded on our previous efforts based on statistical models and algorithms. More specifically, we attempted to solve this problem by analyzing Picasso's poetry corpus using Topic Modeling. Topic modeling is a concept that is often used to describe a set of algorithms that are used to describe a large number of documents that often share a common theme (Blei 2012). In other words, topic-modeling algorithms are statistical

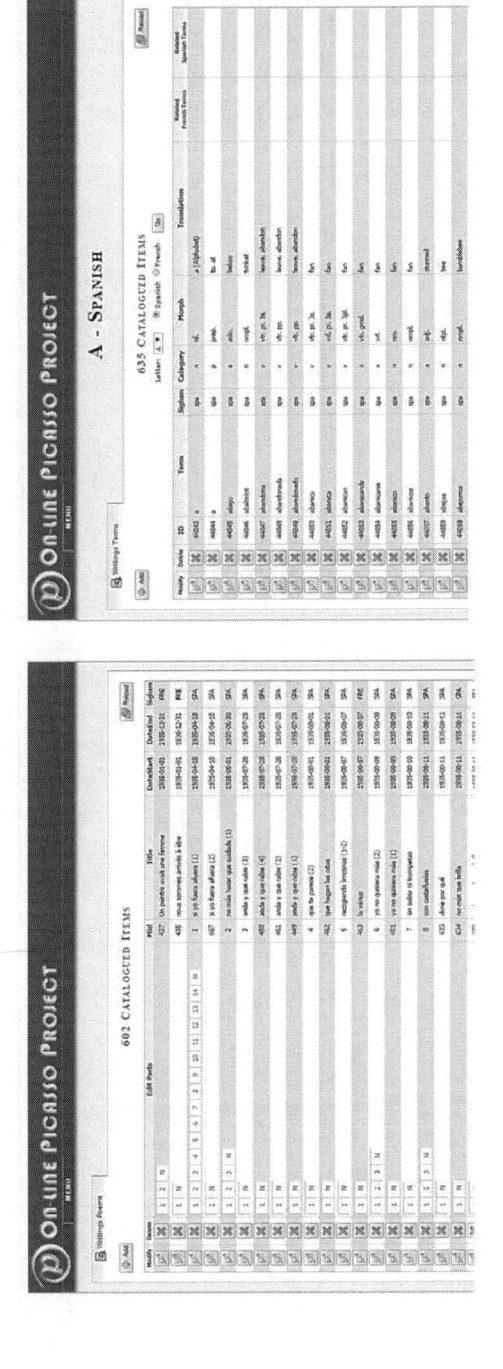

Illustration 1 List of Poems and Spanish Lexicon Specifications

methods that analyze the words in texts to discover the themes that run through them, how those themes are connected to each other, and how they change over time. More importantly, topic modeling as a technique makes no previous assumptions about the text and does not require any prior annotations or labeling of the documents. As a consequence, the topics themselves emerge from the analysis of the original texts. Topic modeling enables us to organize and summarize documents at a scale that would be impossible by human annotation —or that would require large efforts to do so.

Latent Dirichlet Allocation (commonly known as LDA) is the simplest form of topic modeling (see Blei and Jordan 2003). The main idea behind LDA is that the text included in documents does not belong to a single topic exclusively but can instead be linked to multiple topics simultaneously. Formally, a topic can be defined as a probability distribution over a fixed vocabulary. For example, a topic about Spanish literature contains words about literary works in a higher probability, whereas a topic about computer science has words pertaining to engineering in a higher percentage.

LDA can be explained using two steps. First, one randomly chooses a distribution of words over topics. And second, for each word in the document one randomly selects a topic from the distribution over topics in step one. As part of this second step, one also randomly chooses a word from the corresponding distribution over the vocabulary. This process is usually carried out in multiple iterations. Therefore, a topic model with greater iterations is usually considered to provide a better representation of the data (see "methodology" below where we explain choices specific to this analysis). Consequently, the output of an LDA model usually consists of the probability distribution of documents and terms over different topics.

In our case, we specifically chose to use LDA because of its simplicity and, more importantly, because it makes no previous assumptions over the contents of the documents. Our intention was to fully take advantage of the affordances that topic modeling provides as a machine learning technique and discover the relationships within a collection of documents, which falls right under the scope of LDA. For this purpose, the lines for each poem were then tokenized, lowercased, stemmed with a Porter stemmer and had the stop words removed to improve the accuracy of the results. Then we used Python (an interpreted, high-level, general-purpose programming language) and Gensim (a library used for topic modeling) for its implementation of LDA. After running our analysis through different iterations and different numbers of topics, we concluded that this analysis was not providing the level of granularity that we needed—ideally resulting in the highlighting of patterns and trends.

Even though models of small corpora have been attempted and carried out successfully, topic modeling works best with large corpora and text. Being a probabilistic procedure, the use of topic modeling is encouraged with sets of documents that have these characteristics. Picasso's poems, on the other hand, are rather short in their length and thus, the corpus is not substantial in size: it contains 606 catalogued poems—some of which are variations of another. Therefore, we decided to apply a different form of analysis to the corpus of poems focusing on a taxonomy-based approach.

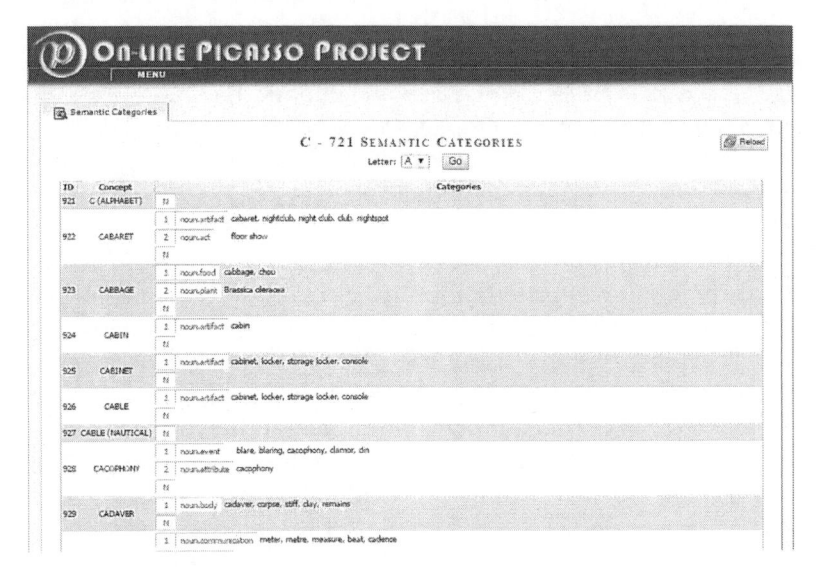

Illustration 2 List of Concepts and Corresponding Semantic Categories

Given the acknowledged semantic interconnections between the concepts Picasso explored in his poetry, we proceeded to classify the uncovered concepts behind the words in order to determine how these concepts could be grouped around specific semantic categories using Wordnet as reference.

By isolating the semantic categories Picasso worked with, we may start to get a clearer picture of how words in his poems relate to each other. These results are only preliminary since we have not yet classified all the concepts into distinct semantic categories and even those we have completed will have to be further refined.

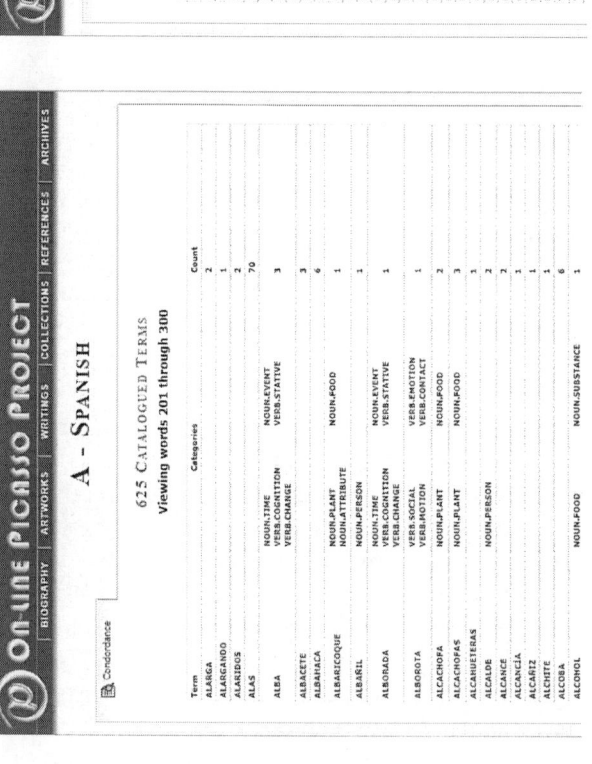

Illustration 3 List of Lexical Items and Corresponding Concepts and Semantic Categories

And yet, we already see that some of the existing semantic categories are linked to a higher number of concepts than others. For example, we found a high number of nominal artifacts in his poems. Some are related to art, such as engraving, fashion, festoon, illumination, image, impression, imprint, ornament, paint, paintbrush, painter, painting, palette; others related to war, such as armor, axe, blade, bomb, bow, bugle, bullet, camouflage, fighter, gallows, gauntlet, knife, knight, rampart, *rapier*. These may appear antagonistic, but in Picasso's world, there is a close relation between destruction in war and creation in art. Similarly, not surprisingly for a painter and writer, nominal communication is another frequent semantic category, with such concepts as advance, advice, agreement, alert, allusion, alphabet, ambiguity, announcement, answer, argument, art, articulation, canticle, fable, language, news, nonsense, note, noun, outcry, parable.

Semantic Domains

Our next goal is to group the uncovered semantic categories into even larger semantic domains: macro categories that would get us closer to main semantic domains that Picasso operated with. The wide range of semantic categories found in Pablo Picasso can be narrowed down to a smaller set of semantic domains that identify major core groups constituting the artist s entire conceptual domain. This is based on the idea of the *archisememe* or *archilexeme*. This term derives from the notion of *archiphoneme* developed by Nikolai Trubetzkoi and others in the Prague School during the years 1926–1935. An *archiphoneme* is an abstract phonological unit consisting of the distinctive features common to two phonemes that differ only in that one has a distinctive feature lacking in the other.

A semantic domain is a linguistic notion that recognizes that languages tend to divide up the spectrum of concepts differently. Sometimes the domain of a word is broader in one language than its definition is in another. For example, in English we can describe a "horse" as a "mare," "stallion," or "colt." In other languages, such as Filipino, there is only one word, i. e., the generic term for "horse." Other times, the domain of a word is much smaller in English than in other languages. For instance, Eskimo dialects have a wide range of terms for different types of "snow," while they lack a single generic word for the entire spectrum of "snow" as we have in English. Then there are cases when the domain in a language covers parts of two or more domains in another language. Again, using Filipino as an example, "orange" in it is split between "yellow" and "red," lacking

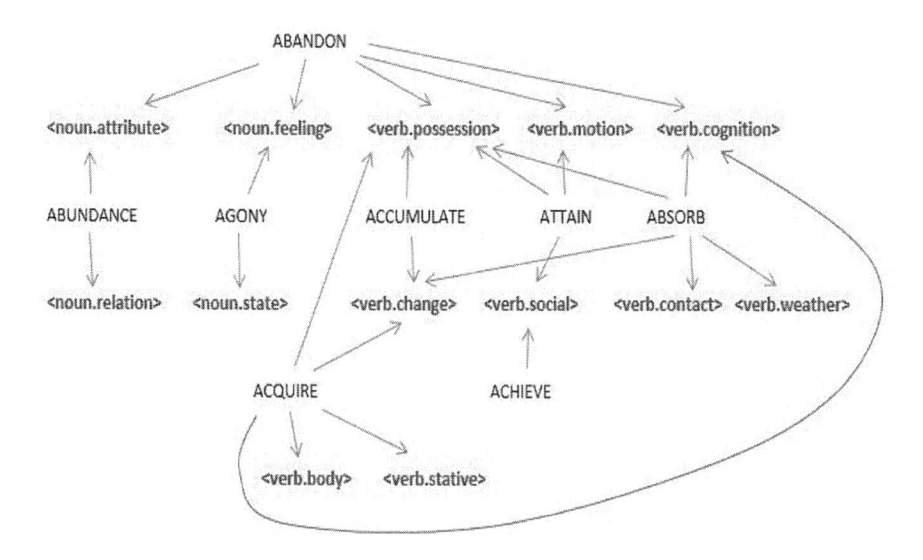

Illustration 4 Example of Semantic Domains with Relations between Concepts and Semantic Categories

the term "orange" that we find in English. Using the bilingual lexicon derived from Picasso's poetry, we devise a mechanism to extricate the set of semantic domains in his literary creation using the English translations for the Spanish and French terms as our basis.

The final goal is to group the uncovered semantic categories into macrocategories that would get us closer to main semantic domains that Picasso operated with. By isolating the semantic categories Picasso worked with, we may start to get a clearer picture of how words in his poems relate to each other.

Categorial and Morphological Distinctions between Concepts

Having identified the concepts in Picasso's poems, we next explored how these concepts differed from language to language (Spanish vs. French) or if there was a certain correlation between concepts and lexical categories or between concepts and certain morphological features (tense or mood, for instance, in the case of verbs).

In order to facilitate the identification of this correlation, we exported the tables into a SQLite database. SQLite is a small, fast, and self-contained SQL database engine with high-reliability and a full set of features. We used SQLite mainly for is portability— allowing us to manipulate and access the individual records locally. Then, we used Python to perform a series of transformations to the records and its lxml library to output the poems into Extensible Markup Language (XML) files—which in turn transformed our data from a relational to a non-relational database. We used this transformation to parse the resulting XML files with Beautiful Soup: a Python library to parse XML. As a final step, we used Plotly: a Python graphing library to create interactive graphs and visualizations from the distinctions between concepts.

The reason why we chose these tools to analyze Picasso's texts is that they allowed us to use a more flexible and agile programming style—along with a data model that is easier to use and understand. The tools are also based on Python, which brings forth an advantage in that their integration is almost seamless between each other. In our opinion, this integration facilitates the development process considerably.

Making use of these tools, we examined how Picasso implemented subtle oppositions between words in French and Spanish within specific concepts to build his poems. We also delved further into these contrasts in order to determine how concepts are either demarcated or left open in his poems. Where word-concept relations overlap in Spanish and French, common conceptual domains would be established between the two languages. In cases where word-concept correlations differed substantially, we would have a differing conceptual domain. We employed this approach to answer the question of why Picasso chose to write in a specific language about some specific content.

An example of his choice of words may be found in the concept, "kill." He used four words (and their morphological derivatives) in French for this concept: *abattent* (knock), *égorge*, *égorgeant*, *égorgée*, *égorgées* (slit); *éteignant*, *éteindre*, *éteint*, *éteinte*, *éteints* (extinguish); and *tue, tuer, tuera, tuez-le* (slay). These words impose a clear lexical demarcation within that concept. For Spanish, however, Picasso chose one single word (and its morphological derivatives) for that same concept: *matar, mataran, mate, maten, mato*. That is, he left the concept more ambiguous. An opposite situation occurs with the concept "anguish," where three words (and their morphological derivatives) are used in Spanish: *angustia, angustias* ("passive"); and *congoja, congojas*; or *acongoja* ("active"). Here, Picasso chose words that further specified the patient's role in the feeling, clearly demarcating the concept in its lexical implementation. In French, however, he selected only one word: *angoisse(s)*.

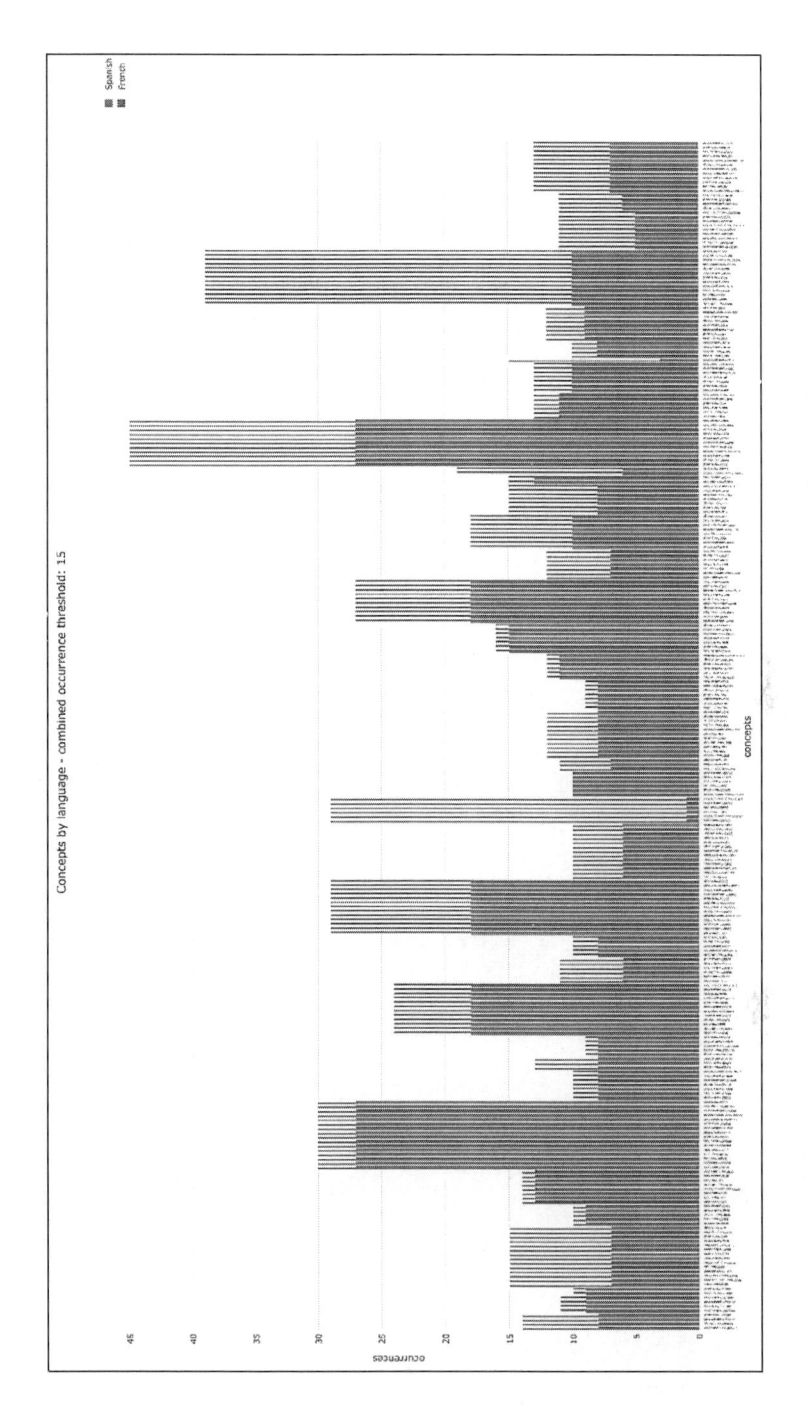

Illustration 5 Concepts grouped by language shown with a threshold of 15 combined occurrences

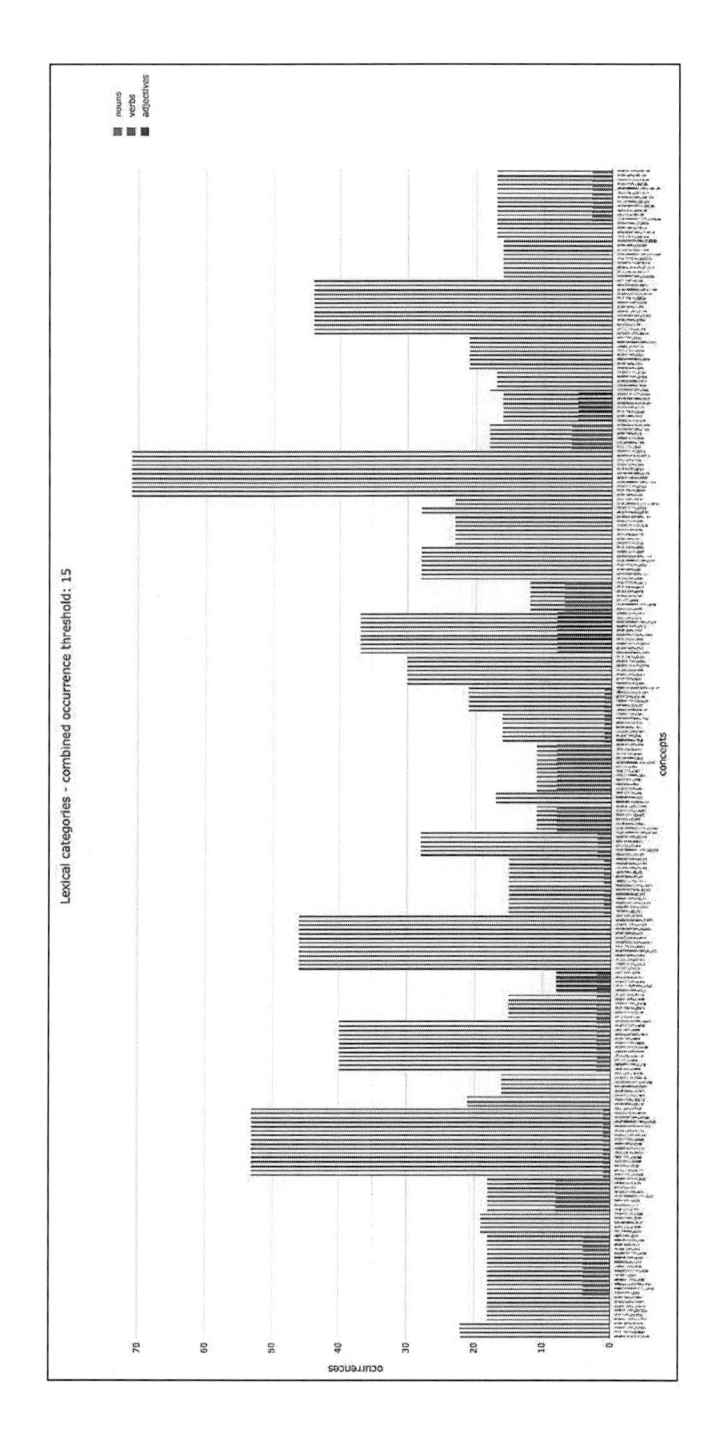

Illustration 6 Lexical Categories and related parts of speech

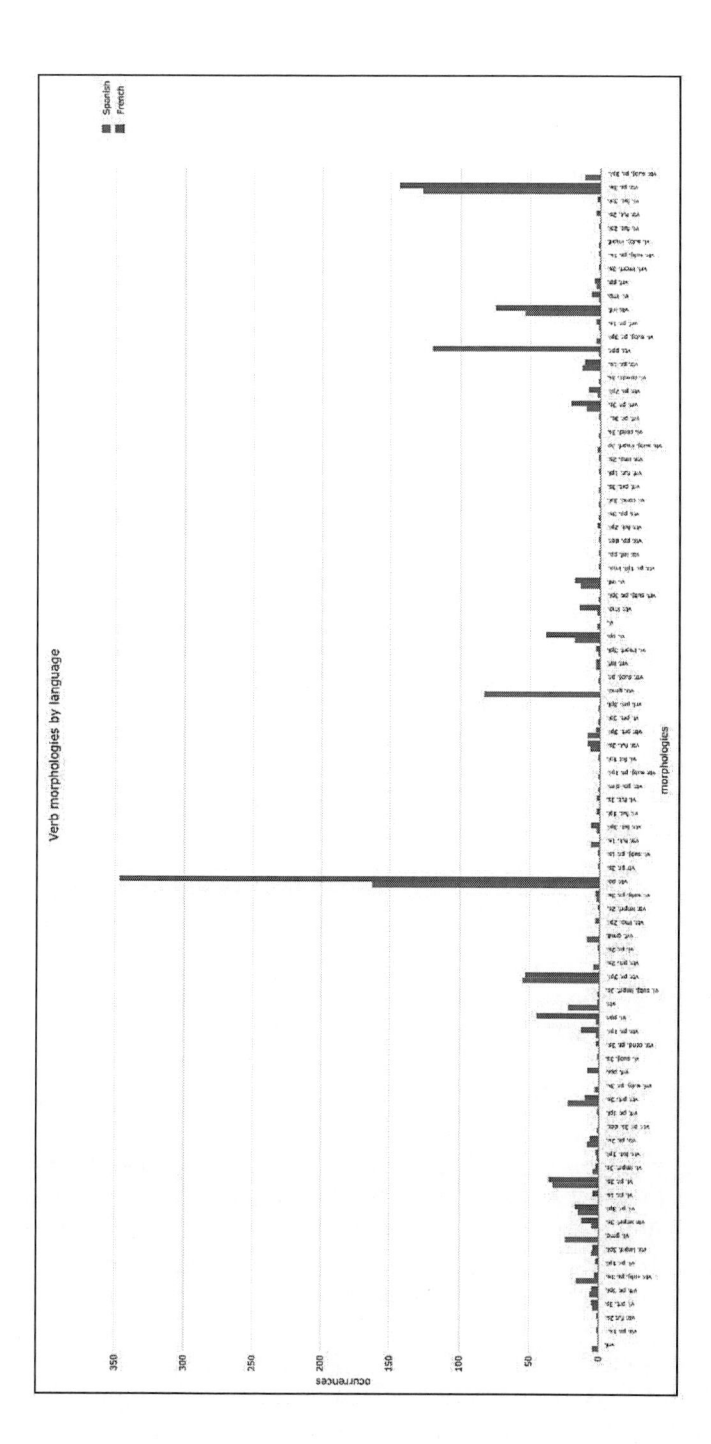

Illustration 7 Verb morphologies by listed by language

Encoding Graphic elements

One thing that remains to be explained is how the graphic components in Picasso's poetry contribute towards its literary value. Picasso's poetry is similar to that to other poets' poems, William Blake's, for example, in that graphic elements are used to enhance the text in both cases. Any account of this type of poetry should include an explanation for the observed correlation between a poem and its accompanying graphic elements. The difference is that all graphic elements in Blake's poetry are decorative in nature while those in Picasso's are, for the most part, triggered by linguistic factors, such as word-string separation, word-deletion, word-insertion, etc.

Given the linguistically-triggered graphic nature of Picasso's poetry, we treat his manuscripts as Visually Complex Documents, where distinct layers of text and images form a representation in which spatial arrangement and graphical attributes provide components of the document's meaning in conjunction with the actual words or images of the document. Effective support for analysis and interpretation of these documents requires features that help users to identify and represent relationships between a document and supporting material and to decompose the document to help clarify spatial, temporal, or other characteristics that affect its meaning.

Similarly to the different "planes of consistency" of collages, Visually Complex Documents present distinct layers of text and images that constitute integral parts of the document's representation. Following this premise, we are currently exploring solutions for encoding Picasso's poetry using the Guidelines from the Text Encoding Initiative (TEI). The TEI Guidelines for Electronic Text Encoding and Interchange define and document a markup language for representing the structural, renditional, and conceptual features of texts. They focus on the representation of primary source materials for research and analysis. The TEI guidelines are expressed as a modular, extensible XML schema, accompanied by detailed documentation, and are published under an open-source license.

In our case, we are using the TEI Guidelines for linking the encoded documents, its digital facsimiles and specific zones in its representation in a Scalable Vector Graphic (SVG). SVG is an XML-based vector image format for two-dimensional graphics. We chose to use SVGs because they allow us to have the encoded document and its representation stored both as XML files. When we couple these representations with the TEI Guidelines, the resulting documents can be read and understood by computer programs on a structural and conceptual level. With this approach, we can start to address three

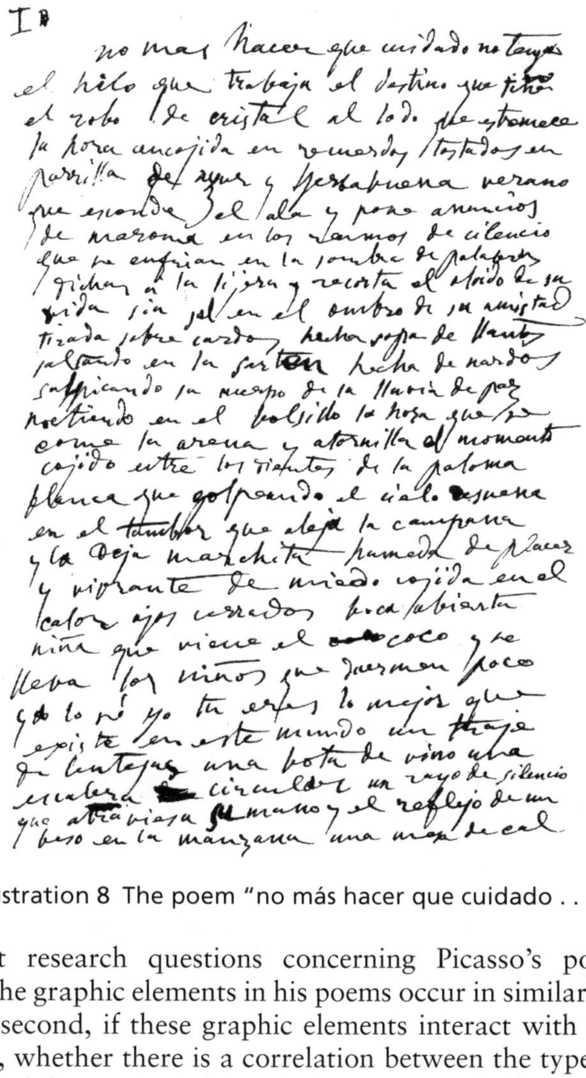

Illustration 8 The poem "no más hacer que cuidado . . . (1)"

important research questions concerning Picasso's poetry: first, whether the graphic elements in his poems occur in similar contexts in all texts; second, if these graphic elements interact with each other; and third, whether there is a correlation between the type of graphic element and the position they occur in. For instance, we can examine if blotches occur primarily before or after specific lexical categories (verbs, nouns or adjectives).

We are currently in the process of publishing a preliminary version of the poems encoded using the TEI Guidelines. As an example, we use a facsimile and a fragment of the encoded version for *"no más hacer que cuidado . . . (1)"*—one of the simpler poems in terms of encoding complexity. We are aiming for completeness, so we are carrying out the encoding process according to the level of detail that is required, going from the simpler to the more complex poems. During this work in progress, we have found that TEI has some

```xml
<div type="page" xml:id="p16" n="1">
    <figure n="OPP.35:054"/>
    <l n="1">I <del rend="crossout">PP</del></l>
    <l n="2">no más hacer que cuidado no tenga</l>
    <l n="3">el hilo que trabaja el destino que tiñe</l>
    <l n="4">el robo de cristal al lodo que estremece</l>
    <l n="5">la hora encogida en recuerdos tostados en</l>
    <l n="6">parrilla de azur y yerbabuena verano</l>
    <l n="7">que esconde al ala y pone anuncios</l>
    <l n="8">de maroma en los ramos de silencio</l>
    <l n="9">que se enfrían en la sombra de palabras</l>
    <l n="10">dichas a la ligera y recorta el olvido de su</l>
    <l n="11">vida sin sal en el hombro de su amistad</l>
    <l n="12">tirada sobre cardos hecha sopa de llantos</l>
    <l n="13">saltando en la sartén hecha de nardos</l>
    <l n="14">salpicando su cuerpo de la lluvia de paz</l>
    <l n="15">metiendo en el bolsillo la hora que se</l>
    <l n="16">come la arena y atornilla el momento</l>
    <l n="17">cogido entre los dientes de la paloma</l>
    <l n="18">blanca que golpeando el cielo resuena</l>
    <l n="19">en el tambor que aleja la campana</l>
    <l n="20">y la deja marchita húmeda de placer</l>
    <l n="21">y vibrante de miedo cogida en el</l>
    <l n="22">calor ojos cerrados boca abierta</l>
    <l n="23">niña que viene el
        <del rend="crossout">oso</del> coco y se</l>
    <l n="24">lleva a los niños que duermen poco</l>
    <l n="25">ya lo sé y tú eres lo mejor que</l>
    <l n="26">existe en este mundo un traje</l>
    <l n="27">de lentejas una bota de vino una</l>
    <l n="28">escalera <del rend="crossout">en</del>
        circular un rayo de silencio</l>
    <l n="29">que atraviesa su mano y el reflejo de un</l>
    <l n="30">beso en la manzana una mesa de cal</l>
    <ab n="31">(cf. Rothenberg &amp; Joris 2004, 20).</ab>
</div>
```

Illustration 9 Fragment of the TEI encoding for "no más hacer que cuidado . . . (1)"

limitations in terms of its expressive capabilities to encode graphic features and stratified text. We are not alone in making this claim—Scholger proposed a practical implementation to interconnect text and images (Scholger 2017).

Conclusions

We have established four points in our analysis. First, as it is safe to assume, all poets limit themselves to a number of topics as they compose their poems. We know that the European conflict, the crisis in his own personal relations and the immediate objects in his surroundings represented the backdrop of many of Picasso's compositions. In this respect, our analysis has allowed us to more precisely delimit the lexical manifestation of these themes, enabling us to see interrelations between words within particular topics. We have also analyzed how concepts in Picasso's poems with each other within a complex conceptual network. As a result, through the use of a carefully-defined taxonomy of concepts, we have been able to identify and categorize representative themes and correlations across different languages.

Second, our research has allowed us to see correlations between concrete concepts as identified by certain lexical terms and different languages, which becomes particularly interesting in the case of a bilingual poet such as Pablo Picasso. For example, psychological concepts (such as madness) are handled preferably in French; while more physical references to his immediate surroundings (such as scorch) are circumscribed to Spanish terms. However, in cases where both languages are used to communicate a similar concept, Picasso chooses Spanish when he intends to apply a more folkloric tone (for instance, maggot). Using the English lexical list of terms, we were able to highlight and identify the interconnections between his poems in different languages.

Third, we have determined that, in Picasso's poems, certain semantic categories are predominant in each of the two languages he used, Spanish and French. For instance, Picasso is more inclined to refer to food items and everyday objects in his Spanish poems, which thus provides a clear reflection of his physical environment and of the harsh economic situation of this time. On the other hand, given the influence French Surrealist writers exerted on him, his French poems concentrate on more abstract concepts involving politics, religion and sexuality.

Finally, the unique visual characteristics in Picasso's poetry leads us to view his texts as Visually Complex Documents, which, as in the different "planes of consistency" of collages, present distinct layers of text and images that constitute integral parts of the document's representation. To account for similar cases, Haaf and Thomas (2016) created a pure TEI subset for the unambiguous annotation of manuscripts. However, we believe that Picasso's case is more complex, as it is hard to define the boundaries between graphic and verbal elements. Considering that the TEI presents guidelines for encoding machine-readable texts, representing these visual features becomes an important aspect. As a work in progress, we will continue to explore solutions within the Digital Humanities to analyze different aspects of Picasso's poetry.

Notes

1 Cf. Zelevansky and Rubin (1992: 209–210).
2 Cf. Baldassari (2005: 34).

3 Cf. Daix (1993: 234–236).
4 Cf. Hamilton (2012: 81–82).
5 Cf. Bernadac and Piot (1989, 19).
6 Cf. Michaël (2008, 244–245).
7 Cf. Michaël (2008, 244–245).
8 Cf. Michaël (2008, 239).
9 Cited in Rothenberg and Joris (2001: xiv).
10 Joris (2003:117).
11 Deleuze & Parnet (2007: 57).
12 Cf. Cowling (2002: 608–611).
13 Cf. Golding (1968: 118–120).
14 Cf. Schwartz (1971: 98–104).
15 Cf. Seckel (1996: 37–38).
16 Quoted in Rothenberg & Joris (2001: vii).
17 Cf. Wadley (1970: 13–15).
18 Cf. O'Brian (1994: 195).
19 Cf. Urban (2011: 9).
20 Cf. O'Brian (1994: 117).
21 Cf. Tymieniecka (2004: 273).

Bibliography

Anderson, Stephen R. *Phonology in the Twentieth Century: Theories of Rules and Theories of Representations*. Chicago: University of Chicago Press, 1985. Print.

Akamatsu, Tsutomu. *Essentials of Functional Phonology*. Louvain–La-Neuve: Peeters Publishers, 1992. Print.

Audenaert, Neal, Karadkar, Unmil, Mallen, Enrique, Furuta, Richard and Tonner, Sarah. "Viewing Texts: An Art-Centered Representation of Picasso's Writings," *Digital Humanities 2007*, 14–16. Print.

Audenaert, Neal. "Patterns of Analysis: Supporting Exploratory Analysis and Understanding of Visually Complex Documents." IEEE Technical Committee on Digital Libraries. 2008.
http://www.ieee-tcdl.org/Bulletin/v4n2/audenaert/audenaert.html

Baldassari, Anne, ed. *The Surrealist Picasso*. New York: Random House, 2005. Print.

Bernadac, Marie-Laure. "Le crayon qui parle." *Picasso poète*. Musée Picasso, Paris, November 8, 1989 to January 29, 1990. Paris: Réunion des musées nationaux.

Bernadac, Marie-Laure and Christine Piot, eds. *Picasso. Écrits*. Paris: Réunion des musées nationaux / Gallimard, 1989.

Blei, D. M., Ng, A. Y., and Jordan, M. I. "Latent dirichlet allocation," *Journal of Machine Learning Research*, 2003, vol. 3, 993–1022. Print.

Cowling, Elizabeth. *Picasso: Style and Meaning*. New York, NY: Phaidon, 2002. Print.

Culicover, Peter W. "Parataxis and Simpler Syntax." Ms. The Ohio State University and Eberhard-Karls Universität, Tübingen, 2016. Print.

Culicover, Peter W. and Ray Jackendoff. *Simpler Syntax*. Oxford: Oxford University Press, 2005. Print.
Daix, Pierre. *Picasso: The Man & His Work*. New York: Praeger, 1965. Print.
——. *Picasso: Life and Art*. New York: Harper-Collins, 1993. Print.
Daix, Pierre and Joan Rosselet, eds. *Picasso: The Cubist Years, 1907–1916: A Catalogue Raisonné of the Paintings & Related Works*. Boston: New York Graphic Society, 1979. Print.
Deleuze, Gilles and Félix Guattari. *What Is Philosophy?* New York: Columbia University Press, 1996. Print.
Deleuze, Gilles and Claire Parnet. *Dialogues II*. New York: Columbia University Press, 2007. Print.
Fabb, Nigel. "The Non-Linguistic in Poetic Language. A Generative Approach [Abstract]." *JLT Articles* 4 (1), 2010.
http://www.jltonline.de/index.php/articles/article/view/246
Felluga, Dino Franco. "Modules on Lacan." 2002.
https://www.cla.purdue.edu/english/theory/psychoanalysis/lacanstructure.html
Golding, John. *Cubism: A History and an Analysis 1907–1914*. New York: Harper & Row, 1968. Print.
Haaf, Susanne, and Christian Thomas. "Enabling the Encoding of Manuscripts within the DTABf: Extension and Modularization of the Format." *Journal of the Text Encoding Initiative*, no. Issue 10 (December 2016).
https://doi.org/10.4000/jtei.1650
Hallward, Peter. *Out of This World*. London: Verso, 2006. Print.
Hamilton, James W. *A Psychoanalytic Approach to Visual Artists*. London: Routledge, 2012. Print.
Jackendoff, Ray. *Foundations of Language: Brain, Meaning, Grammar, Evolution*. Oxford University Press, 2002. Print.
Jackendoff, Ray and Eva Wittenberg. "What You Can Say Without Syntax: A Hierarchy of Grammatical Complexity," pp. 65–82. *Measuring Grammatical Complexity*. Frederick J. Newmeyer and Laurel B. Preston, eds. Oxford: Oxford University Press, 2014. Print.
Jakobson, Roman. *Framework of Language*. 1st edition. Ann Arbor: Michigan Slavic Publications, 1980. Print.
Joris, Pierre. *A Nomad Poetics: Essays*. Middletown, CT: Wesleyan University Press, 2003. Print.
Klages, Mary. "Jacques Lacan," 1997.
http://www.Colorado.EDU/English/ ENGL2012Klages/ 1997lacan.html
"Lxml – Processing XML and HTML with Python," 2018.
http://lxml.de/
Mallén, Enrique. *The Visual Grammar of Pablo Picasso*. Berkeley Insights in Linguistics and Semiotics 54. New York: Peter Lang, 2003. Print.
——. "The Multilineal Poetry of Pablo Picasso." *Interdisciplinary Journal for Germanic Linguistics and Semiotic Analysis*. 14.2. 1–35. Fall 2009. Print.
——. *A Concordance of Pablo Picasso's Spanish Writings*. New York: Edwin Mellen Press, 2009. Print.

———. The Fichtean Anstoß and Pablo Picasso's Poetry. *Revista Académica liLETRAd*, 1.251–261. 2015. Print.
———. ed. *Online Picasso Project*. Sam Houston State University. 2018. http://picasso.shsu.edu (accessed: 7.9.2018).
Mallén, Enrique, Neal Audenaert, Unmil Karadkar, Richard Furuta and Sarah Tonner. "Viewing Texts: An Art-Centered Representation of Picasso's Writings." Digital Humanities Proceedings: University of Illinois, Urbana-Champaign, 2007. Print.
Meneses, Luis, Monroy, Carlos, Furuta, Richard, and Mallén, Enrique. "Computational Approaches to a Catalogue Raisonné of Pablo Picasso's Works," *Interdisciplinary Journal for Germanic Linguistics and Semiotic Analysis*, 2011.
Meneses, Luis, Monroy, Carlos, Mallén, Enrique, and Furuta, Richard. "Picasso's Poetry: The Case of a Bilingual Concordance," *Digital Humanities* 2008, 157–159. Print.
Meneses, Luis, Estill, L. and Furuta, Richard. "'This was my speech, and I will speak it again': Topic Modeling in Shakespeare's Plays," *Joint CSDH/SCHN & ACH Digital Humanities Conference*, 2016.
Michaël, Androula. *Picasso poète*. Paris: Beux-arts de Paris, 2008. Print.
Most, John. "Picasso as Poet." *Jacket Magazine*. no. 30. July 2006. http://jacketmagazine.com/30/most-picasso.html
"MySQL" 2018. https://www.mysql.com/
O'Brian, Patrick. *Pablo Picasso: A Biography*. New York: W.W. Norton & Company, 1994. Print.
Phillips, John. "Lacan and Language." 1999. https://courses.nus.edu.sg/course/elljwp/lacan.htm
Rehurek, R. "Gensim: Topic Modelling for Humans." goo.gl/UCLX3r 2017. [Accessed: 12-Apr-2017].
Rossum, Guido van. "Python Tutorial, Technical Report CS-R9526." Amsterdam: Centrum voor Wikunde en Informatica (CWI), 1995. https://ir.cwi.nl/pub/5007/05007D.pdf
Rothenberg, Jerome and Pierre Joris, eds. *The Burial of the Count of Orgaz and Other Poems*. Cambridge, MA: Exact Change Publishers, 2001. Print.
Rubin, William. *Picasso and Braque: A Symposium*. New York: The Museum of Modern Art, 1992. Print.
Sabartés, Jaime. "La literatura de Picasso." *Cahiers d'art 1930–1935*, vol. X, 7–10, January 1936, 89, 90. Print.
Scholger, Martina. "Taking Note: How to Represent Graphics in TEI?" presented at the TEI 2017, Victoria, British Columbia, Canada, November 11.
"SQLite Home Page," 2018. https://www.sqlite.org/index.html
Taylor, John R. *Linguistic Categorization*. New York: Oxford University Press, 2003.
Tymieniecka, Anna-Teresa. *Does the World Exist? Plurisignificant Ciphering of Reality*. Volume 79. Berlin: Springer Science & Business Media, 2004. Print.

Urban, William John. "Giving Fichte a Chance: A Žižekian Defense of the I." *International Journal of Zizek Studies*. Vol 5, No 3, 2011. 1–16. Print.
Wadley, Nicholas. *Cubism*. New York: The Hamlyn Publishing Group, 2970. Print.
Zelevansky, Lynn & William S. Rubin, eds. *Picasso and Braque: A Symposium*. New York: Museum of Modern Art, 1992. Print.
Waugh, Linda R. "The Poetic Function in the Theory of Roman Jakobson." *Poetics Today* 2 (1a), 1980: 57–82. https://doi.org/10.2307/1772352
Žižek, Slavoj. "Deleuze and the Lacanian Real." *The Symptom* 11. (Spring 2010). 346. http://www.lacan.com/zizrealac.htm

CHAPTER

9

Ramón J. Sender's Sublime Visions of Freedom in *Relatos fronterizos* (1970)

Montse Feu

After having served as an officer in the Spanish Republican Army (1936–1939), Spanish novelist and essayist, Ramón J. Sender (1902–1982), fled to Mexico at the end of the Spanish Civil War. He moved to the United States in 1942 and published numerous articles and books, among them *Relatos fronterizos/Border Stories* (1970). The collection of short stories maintains his recurrent exilic autobiographical projections with new transnational concerns. Protagonists are on the move: they are traveling, migrating, crossing borders, staying in hotels or visiting someone. Sender observes the bourgeois characters with the frivolous disdain of a *flaneur*[1] but offers his solidarity to subjugated characters and qualifies their insights on repression as sublime. Characters from Europe, Latin America and the United States exhibit perceptive awareness of the oppression they suffer. His publications in U.S. Spanish-language periodicals and his political involvement at the time help discern the mixture of themes and styles in *Relatos fronterizos*, which are *flânerie*, antifascist exile, and denunciation of civil right infringements.

Sender and the American Literary Agency

After his arrival to the United States, Sender started contributing to the American Literary Agency (ALA), which placed journalistic essays in numerous newspapers in the Americas. The syndicating agency, founded in New York City in the late 1940s by another Spanish Civil

War exile, Joaquim Maurín Julià, provided the opportunity for a Hispanic perspective on featuring U.S. news and society.[2] Sender's literary column "Los días y las horas" (The Days and the Hours), among other pieces, was featured in several newspapers in Argentina, Bolivia, Colombia, Dominican Republic, Ecuador, Honduras, Mexico, Peru, Republic of Panama, El Salvador, Uruguay, and Venezuela (Mainer 202).[3] In the United States, ALA also placed Sender's articles in *El Diario de Nueva York*, *Temas* (New York), *La Prensa* (San Antonio), and *La Opinión* (Los Angeles) (Caudet, *Correspondencia* 78, 106, 107). Between 1953 and 1982, Sender published more than 825 articles through the ALA (Mainer 17).[4] In 1958, Maurín Julià told Sender that his articles reached one million readers through ALA.[5] For his newly-found audience in the Americas, Sender wrote about a broad range of political, social, and cultural themes related to the United States (King 226).[6] Many of these chronicles were compiled in *Ensayos de otro mundo* (1970) (Caudet, "Sender en Albuquerque" 141–158, 145).

Sender's exile and journalistic experiences transferred into his fiction. *Relatos fronterizos* offers a distinguishable narrator who confidently observes and describes North America and the ALA commissions surely helped Sender accomplish this *flânerie*.[7] The forty-six books that he wrote while in exile in Mexico and in the United States portray American themes as well. The grid below, adapted from Marielena Zelaya Kolker's *Testimonios americanos de los escritores españoles transterrados de 1939*, illustrates Sender's transnational approach to writing.

Title	Setting and time	Genre
Relatos fronterizos (1972)	United States, Latin America, Europe, 1950s–1960s	Short Stories
Nocturno de los catorce (1969)	Mexico and the United States, 1939–1960	Short Stories/ Essays
Novelas ejemplares de Cíbola (1961)	Southeastern United States, 1950–1960	Short Stories
Mexitayotl (1940)	Tenochititlan Pre-Columbus Prehistory	Short Stories
Túpac Amáru (1973)	Peru, 1778	Novel
Tanit (1970)	United States/ New York City, 1968	Novel
El bandido adolescente (1965)	New Mexico, 1865	Novel

La aventura equinocial de L. de Aguirre (1964)	Amazon River, 1558	Novel
Los tontos de la Concepción (1963)	Arizona, 1778	Novel
Epitalamio del Prieto Trinidad (1942)	Mexico, 1939	Novel
H. Cortés (1940)	Tenochtitlan, 1521	Theater

For the literary world, Sender proclaimed himself to have lost his conviction in any sort of political radicalism and to have resigned himself to a reformist democracy (Barreiro 2012).[8] Possibly for this reason, he reedited his novel about Spanish anarchism, *Siete domingos rojos* (1932), in 1973. The novel was published again in 1974 under the title, *Las tres sorores,* as the definitive version. While the original advocated for immediate social revolution, the later versions eliminated or substituted revolutionary words and acknowledged instead the difficulty in achieving liberty at the individual and social level (Salguero Rodríguez 12). More tellingly, some of his later novels portrayed defeated protagonists. For example, *En la vida de Ignacio Morel*, which garnered the prestigious Premio Planeta in 1969, is about the transformation of its protagonist, a writer, into a grotesque puppet of his own making. Similarly, his surrealist novel, *Nocturno de los 14* (1970), narrates the suicide of fourteen of the narrator's friends.

Sender and the Spanish Civil War Exile Periodicals

Before the Spanish Civil War, Sender was a politically-committed writer of the Left. In 1932, for example, he published an article expressing his disaffection of bourgeois intellectuals and in support of the new revolutionary movement prior to the war (Sender, "La cultura y los hechos económicos"). In the 1930s, Sender was a regular contributor to anarchist periodicals in Spain, in particular, *Solidaridad Obrera* in Barcelona.[9] In exile in Mexico and in the United States, despite his somber statements to the literary world, he still corresponded with Spanish anarchists. This was the case of Progreso Alfarache, who directed *Comunidad Ibérica* in Mexico. Sender regularly published articles about anarchism, art and literature in *Comunidad Ibérica* and *CNT México*. Some of these articles, along with other originals, were published in *España Libre* (New York City). Sender was an honorary member of these periodicals, sent regular donations, and participated as a speaker in their fundraisers and rallies. He also worked with the Medical Bureau of the North American Committee to Aid Spanish Democracy and The Exiled Writers' Committee (of the League of American Writers). For his political involvement, Sender was investigated by the FBI from 1943 to 1983 (Ordaz Romay 265).

In his articles in anarchist exile periodicals, Sender continued to proclaim his belief in the people's right to self-determination and openly proclaimed an anarchist distrust of institutionalized power.[10] He believed in the anarchist utopian aspiration of mutual aid and cooperation, away from the competition fomented by capitalism.[11] Often, he demanded a more combative opposition to Francisco Franco's dictatorship than the one given by the Spanish Republican government-in-exile and accused exiled politicians of passivity and inefficiency. Sender expected that syndicates in exile and in Spain would work together to help build cooperative industry and distribution in a federal Spain.[12] However, his articles about the movement showed a similar evolution to other Spanish anarchists-in-exile who no longer saw violent revolution as a viable option after the Spanish Civil War and focused instead in a daily practice of cooperation with democratic and progressive groups.[13] Also, he felt hopeless for the lasting and extreme state terror in Spain, and his writing focused about anarcho-syndicalist values rather than in any political tactics because "all of our potential leaders have dropped dead by execution."[14]

Sender often elaborated in the idea of two Spains: the traditional and the progressive.[15] In one of these essays, "El español 'fronterizo'" (Border-crossing Spaniard) published in *España Libre*, Sender distinguished between the progressive Spain in exile and the traditional Spain at the time under Fascist rule. Reflecting on the Spanish Civil War diaspora, Sender claimed that exiles had a "sublime frontier quality" (solera fronteriza sublime) inherited from medieval multicultural coexistence of Muslims, Jews, and Christians and exercised in their roaming the world escaping Fascism.[16] Sender published a similar article in *CNT Mexico* the same month, June 1960, "Montesquieu y el español "fronterizo" (Montesquieu and the Border-crossing Spaniard), in which Sender reviewed Montesquieu's characterization of Spaniards as sublime, "Everything in Spain can be ugly and sublime at the same time . . . There is that jump into the abyss."[17] Sender clarified that Montesquieu must have referred to the "border-crossing Spaniard . . . [who had] an easy tendency to the ugly sublime or the sublime ugliness" (Sender, "Montesquieu y el español "fronterizo" 1). In *Valle Inclán y la dificultad de la tragedia* (1965), Sender further explored the concept of fealdad-sublime (ugliness-sublime) in reviewing the grotesque literary technique coined by Ramón del Vallé

Inclán, el *esperpento*, a mix of laughter and fear. For Sender, Ramón Valle Inclán portrayed the bourgeoise under the lenses of the farce and the grotesque to mock their pretenses of honor, culture, love, and justice (82).[18] In *Relatos fronterizos,* protagonists live similar ugly-sublime experiences when their quest for justice is defeated and they experience intensified feelings of being at a cliff's edge.

In the eighteenth century, the aesthetic concept of the sublime stirred the arts and philosophical realms. The Romantic sublime unveiled an experience that opened new horizons of perception. In their observation of the unattainable nature and the infinite, the sublime quality made thinkers aware of their human limitations. Modern authors, such as Victor Hugo and Fredric Jameson, rearticulated the classic rendition of the sublime as supernatural natural beauty into the human experience that brings augmented cognizance, as in the creation of art (Hugo) or the elation of consumerism in the capitalist logic (Jameson).[19] In antifascist exile, Sender integrated the sublime in his *flânerie*. Under his observation, characters suffering social exclusion experience an enlarged consciousness of their marginalization. Sender accompanies these characters with a listening alterego, as a way to sooth the author's nihilistic outlook on the failures of justice after Fascism.

Sender's wife and brother were killed by Spanish Fascists and he gave his children up for adoption to protect them from a life of fear and persecution in exile. Sender lived convinced that Communists would kill him. In a letter to Maurín Julià, Sender explained his reasons, "The Russians set out to finish me off and if something happened to me, I do not want my children to suffer another shock. The Communists have deprived me of one of the most legitimate satisfactions of my life: to live with my children."[20] These traumatic experiences marked Sender's notion of grotesque-sublime in exile. The grotesque reality of war and Fascism in Europe and civil rights infringements in the United States enlarged and deformed reality and metaphorically extended boundaries of perception, resulting in a sublime understanding that simultaneously reaffirmed individual and collective empathy and solidarity, as portrayed in *Relatos fronterizos*.

Flaneur, Exilic,[21] and Sublime Qualities in *Relatos fronterizos*

Some stories in *Relatos fronterizos* mock the bourgeoise and their adoration of money and pretense. "Manuela en Copacabana" is about a prostitute, Manuela, who not only finances Amado's business but helps him in his business negotiations, with the condition that her client will add her name (and inter her body) when she dies in the family pantheon instead of those of his wife's. Manuela buys social acceptance by being buried in a rich family's pantheon. Sender compares the actions of Manuela, who sells her body to obtain social recognition, with those of Amado, a member of the bourgeoise, who sells his family name in order to continue his pretentious life. Manuela asks for roots, if only after death, like exiled authors do with their writing. For Manuela, a dignified place in the world, denied in life, is worth selling all she has: her body; for rich Amado, monetary gratification is more comforting than preserving the memory of his wife. Similarly, the protagonists of "A bordo de un avión/On Board a Plane" and "A pseudo" are shallow characters mainly concerned with appearances. In "Germinal," Sender mocks the airs of greatness of a Spanish Communist exiled in Moscow.[22] In the last story, "Velada en Acapulco/Night in Acapulco," the Mexican bourgeoisie is mocked for their frivolous chatter and their rejection of Fermín Tapia's story. Sender fictionalizes the story of his lost family with Tapia, or Tapioca, who tells his sad story. His wife abandoned him, "when I returned from work one night, I found that the house was abandoned . . . I cried bitterly and not for her . . . but for my children."[23] Sender shows a deep contempt for these characters. In his fictional projections, Sender both attacks his enemies and makes amends with his loved ones.

Another striking rendition of *flânerie* is found in the fifteenth story, "Aquel día en El Paso/That Day in El Paso," which is about a Spaniard traveling from Mexico to the United States. At the border, he refuses to be vaccinated, claiming that he is allergic to certain medicines. The border official gives him a warning that he might be quarantined. The Spaniard is happy with the resolution and shares why North American vaccines seem dangerous to him compared to Mexican ones,

> Mexican bacilli are good . . . they do not have an exaggerated sense of duty. People who exceed in the accomplishment of their duty are dangerous. And the Yankee bacilli, preserved in special refrigerators, prevented from acting, subjected to a cold virtue, that is, at the temperature of the Puritans, are repressed bacilli. Puritans, well-educated, with a rational sense of the efficiency of their means. And also, perhaps, with a notion of the transcendence of their mission . . . to me, the bacilli cultivated by the Yankee laboratories, no thanks. They are rabid and frenzied.[24]

The usage of national archetypes was cultivated in Sender's journalistic chronicles about the United States for ALA and the sense of moral superiority must have been popular among Hispanic readers.

Another example of *exilic flânerie* is found in "En el Grand Canyon/In the Grand Canyon." Sender describes the hotel in the Grand Canyon employing European references, "one would feel like in those provincial Spanish hotels with big patios where babysitters with uniforms and wet nurses with pearl collars would entertain the kids under their guard."[25] In possibly the most sublime scenario of North America, the *flaneur* smirk is even more poignant. The protagonist notices a cliff that reminds him of the sublime quality of his exile condition, forever near the abyss. The story describes at length the sublime qualities of the Canyon but soon the narrator focuses on a sad African young woman staying at the same hotel (*Relatos fronterizos* 60). One day, he overhears her conversation with a friend, "She added that her husband was in Africa and was a political leader of a party and was in difficulties."[26] Days later, the protagonist sees a teletype that is addressed to the young woman in the hotel lobby but destroys it before she finds out about it because, "the machine said (for the international press) that her husband had been shot. I thought I did her a favor by suppressing the testimony."[27]

Sender fictionalizes the execution of his wife, Amparo Barayón, and his brother, Manuel Sender, by the Fascists during the Spanish Civil War.[28] In his literary projection, the African political leader is his alter ego. Sender, who enlisted in the Spanish Republican forces, would have been the one shot and not his family, who would have fled for exile. Sender, who knew the pain of being told that the political enemy had shot the loved ones, makes his fictional alter ego eliminate the teletype in an attempt to prevent or delay the suffering to the young woman (*Relatos fronterizos* 62). The *flaneur* voice in the collection observes, mocks and projects autobiographical facts, emblematic of Sender's literary *oeuvre*.[29]

The sublime qualities move from nature to understanding of the effects of injustice in the stories dedicated to denouncing the civil rights infringements in the United States and Spain. The first story of the collection, "Aventura en Texas/Adventure in Texas," is located on the Mexico–United States border and chronicles his early days in the United States when he crossed from Mexico to Texas. On the bus, the protagonist, Sender's alter ego, is bored: "The trip was long, needless to say. Two days and one night."[30] He starts talking to a little girl who was traveling with her grandmother: "The old woman explained that she was going with the child to New Mexico, where relatives were waiting for them. That someone was waiting for them she said it as if she wanted to warn me."[31] Accustomed to the dangerous scrutiny from others, the Mexican woman has a ready-to-be-delivered protecting narrative. However, they soon become friends sharing the long trip inside the bus. When the bus stops at the Texan city of Pecos, the Spaniard suggests getting some medicine for the little girl because she has a fever. The elderly woman explains to him that neither she nor her granddaughter can enter a local drug store: "No, sir, we cannot go in. They will not let us in the pharmacies."[32] The Spaniard is astonished at the employee's refusal to assist them because they are Mexican: "I could never imagine what it was like 'to be nobody' . . . To be absolutely nobody . . . That is why she [the pharmacist] did not see us, she refused to see us."[33] The Spaniard confronts the pharmacist, and the police are called in, but he cannot do much for the little Mexican girl. The Spaniard reclaims radical democracy with his direct action and solidarity in the public space—an anarchist praxis.

As an exile from Fascist Spain, Sender hoped to find in the United States "systems of social relations in which life flowed with greater happiness and more sense."[34] Instead, he found minorities in inner exile in their own country. Their life seemed as vulnerable as the life of Spaniards under Franco's rule. The discrimination suffered by Mexicans in the southern United States in the 1950s was an overwhelmingly sublime experience for Sender that reinforced his perception of the limited scope of his antifascist fight in Spain and his direct action in the United States,

> I thought that in a country like the United States that had drafted and launched the declaration of human rights, in the homeland of civil liberties, in the most functional democracy known to the history of mankind, what that woman [the pharmacist] said was totally without foundation.[35]

Sender, who met Chicano author Alurista,[36] joined the literary demand for a safe space denied to Latinos in the South. Borrowing from José David Saldívar's examination of Chicano cultural productions, border stories in *Relatos fronterizos* act as literary "place-making" for Latinos.[37]

In another story that criticizes racial oppression, Sender recreates the foundational myth of American racism: the rape of a white woman by a black man. Marginalization takes center stage in "Adiós pájaro negro/Goodbye Black Bird:" Bob, an Afro-American young man, forces his entrance into the apartment of a white university student. In her student apartment, Ray Henderson's song, "Bye Bye Black Bird" (1926), is playing, a song segregationists would play in their demonstrations against the Civil Rights Movement.[38] After raping the young woman twice, Bob asks her to teach him about the history of Muslim thought, which she is studying at the university: "he had his pleasure and now he wanted some wisdom. That's what he said."[39] Bob's violence confronts racial, educational and institutional politics of discrimination.

When Bob accidentally drops a book, the young woman seizes the opportunity to alert her neighbor to call the police. The song, "Bye Bye Black Bird," is playing as the police arrives and lights ups the windows of the apartment. Bob, who recognizes himself as the black bird of the song thinks to himself that it, "was too much for two orgasms and a gramophone record. Well, and a lecture on Muslim philosophy."[40] Sender renders a tragic end for Bob in cinematographic images, "They hit him in the head. He fell on the stairs, and when he was dead, he continued to descend, sliding, until he was next to the blue water of the pool, blue and hot water illuminated from below."[41] Sender alerts the reader with the song title what will happen in the story, making them participants (for understanding the alert) and observers (as readers) of the state violence against black men in the United States.

In "Pantera negra/Black Panther," another story that covers discrimination, a street vendor arrives at the narrator's apartment and engages in a long conversation with him. The salesman, who is also a Black Panther, talks about his experience as a bus driver in the outskirts of the city.[42] Without social power, bus riders find ways to make their underground existence more tolerable with small rebellious acts: not paying for the bus, having a small hidden serpent as pet, hitting others pretending not to see them (blind bus riders). They are off limits of the sanitized, routinized, highly policed city space. The Black Panther describes some of his bus riders as economically-challenged, but mainly deranged,

> diminished and deteriorated people . . . When the one who drives the bus is a black man, like me, they dare to let go . . . A lady used to come with a moth-eaten hat, hairs on her brow, grimy hands, smelling of stale bacon. And when she was to pay, she would open her black rubber bag and show me bundles of hundred-dollar bills and she would offer them to me. She wore old men's shoes, wrinkled and torn socks, a jacket from the last century, and as I say, she smelled like a wet dog.[43]

The lady calls herself Necessary Angel, claiming that the author of the book said so, "the last book he wrote was entitled *The Necessary Angel*. That angel was (my poor Wallace said) myself."[44] In 1951,

Wallace Stevens published *The Necessary Angel*, a book of poems about reality and the imagination as necessary joyful experiences for humans. Sender's reference to the publication is an ironic take on the harsh realities for those who live in the margins and illustrates the challenge of being constantly put in the position of explaining one's existence and one's reality with the rhetoric tools of the status quo. Both the Black Panther and Necessary Angel struggle for self-representation in the search for a reality they can call theirs. Meanwhile, they express their frustrations outside the ordered vision of public space. With the reference to the publication, Sender sought to refer to a pre-figurative free world without the predetermining power of language.

The narrator returns to the border location where Sender escaped Fascist Spain in the eighth story, "Despedida en Bourg Madame/Farewell at Bourg Madame." Two peasants reflect about their new identity as migrants and as border-crossing Spaniards. The narrator tells readers, "I also left Spain a few years earlier by the same place on the border,"[45] and shares his wandering experience: "I will leave my bones in some of the crossroads of the world, like so many other Spaniards."[46] Once the peasants have crossed, they eat bread and wine. With this Catholic symbolic communion, Sender blesses the migrants for having survived their escape on foot and marks their first steps in a free country by a symbol that shows the strong communion with the people who remain subjugated under Fascism. The sublime quality of the Pyrenees enhances the metaphysical sublime meaning of the act of crossing the border. The narrator tells the peasants: "I have lived since then on the border. Not the physical border but the other one that separates life from death, in the cliff's edge. Now, I often see a butterfly with golden wings crossing it without difficulty."[47] In the sublime mountains, the Spaniards experience a clearer understanding of their new acquired identity as refugees. The act of crossing provides them with a sublime vision of the ugliness of Fascism and exile.

In one dark story, Sender examines what shapes individual freedom in more complex ways, playing with a portrayal that contravenes psychological normality. "Chessman" explores the convict life of a U.S. sexual criminal, Caryl Chessman, sentenced to death for various sexual offenses in 1948. In prison, Chessman writes novels narrating his murders. With the profits, he pays his lawyers. Liberated from the moral discourse of governance, Chessman writes about his murders and sexual offenses. Sender is startled about Chessman's grotesque ability to monetarize his transgressions.[48] The narrator, who requests to visit the convict to listen to his story, reads compulsively about him and compares the convict's literary predisposition with that of the Spanish 1898 literary generation,

> Chessman was skinny like Azorín, skeptical like Baroja, pseudo-lighted as Unamuno, vociferous as Maetzu, distant and unconventional as Valle Inclán, and like him, Chessman liked truculence with double lyrical background. Almost all the Generation of '98 writers were in prison or in exile, that is, that for one reason or another suffered persecution.[49]

Compared to the Generation of 1898, which Sender considers to be both disaffected and defeated bourgeois, Chessman recreates the grotesque/*esperpento*, as established by Valle-Inclán, when the convict profits from his violence: "I saw Chessman deteriorated and wilted, thinking that he was going to impersonate stubbornness in that circus of hilarity. The monstrous superclown."[50]

Conclusion

This combination of themes is a constant throughout Sender's *exilic* narrative and continues in *Relatos fronterizos*. His syndicated columns for the American Literary Agency provided the exile author with a new readership in the Americas. Although Sender juxtaposes European and American themes, *Relatos fronterizos* builds on the intersections of literary and political experiences in the Americas. From bourgeoise disengagement, to biographical projections, to sublime understanding and empathy, and newly-found friends, *Relatos fronterizos* reads as a kaleidoscopic investigation of individual sufferings, contestations, and solidarities.

Beyond a social literature that calls for solidarity with the dispossessed and marginalized, Sender presents marginal characters that possess sublime visions on subjugation and freedom. The wandering and liminal characters are split off from the geographical, historical, political, cultural, and national expressions of sovereignty. They cross not only geographical but also political and societal margins when they act in ways that rebel against systems, laws, and geographies that rule them and oppress them. As outlaws or outsiders, these protagonists are aware of their exclusion. On the margins of social, political, legal and medical normality, Sender recreates characters who acquire sublime (even if tragic, ugly, and grotesque) foresights.

The simultaneous use of ugly and sublime qualities in *Relatos fronterizos* avoids mythical representations of the protagonists; rather the narrator humanizes them through other characters' validation, listening, and friendship, or their own criminal acts. In this regard, the sublime and border settings are domains of both violence and solidarity. Sender restores some justice by the practice of friendship, solidarity, acts of rebellions and direct actions, and in the writing of their stories. In his U.S. exile, Sender documents social exclusion, which he did not see to end.

Notes

1. According to *Wikipedia*, "*flâneur*, from the French noun *flâneur*, means "stroller", "lounger", "saunterer", or "loafer". *Flânerie* is the act of strolling, with all of its accompanying associations. A near-synonym is 'boulevardier'. He is an ambivalent figure of urban riches representing the ability to wander detached from society with no other purpose than to be an acute observer of society."
2. By 1954, ALA worked with thirty-five newspapers in Latin America (Anabel Bonsón Aventín, *Joaquín Maurín, 1896–1973: el impulso moral de hacer política*. Huesca: Diputación de Huesca. Instituto de Estudios Altoaragoneses, 1995, 367; Francisco Caudet, *Correspondencia Ramón J. Sender – Joaquín Maurín (1952–1973)* (Madrid: Ediciones de la Torre, 1995), 33; Joaquim Roy, *Maurín als Estats Units*. Barcelona: Centre d'Estudis Internacionals. Universitat de Barcelona, 1989, 3.
3. See also Charles King, "Sender's Column: Los libros y los días," 1975–1982." Mary S. Vázquez (Ed), *Homenaje a Ramón J. Sender*. Newark: Juan de la Cuesta, 1987, pp. 201–225.
4. See also Charles King, "Sender's Column: Los libros y los días," 1975–1982." Mary S. Vázquez (ed.), *Homenaje a Ramón J. Sender*. Newark: Juan de la Cuesta, 1987, pp. 201–225.
5. ALA grew to syndicate authors such as Raúl Andrade, Miguel Ángel Asturias, Alfonso Reyes, Germán Arciniegas, Waldo Frank, José Vasconcelos, Ramón Gómez de la Serna, and Uslar Pietri (Caudet, *Correspondencia* 13, 46, 178); Victor Albà, "Los refugiados españoles en la prensa francesa (1945–1947)," *Emigración y exilio. Españoles en Francia 1936–1946*. Eds. Cuesta and Bermejo. Madrid: Eudema, 1996, pp. 144–152, 146; Other exiled Spanish intellectuals also contributed, including Luis Araquistáin and Salvador Madariaga.
6. For example, Charles L. King's annotations of Sender's articles published from 1975 to 1982 show essays on anticommunism, anti-Semitism, free speech, new technologies, racial discrimination, the Vietnam War, U.S. literature, electrical blackouts, Emily Dickinson, Joseph Heller's *Something Has happened*, Karl Hess's *Dear America*, Hispanic American Women Writers, Chicano literature, and Frieda Lawrence (who was living in Taos, New Mexico).
7. The CIA financially supported left-wing anticommunist agencies such as ALA. See José-Carlos Mainer, "El héroe cansado: Sender en 1968–1970," in *El lugar de Sender. Actas del I Congreso sobre Ramón J. Sender*. Eds.

Ara Torralba and Gil Encabo. Huesca: Instituto de Estudios Altoaragoneses, 1995, pp. 27–44, 30.

8 See Javier Barreiro, "Ramón J. Sender y Francisco Carrasquer: El reencuentro literario de dos libertarios del Cinca," *Alazet 24. Boletín Senderiano* 21 (2012): pp. 275–286.

9 See José Domingo Dueñas Lorente, Ramón J. *Sender, Periodismo y compromiso (1924–1939)*. Huesca: Colección de Estudios Altoaragoneses, 1994.

10 See Sender, "La sociedad con la que uno sueña" *CNT México* Julio 1958: 1; Sender "Falacia de los partidos políticos." *Comunidad Ibérica*. Sept.–Oct. 1964: pp. 16–20; Sender, "De la influencia católica al anarquismo español" *España Libre* 16 Aug. 1957: 5; Sender, "Réplica a los arguyentes" *Comunidad Ibérica*, Nov.–Dic. 1967: pp. 30–32.

11 Sender, "De la influencia católica al anarquismo español" *España Libre* 16 Aug. 1957: 5; Sender "Un poco más sobre lo mismo" *CNT México* Aug. 1958: 4.

12 See, "*España Libre*: Anarchist Literature and Antifascism, 1936–1977." *Writing Revolution: Hispanic Anarchism in the United States*. Champaign: University of Illinois Press (2019), pp. 245–257.

13 See Sender "Las bestias moribundas se levantan." *CNT México* March 1957: 4. Sender, "Generalidades sobre un futuro próximo" *CNT México*, Sept. 1958: 4. Sender, "Sobre federalismo" *Comunidad Ibérica*, May–June 1964: 12; Sender, "Dos palabras sobre cien problemas" *Comunidad Ibérica*, Apr. 1967: pp. 5–6; Sender, "Réplica a los arguyentes" *Comunidad Ibérica*, Nov.–Dec. 1967: pp. 30–32.

14 "Todos nuestros jefes potenciales han caido a balazos Sender" ("No volver a las andadas" *Espana Libre* 19 August 1960: 1).

15 See Sender, "¿Por qué no? Una joven España." *CNT México* March 1959: 1; Sender, "cuento de nunca acabar. España del Castillo y del Valle" *CNT México* March 1958: 1.

16 See Sender, "Montesquieu y el español "fronterizo," *CNT México* May–June 1960, 1; Sender, "El español "fronterizo," *España Libre*, June 17, 1960, 3.

17 "Todo en Espana puede ser feo y sublime a un tiempo . . . [En España] hay ese salto al vacio de lo sublime . . . " Sender, "Montesquieu y el español "fronterizo," *CNT México* May–June 1960, 1.

18 Sender's reference to the frontier quality of exiles is intriguing considering that he applies this quality to exiles in the early development of critical approaches with geographical scholarship in the 1950s, anthropological approaches in the 1970s, and ethnic studies research in the 1980s.

19 See Victor Hugo's *Preface to Cromwell* (1827); Fredric Jameson, "Baudelaire as Modernist and Postmodernist: The Dissolution of the Referent and the Artificial 'Sublime.'" In *Lyric Poetry: Beyond New Criticism*. Ed. Hosek, C.; Parker, P. Cornell University Press, 1985, pp. 247–263.

20 "Los rusos se propusieron acabar conmigo y si ocurriera algo no quería

que mis hijos sufrieran otro shock. Los comunistas me han privado de una de las satisfacciones más legítimas de mi vida: vivir con mis hijos" (Sender in Caudet, *Correspondencia* 190–1).
21 *The Free Dictionary* on-line defines exilic as "ex·ile
  a. the condition or period of being forced to live away from one's native country or home, especially as a punishment.
  b. The condition or period of self-posed absence from one's country or home: *a writer living in exile in protest.*
  2. One who lives away from one's native country, whether because of expulsion or voluntary absence."
22 This approach is reminiscent of the work of another well-known Spanish exile in the United States, Luis Buñuel. See Luis Buñuel, *Belle de jour* (1967) and Buñuel, *Le charme discret de la bourgeoisie* (1972).
23 "cuando regresé del trabajo cierta noche me encontré con que la casa estaba abandonada. Había huido con los dos niños . . . Yo lloraba amargamente y no por ella . . . sino por mis hijos" (*Relatos fronterizos* 327).
24 "los bacilos mexicanos son buena gente . . . tampoco tienen una exagerada conciencia del deber. Es peligrosa esa gente que se excede en el cumplimiento del deber. Y los bacilos yanquis, conservados en neveras especiales, impedidos de actuar, sometidos a un virtuoso frío, es decir, a la temperature de los puritanos, son bacilos reprimidos . . puritanos, bien educados, con un sentido racional de la eficacia de sus medios y también, quizás, con una noción de la transcendencia de su misión. . . . a mí, los bacilos cultivados por los laboratorios yanquis, no. Están rabiosos y frenéticos" (*Relatos fronterizos* 270–1).
25 "uno se sentía como en aquellos hoteles españoles de provincias con grandes patios interiores donde niñeras uniformadas y amas de leche con sartas de perlas en el cuello entretenían a los pequeñuelos que estaban a su cargo " (*Relatos fronterizos* 52).
26 "Añadía que su marido estaba en África y era jefe político de un partido y andaba en dificultades" (*Relatos fronterizos* 60).
27 Con todos sus errores la máquina decía (para la prensa internacional) que al marido de la negrita lo habían fusilado. Yo creí hacerle un favor suprimiendo el testimonio" (*Relatos fronterizos* 62).
28 See, Rodríguez, José-María Salguero. "El primer Sender (y IV). La Guerra Civil." *Alazet. Revista de Filología* 10 (1998): 129–157, 153; and Ramón Sender Barayón, *A Death in Zamora* (Albuquerque: University of New Mexico Press, 1989).
29 Sender's autobiographical projection in his novels has been explored before. See Francisco Ernesto Puertas Moya, "Palabras de memoria: autobiografía dialógica de Ramón José Sender," in José Domingo Dueñas Lorente. *Sender y su tiempo. Crónica de un siglo. Actas del II Congreso sobre Ramón J. Sender.* Huesca: Instituto de Estudios Altoaragoneses, 2001, pp. 225–236.
30 "El viaje era largo, ni que decir tiene. Dos días y una noche" (*Relatos fronterizos* 9).

31 "La anciana me explicó que iba con la niña a New Mexico donde tenían parientes que las esperaban. Eso de que las esperaban lo dijo como si quisiera advertir" (*Relatos fronterizos* 11).
32 "No señor, no se puede. No nos dejan entrar en las farmacias. — ¿A quiénes? — A los mejicanos" (*Relatos fronterizos* 12).
33 "Nunca había podido imaginar lo que era "no ser nadie" ... No ser absolutamente nadie ... Por eso ella [la dependienta] no nos veía, se negaba a vernos" (*Relatos fronterizos* 14).
34 José Carlos Mainer, "El héroe cansado: Sender en 1968–1970," p. 29.
35 "Pensaba yo que en un país como los Estados Unidos que había redactado y lanzado por el mundo la declaración de los derechos del hombre, en la patria de las libertades civiles, en la democracia más funcional que ha conocido la historia de la humanidad lo que aquella mujer decía era del todo sin base" (*Relatos fronterizos* 12).
36 Alurista wrote a handwritten dedication to Sender in his book, *Timespace huracán. Poems, 1972–1975* that showed his respect for the exiled author, "Pa'l maestro Ramón, de corazón, su carnal y servidor, Alurista." Víctor Fuentes found the book and the dedication in Sender's library (Víctor Fuentes, "Constantes y Variaciones exílicas en la obra (americana) del último Sender." In José Domingo Dueñas Lorente. *Sender y su tiempo. Crónica de un siglo. Actas del II Congreso sobre Ramón J. Sender*. Huesca: Instituto de Estudios Altoaragoneses, 2001, pp. 211–222, 217.
37 Jose David Saldívar, *Border Matters: Remapping American Cultural Studies* (1997).
38 Renata Adler, "Letter from Selma," *The New Yorker*, 24 Sept. 2013.
39 "[h]abía tenido su placer y ahora quería un poco de sabiduría. Eso dijo" (*Relatos fronterizos* 29)
40 "Pensaba Bob que aquello era demasiado por dos orgasmos y un disco de gramófono. Bueno, y una conferencia sobre filosofía musulmana" (*Relatos fronterizos* 35).
41 "le acertaron en la cabeza. Cayó en las escaleras, y ya muerto siguió bajando, resbalando, hasta quedar al lado del agua azul de la piscina, agua azul y caliente iluminada por abajo" (*Relatos fronterizos* 37).
42 Andrew Cornell examines the various contributions anarchists made to the Black Freedom Movement in *Unruly Equality. U.S. Anarchism in the 20th Century*. Oakland: University of California Press, 2016.
43 " ... son gente disminuida y deteriorada de aquí -se tocaba la frente- [...] gente rara, casi todos [...] tienen los nervios hechos un lío. Cuando el que conduce el bus es un negro, como yo, se atreven a dejarse ir y cada cual saca sus mañas. No falta algún majareta perdido ... Una señora solía venir con un sombrero apolillado, los pelos sobre la ceja, las manos mugrientas, oliendo a tocino rancio. Y al ir a pagar abría su bolso de hule negro y enseñaba fajos de billetes de cien y me lo ofrecía [...] Llevaba zapatos viejos de hombre, las medias arrugadas y rotas, una chaqueta del siglo pasado, y como digo, olía a perro mojado" (*Relatos fronterizos* 218–220).

44 "el último libro que él escribió se titulaba el *Ángel Necesario*. Ese ángel era (decía mi pobre Wallace) yo misma" (*Relatos fronterizos* 236).
45 "Yo también salí de España algunos años antes por aquel mismo lugar de la frontera . . . " (*Relatos fronterizos* 109).
46 "Dejaré mis huesos en alguna de las encrucijadas del mundo, como tantos otros españoles" (*Relatos fronterizos* 112).
47 "Uno ha vivido realmente, desde entonces, en la frontera. No la frontera geográfica sino la otra, la que separa la vida de la muerte. Al borde del abismo. . . . Al borde del precipicio vivo todavía, ahora, y veo con frecuencia cómo una mariposa de alas doradas vuela sobre él y lo cruza sin cuidado" (*Relatos fronterizos* 127).
48 For the grotesque in other works of Sender, see Jean-Pierre Ressot, "Apología de lo monstruoso." In José Domingo Dueñas Lorente. *Sender y su tiempo. Crónica de un siglo. Actas del II Congreso sobre Ramón J. Sender.* Huesca: Instituto de Estudios Altoaragoneses, 2001, pp. 413–422.
49 "Era Chessman flaco como Azorín, escéptico como Baroja, seudoiluminado como Unamuno, vociferante como Maetzu, distante e inconvencional como Valle Inclán, y como él amigo de las truculencias con doble fondo lírico. Casi todos los del 98 estuvieron en la cárcel o en el exilio, es decir, que por una razón u otra padecieron persecución . . . " (*Relatos fronterizos* 71).
50 "Veía yo a Chessman desgringolado y lacio, pensando que él iba a ser en aquel circo el tozudo de la hilaridad. El superclown monstruoso" (*Relatos fronterizos* 71).

Bibliography

Barreiro, Javier. "Ramón J. Sender y Francisco Carrasquer: El reencuentro literario de dos libertarios del Cinca," *Alazet 24. Boletín Senderiano* 21 (2012): pp. 275–286. Print.

Caudet, Francisco "Sender en Albuquerque: la soledad de un corredor de fondo," *El lugar de Sender. Actas del I Congreso sobre Ramón J. Sender.* Eds. Ara Torralba and Gil Encabo. Huesca: Instituto de Estudios Altoaragoneses, 1995. Print.

Caudet, Francisco. *Correspondencia Ramón J. Sender – Joaquín Maurín (1952–1973).* Madrid: Ediciones de la Torre, 1995. Print.

King, Charles L. "Los libros y los días," 1975–1982: An Annotated Bibliography" in Mary S. Vázquez, *Homenaje a Ramón J. Sender.* Newark, Juan de la Cuesta, 1987, pp. 201–226. Print.

Mainer, José Carlos. "Prólogo. Resituación de Ramón J. Sender," José-Carlos Mainer (ed) *Ramón J. Sender. In Memoriam. Antología Crítica.* Zaragoza: Diputación General de Aragón 1983, pp. 7–23. Print.

Ordaz Romay, M. Ángeles. "Características del exilio español en Estados Unidos (1936–1975) y Eugenio Fernández Granell como experiencia significativa," Diss. Universidad de Alcalá, 1999. Print.

Salguero Rodríguez, José-María. "El primer Sender (III). Anarquismo y religión," *Alazet* 9 (1997): pp. 139–174, 148. Print.
Sender, Ramón J. "La cultura y los hechos económicos" *Orto* 1 (1932), pp. 25–28. Print.
———. *Vallé Inclán y la dificultad de la tragedia*. Madrid: Editorial Gredos, 1965. Print.
———. "Montesquieu y el español 'fronterizo,'" *CNT México* May–June 1960, 1. Print.
———. "El español 'fronterizo,'" *España Libre*, June 17, 1960. Print.
———. *Relatos fronterizos*. Mexico: Editores Mexicanos Unidos, 1970. Print.
Zelaya Kolker, Marielena. *Testimonios americanos de los escritores españoles transterrados de 1939*. Madrid: Ediciones Cultura Hispánica, 1985. Print.

CHAPTER
10
Pérez-Reverte at the Early Twenty-First Century Crossroads of Spanish History and Literature

Stephen Miller

Following a twenty-one-year career as a war reporter in print and television, Arturo Pérez-Reverte (APR) left it in 1994 and dedicated himself full time to researching and writing novels. By that date he already had published three long narratives: *El husar* (1986), which is an anti-epic, Goya-esque disasters-of-war view of the fate met by a separated Belgian cavalry officer in the aftermath of the Spanish victory against the French at the Battle of Bailén in 1808; *El maestro de esgrima* (1988) tells the story of Spain's last great fencing master and his last pupil in later nineteenth-century Madrid when duels are fought with pistols, not swords; and *La tabla de Flandes* (1990), a mystery novel in which a fifteenth-century Flemish painting on wood panels contains the clues to a murder committed at that time but which only in the novel's late twentieth-century present is fully understood and solved.

According to the narrative of APR's career offered by Gregorio Salvador in his *"Contestación"* to APR's discourse on the occasion of his reception into the Spanish Royal Academy of the Language (RAE) on June 12, 2003, APR's breakthrough book as novelist was his fourth novel, *El club Dumas* (1992), as in a club of those united by their love for serial novels of the kind produced by Alexandre Dumas (1802–1870). Noteworthy, however, is a curious bifurcation in APR's reception described by Salvador. On one hand, Salvador observes that with this fourth novel, APR "se consagra como novelista arrollador, como autor siempre instalado en las listas de libros más vendidos/he consecrates himself as an overwhelming novelist, as an author always installed on the best-selling book lists" and that his fiction "empieza a traducirse y a traspasar fronteras/begins to be translated and to cross borders" (57). On the other hand, the Spanish critical establishment sees his work differently: "la crítica española se muestra remisa a reconocerle méritos literarios, considerándolo un escritor de novelas populares cuyo éxito se basa en ser una cara conocida de television/ Spanish criticism is reluctant to recognize his literary merits, considering him a writer of popular novels whose success is based on being a familiar face of television" as war reporter and subsequent activities (57). This lack of critical acceptance continues among some in the literary establishment. For these, who have their minds made up and do not deign to spend time reading or considering APR's literature, his writing has the importance of any other element of the pop culture, which for them is an uninteresting alternative reality for the great unwashed and vulgar. However, as Salvador reiterates, this attitude back in the mid-1990s became more difficult for the majority of the literary establishment to accept once APR had published *El capitán Alatriste*. This volume became the first—to date—in a seven-volume, 1996–2011 series of novels set around Diego Alatriste, a Spanish soldier of fortune during the time of the Thirty Years War (1618–1648), a period coinciding with the latter decades of Spain as a dominant power in Europe and of its Golden Century in literature and art. Not only are the politics of King Philip IV and the Spanish Inquisition set front and center in the novels, as are such figures as the writer, Quevedo, above all, but also the likes of the dramatist, Calderón de la Barca, and the court painter, Velázquez, who alternate between having major or cameo roles in the action. Such was the overwhelming public, and gradually critical, acceptance of this series, as well as the consequent expanded readership for all his earlier and new works, that APR entered the twentieth-first century with a not-to-be-disputed prominence. Hence, when he was sponsored for membership in the RAE, elected to and formally took his seat, on the aforementioned date in 2003, APR was a generally—not universally—acknowledged major figure in Spanish literature and historical studies. His heavily-researched entry discourse, "El habla de un bravo del siglo XVII," documents the work involved in faithfully recreating the speech of that time's underworld, in which the often-shadowy Alatriste and his friends move. When not at war in the Low Countries, Diego and his colleagues, only some of whom are faithful friends, must hire out—often to the aristocracy and even to the Philip IV's agents—to perform secret activities in Spain and abroad. These confidential missions are, besides, of questionable morality and legality. They are the "dirty work" of empire, the Court and/or the Catholic Church and often leave one societal force competing against another. By undertaking these missions—or, on occasion, not—Altatriste and his closest associates are put at risk as they negotiate the interstices of the conflicting goals of those who contract them and of those against whom they labor. APR's ability to create the multi-dimensional fictional characters who foreground the history, and then experience the societal issues of earlier seventeenth-century Spain, are what won him the ever-greater popular success, and then the notable acceptance, by the literary and historical Spanish establishment, which led to his 2003 entrance into the RAE.

From the vantage point of 2019, it is clear that in the interim since 2003, APR has not disappointed his readers, most of the literary and historical establishment, nor publishers, nor the RAE.[1] Besides, because of his exhaustive research for his fictions, he is a first-call for the antiquarian and rare book dealers who, more prosaic versions of book-sleuth, Lucas Corso, in *El club Dumas*, know of the interests and proclivities that make the very well-heeled APR a highly-valued client.[2]

Several aspects of APR's personal history and profile as literary author and major Spanish cultural figure were already clear by his 2003 entrance into the RAE but, since then, have been amply confirmed and reinforced. In this essay, some of these aspects shall be identified and afterwards be discussed ad seriatim. This listing includes the following activities and characteristics: 1) APR's twenty-one years as a combat reporter across the world; those two decades transformed him from a young man of peripheral Spain (Cartagena on the southeast coast of the Peninsula) into the most cosmopolitan and deeply-experienced of all the contemporary Spanish creative writers—and perhaps, in all of Spanish history; 2) his never-forgotten schoolboy work translating from the Latin of Caesar and the Greek of Xenophon, as commented upon by Gregorio Salvador (55–56, 65) (from that time forward, APR became a student of history, particularly as focused by war, and that of his own country); 3) APR's status as a life-long reader of fiction who knows both the canon and that literature which inspires him most to create more literature; 4) APR's devotion to the pictorial art of the West from the late Middle Ages through the present (this taste extends to photography, perhaps most especially, to war photography, some of which he himself produced early in his reporting career); 5) APR finds marginal characters, be they an Alatriste, a graffiti tagger, or a secret agent, endlessly fascinating and compelling; for him, the best among them decide when to put all they have and are on the line, and in so doing, reveal much about societies so much less-demanding of themselves than the individuals he most admires. Life-and-death action obliges him and his characters to inquire, to try to learn what those epiphanies reveal about the meaning of everything; the game of chess and the science of geometry become the analogs of such questing. Somehow, APR repeatedly speculates, were we to be able to understand the geometry and chess of our lives, that we truly would achieve life. This is a kind of non-dogmatic conviction that seems to underlie all APR's work. Against the nihilism of so much of the world he portrays, APR has a subtle faith that there is a meaning to everything if we were just able to penetrate with precision, discover finally how and why everything comes together.

To take up, then, the first of these six themes in APR's literature, he writes a lot about violence, war and death. The entire *Alatriste* series is a prime example, but the six volumes treating the Spanish War of Independence (1808–1814,) which APR published between 1987 and 2010, are as well. With the exception of one of these six volumes (*La sombra del águila/The Eagle's Shadow*), they cover, in highly-original manner, the actions and dates of that war as established by Benito Pérez Galdós in the First Series, in ten volumes, of his *Episodios nacionales* (1873–75).[3] Also in this context, APR's two volumes, based on his correspondent's experience of the Yugoslav Wars (1991–2001), waged between Christians and Muslims, which led to the breakup of that country into ethnic republics, *Territorio comanche* (1994) and *El pintor de batallas/The Painter of Battles* (2006), must be cited. Unlike Galdós and much more like Hemingway,[4] APR writes of violence, war and death based on more than two decades of personal experience. And, while in no place known to me, does he analyze the effect of those decades upon himself, it seems clear that the obsession he has with battles and warriors formed him profoundly. For example, in a short opinion for the criticism website, *Bibliópolis*, José Joaquín Rodríguez ultimately greatly praises *Territorio comanche,* but first characterizes his own attitude toward APR before having read that autobiographical novel of APR and war photographer, José Luis Márquez, as they experience one particularly dangerous afternoon in the Yugoslav Wars, which they had been covering for many months. Rodríguez begins by repeating a relevant-for-our-purposes stereotypical characterization of APR by those, including originally himself, who do not react well to APR—nor to Hemingway in his day: "el aire de 'yo he vivido mucho' que adopta/the air that 'I have lived a lot' that he adopts" and that, as a result, "como si él, por haber estado en la guerra, fuese más hombre/as if he, because he had been in war, was more of a man." What most people—how lucky for us—can only imagine, for writers like APR, these are ingrained reflexes that condition everything they are and do. The only importance of words for them is to help themselves and others to really understand what humankind is capable of when the restraints of reason and decency are lifted. They are disgusted by those, e.g., politicians and all other manner of con artists, who use words to shape the narratives in which they emerge as heroes and saviors and which serve to bend the unwary and innocent to their ends. Hence, in APR, it is actions, and those actions analyzed as sincerely and completely as possible, that matter, not the display of words used to create alternate, self-enhancing ruses.

While Gregorio Salvador recalls the young APR translating the historical war narratives of Caesar and Xenophon, Salvador neither attempts to plumb those experiences nor enter into any extended speculations on the effect of them on APR, the future writer. Nonetheless, as any veteran translator of those kinds of texts remembers, the meaning squeezed from them related directly to epiphanies of emotion-filled understanding that lasts lifelong. When the "historical-personal" enormity of such words as "Veni, vidi, vici" or "Iacta alea est" is first comprehended, the impression becomes a parameter of one's life and more so if, like APR, one runs off to be a war correspondent when still little more than a child. No matter how many youth have had such translator epiphanies, so very few are moved to want to participate in the world they expose, and not from the relative safety of being an order-following soldier but rather as a free entity whose only constraints to going under fire are the ignorance and inexperience which youth has in most abundant supply, and which news organizations are happy to indulge. At the same time, such a young man as APR went to war thinking there was some great plan to be experienced and understood. The likes of Caesar and Philip the Great were consequential people, men of vision and epoch-making leaders. Despite all their limitations, they became world-historical figures, the protagonists of the worlds they made. How different, though, APR's wars and their leaders were! No world-historical figures strode or presided over APR's battlefields, just the combination of miserable warlords, politicians and inexperienced idealists who substituted either their self-serving aims or their well-meaning principles for the previous generation's crusades for world domination . . . or saving the world from them. The youthful APR was conditioned by epic figures and times, yet he, beginning in the Spain of the dictator Franco, lived and learned from much smaller ones. Perhaps that is one of the reasons why in the *Alatriste* series first, and then in his recent *Una historia de España* (2019, a recompilation of a chronologically ordered series of newspaper columns first published in *XL Semanal* between 2014 and 2018), APR constantly draws a fundamental comparison. On one hand, there are individuals characterized above all by personal worth and values; on the other, there are the incompetents, cheats, sharpers and manipulators put into places of authority and power by birth, luck or their own ambition, with a talent for self-promotion and a lack of scruples of any kind. The protagonists favored by APR in his fiction are those who make themselves responsible for the meditated actions for which they stand by and accept responsibility, come what may. Nevertheless, in APR's world, there are no larger-than-life heroes, just individuals who, guided by their own lights, do what they feel they must. Fully post-modern, APR's protagonists lack any hope for big societal projects and do well to remain faithful to themselves and to those who depend upon them.

In his 2003 "*Contestación,*" Gregorio Salvador neatly summarizes what APR has stated often in different contexts over time concerning his writer-as-reader self-identification and how that equation influences his writing. To this effect, Salvador quotes APR: "Escribo como lector/I write as a reader" of fiction (56). And, this means concretely that he follows the practice of writers like Galdós, Stevenson, Dumas and Stendhal. In these classic 19th-century literary authors, who sold enough copies of their novels to live by their pens, APR sees the "secreto/secret" to his own narrations. They employ the same "mecanismos de la narración clásica/mechanisms of classic narration" as the above-named storytellers. This means plots structured by "planteamiento, nudo, desenlace/approach, climax, outcome" presented in simple, straightforward prose (56). Consequently, both he and the reader can concentrate, almost seamlessly, on the structures of actions and character wherein "el honor, la amistad, la aventura, el mar, el peligro, el tesoro, el laberinto, el enigma/honor, friendship, adventure, the sea, danger, treasure, the labyrinth, enigma" are explored, experienced, perhaps savored, and most certainly, better-appreciated than before the writing and the reading. With the most obvious and singular exception being *Territorio comanche*, APR does not write autobiographical fiction. Instead, he creates characters who he puts into situations that allow he himself and his reader opportunity to live vicariously the situations, themes, places and times valued by both.

When circumstances indicate, the creation of variously illustrated texts become highly germane to what we can call the "project-APR." Nineteenth-century masters all saw at least some of their most famous titles illustrated in the century, which was already by 1842, denominated as "the age of graphically-illustrated books."[5] The first editions of *La tabla de Flandes, El club Dumas, La sombra del águila, Ojos azules/Blue Eyes,* as well as all seven volumes of the *Alatriste* series, were illustrated in various ways and several of these volumes have subsequently been adapted by other authors into the format of graphic novels. Such are the fashions in the literary world that many professors—many fewer readers—scorn such editions as child-book literature. Yet for the realist artist—and APR is fundamentally a realist despite his often sophisticated narrative techniques—the key is to make the world of dress, objects and settings in which his characters move as present as possible to the reader. Hence, Sir Walter Scott for his novels and Frederick Remington for his narrations, paintings, prints and bronzes had important antiquarian collections which helped document their lexical and plastic work. William Makepeace Thackeray illustrated many of his own novels. The young Galdós created graphic narrations of Canary Islanders in Las Palmas and in Madrid. Then he created a corps of illustrators for the first two series of his *Episodios nacionales*, while himself contributing a few architectural drawings for them. The relations between Dickens and Twain on the one hand and among their several illustrators on the other have been heavily-documented and studied. APR's supervision of the *Alatriste* series included a gradual change from the sole illustrator of the first three volumes (Carlos Puerta) to a second illustrator (Joan Mundet), who supplemented Puerta's work with about a quarter of the illustrations for the fourth volume. Mundet then did all the illustrations for volumes 5 through 7, as well as all-new illustrations for the first four volumes in *Todo Alatriste*, the 2016 single-volume collection of all seven volumes of the series. At the same time, as Galdós stated in the prologue to the luxurious, ten-volume edition of the *Episodios ilustrados*, there are works that do not need illustration. And APR does not to my knowledge reveal why he published *El pintor de batallas* with no edition of the novel illustrated, a work whose constant intertexts are paintings over five centuries and photographs from more than 100 years that document, portray and interpret the destruction and death that come from war. Nonetheless, so striking are the mentions and even *ekfrases* of some of these paintings and photos that there is a noteworthy, disinterested website that brings together as many of these graphic intertexts as possible: http://perso.wanadoo.es/pintordebatallas. Reflection, though, suggests that to illustrate a comparatively-short novel (barely more than 300 pages of normal-sized and spaced type) with many score paintings and photos might distract from the novel itself. Something similar seems to be the case with the graphically-gifted author, John Updike, for his *Seek My Face* (2002), whose implicit graphic intertexts are numerous works by marketing genius, Andy Warhol, and by the art-consumed Jackson Pollock. In these novels, neither APR nor Updike wishes to document his words. Rather, both count on readers with enough relevant, stored, mental images so as to engage in a continuous segue; the verbal/mental action of the respective novels is a volume-long meditation on the relation between life and art, of how the latter tries at its best to capture and understand the former.[6] In the end, then, APR, who has for decades welcomed film versions of his work, over which he has been content to exercise little or no control,[7] is artistically centered by creating as deep an experience for his public, amply understood, as possible. For this reason, in my opinion, he is so open to exploring and seeking the help of as many different artistic means and media as relevant to that end. This attitude derives, of course, from his semi-naive viewpoint as reader and more generally, of audience for art. What matters is the success of the work, the feelings it evokes of having experienced something of value during its contemplation, of having spent one's time well.

In some senses, APR's preference for marginal protagonists may be best introduced through the imposing mastiff named *Negro/Black*, as he, first-person narrator, tells the reader of his life and last great adventure. He is a retired, champion fighting-dog who feels forced back into action in the vain effort to save a canine friend who has fallen into the hands of a band of to-the-death-dog-fight organizers somewhere in extra-urban Madrid. Beginning with a citation from Cervantes' *El coloquio de los perros* (9), the short novel listens to Negro show just how inhumanely dogs, by their nature loyal to their human masters, are stolen from them and turned to deadly blood "sport" by dehumanized people. Negro possesses elements of human cultural learning and can trace his bloodline going back to Roman times in the *circenses* of the Coliseum. Not so differently, then, from the brave, but down-on-his-luck soldier-for-hire, Alatriste, Negro is a good creature for whom society does not provide a good place. Intelligent, observant and loyal to those in whose service they must labor, both Negro and Alatriste are marginal figures who merit much better than they receive. But, it is precisely their perspective on the larger societies in which they live that lets APR create the readerly experience of the distances and contours between what is right and what society allows or actually calls for.

Brothers-in marginality of Negro, Alatriste and, for that matter, all the Spanish *Tercios* in Flanders, are the abandoned-to-his-fate, Belgian Sub-lieutenant, Frederic Glüntz, following the rout of the French at Bailén in *El húsar*; the Spanish soldiers forced by Spanish royalty's ineptitude into the Russian campaign of Napoleon in *La sombra del águila*; the reporters-at-their-own-risk of *Territorio comanche* and *El pintor de batallas*; Manolo, the convict-turned-truck-driver/white knight, who is disposed to give his life for the equally-luckless, oft-betrayed, young María in *Un asunto de honor/A Matter of Honor*;

and, most recently, the late 1930s secret agent, Lorenzo Falcó, who will be disavowed and abandoned by his Nationalist handlers, should it be to their convenience. These characters, despite themselves and society, have, in APR's world, more to show about the good and the beautiful than any official representative of the society that first uses and abuses them, and then leaves them, at best, to uncertainty and to either the barest or no hope of a future. APR does not moralize about these figures but their situations give the reader the vicarious experience of good and of evil, the possibility coming to provisional conclusions at least about light and the darkness always looming around human society.

In APR's world, there is a kind of non-divine, non-personal providence. It is a feeling that, no matter the chaos and the violence, there is, in fact, some hidden chess-like geometry that underlies it all, which, if perceived, could explain it all. In life, practical men try to learn the schemes of this "providence" for all manner of purposes, some legitimate and some not. It is perhaps, though, in *El pintor de batallas* where APR probes these structures most deeply. It seems that it is in pictorial art where the humanly most meaningful representations of these structures can be found. Faulques, the protagonist and former prize-winning combat cameraman, suffers the loss of Olvido,[8] the much-younger Italian combat reporter who steps on a mine and is killed in the war in Bosnia. Ten years after her demise, Faulques still struggles with the issue of his responsibility for her death. On the eve of her leaving him for at least a period of independence, they are in a Bosnian war zone, but sitting at rest, since not under fire. At one point, Olvido stands and moves towards something in the nearby grass that attracts her. The more experienced Faulques realizes too late to warn her to stop and a mine detonates, fatally for her. The question Faulques poses concerns whether his hesitation in warning her was just a matter of reflex delay or did her purpose of leaving him delay, for just a split-second, his reflex to warn her?

It is not clear to me that *El pintor de las batallas* offers a categorical answer to this question. Instead, much of the narration is a recounting of Faulques' apprenticeship to/by Olvido, going to museums throughout Europe and the Americas and having her teach him how to read paintings of war from the Middle Ages to the twentieth century. Faulques observes, "Olvido tenía los ojos adiestrados desde niña; el instinto de leer un cuadro como quien lee un mapa, un libro o un pensamiento de un hombre/ Olvido had her eyes trained from childhood; the instinct to read a picture as one who reads a map, a book or a thought of a man" (91). As a corollary ability, she observed that the photography-saturated world produces more images than it can handle. Something like so many occasions in life itself, the photos are unintentional, non-purposed in their infinite variety when compared to works of meditated pictorial art rendered by great masters. Especially after Olvido's death, Faulques becomes convinced of the correctness of her thought and sets out to paint a great circular mural on the interior walls of a centuries-old watchtower looking out over the Mediterranean to warn of once-invading Moors. Although he is a far better photographer than painter, painting becomes Faulques' highly intentional way to seek understanding. Chess as one kind of game and geometry as one kind of science create, as well as order, the world. The painter of the kind identified by Olvido and which Faulques is striving to be studies the games and patterns in life and in art. In the greatest art, the kind in which Faulques has been schooled and to which he aspires to create, the epiphanic moment is to reveal something of the underlying order of things, an order best appreciated when contemplating that most horrible, but tremendous human activity of waging war.

Since Faulques is dying of what seems to be a stomach cancer, his work on the mural is never complete but does reach an endpoint. That occurs when he goes for his daily swim in the Mediterranean one day but instead of returning to shore, he continues, the reader understands, swimming out to sea until exhaustion takes over and he drowns. Not clear to this reader at least is if Faulques ever achieves an ultimate understanding of life, death and the world through the work on his mural. Maybe he has a good-enough realization. However, it remains ironic that it is Faulques, who could sense the presence of the hidden land mine, not Olvido, the great reader of paintings. Is art too processed, too distant from life to be useful for understanding life in the world? Very hard to say based on the novel. But those are the questions APR poses in *Pintor* and so many others of his volumes.

At the writing of this essay, in mid-2019, Spain is at a real historical crossroads between total democracy and more-limited constitutional organization, specifically that of the Constitution of 1978, as interpreted by Spain's equivalent of the Supreme Court in the United States. The question is posed: should Spain continue as the Iberia-wide entity it now is or should it become geographically and culturally diminished by successful separatist movements in the Catalonian and Basque regions? In numerous newspaper columns and media interviews, APR has made clear that he favors the historical Spain that his *Una historia de España* traces back to pre-Roman times. And his pedagogic volume, *La Guerra Civil contada a los niños*, affirms the same unity. So too, do the *Alatriste* novels which have Castilians, Andalusians, Basques and Catalonians all living and warring together as Spaniards. This is not to say that APR views "Greater" Spain now and through history as problem-free, just that, having lived revolutions and wars of independence around the world for twenty-one years as a reporter, he views Spain, indeed Europe, as privileged lands where people have the best possible chance at living quality lives. His literature in its historical and its contemporaneous settings pits its marginalized protagonists against the status quo, which is more often corrupt than not. Yet, much like Galdós, APR presents the world and its structures not so much to criticize them but so that the reader can arrive at individual assessments as to what should and may be done. APR well understands the desire for an overarching schema that makes everything clear. But his work seems to indicate skepticism as to the existence of such a schema. Art can only prepare those who enjoy and reflect upon it to take practical actions. At the same time, with Olvido's as a cautionary tale, APR indicates that understanding must be a carefully observant journey, not a packaged, individual synthesis. While the journey ends for the individual with death, for society, it is a different matter. For the widely known—and respected—APR, his ultimate audience is the society of his time. He seems to urge that the journey he has in mind should be made by socio-political entities that have stood the test of the centuries in creating ever-bettering bodies politic. The revolutions and civil wars of the Third World, which he has seen first-hand, have not created perfect societies. To the contrary. Hence, APR seems to say, the test of any society is its ability to hold up the mirrors of its history and art and determine where to go forward based on the facts and aspirations of its past and present. If Pérez Reverte's art is successful, it will continue to be what it has become since the 1980s, one of the meditations and markers of what Spain has done right and wrong, especially for the past four hundred years. But, it is the larger society, only some of it formed by his readers, that will determine what of that past will be modified and continue and what parts will not. Pérez-Reverte knows exactly what he thinks on these matters, but, as with those who want to adapt his writing to filmic and other graphical formats, he limits himself in trying to direct both his readers' and his adapters' activities.

Notes

1 The article by Pozuelo Yvancos, a university professor in Spain and frequent literary critic for the newspaper *ABC*, cited in the Bibliography, originally published on 2 June 2018, confirms everything about APR's literary standing sixteen years after Salvador's "*Contestación*," while also returning to emphasize some of the points made by Salvador. See also, in this vein, the 2009 collection of some twenty essays by professors and

interview with APR edited by Belmonte and López de Abiada cited in the Bibliography.

2 Perhaps the most complete example of APR working with such merchants is found in *Hombres buenos/Good Men* (2015), where the meta-narration of the novel details precisely his painstaking interactions with purveyors of books and maps, as well as fellow academicians and librarians of the RAE, to document facts relative to the Madrid, Paris and land route between those cities in the late eighteenth-century setting of the novelesque action.

3 All titles by me cited in the Bibliography study this Galdós-APR relation. In his "*Contestación*" Salvador cites Galdós as one of the formative and continuing influences in APR (55, 56, 63).

4 APR is no fan of Hemingway. In a manner that is novelistically gratuitous and demeaning to himself, APR caricatures and degrades Hemingway in the third of his series of the secret agent, Lorenzo Falcó, novels: *Sabotaje* (2018). That said, both writers have "done" war in various continents and, either as soldier or reporter-defending-himself, had to take up arms and use them. Unlike Hemingway, but much like, it seems, the novelist—my friend, student of Galdós and decorated Korean War combat veteran, Rolando Hinojosa, APR retained his sanity despite what he saw and did. Hemingway, in some ways like the sadly, painfully, slowly dying first responders to the 9/11/2002 slaughter at the World Trade Center Towers in Lower Manhattan, succumbed, as a suicide in his case, to the cumulative effects of his wounds and experiences only years after the traumas. Something of the same happens, arguably, with APR's own Andrés Faulques, a war photographer, in *El pintor de batallas*.

5 Anon., "Notice to the Abbotsford Edition," 3. To this general theme, I have dedicated many studies, one of which is cited in the Bibliography ("Pérez-Reverte entre la ekfrasis y la ilustración del texto narrativo: *El sol de Breda* y *El pintor de batallas*"). My principal work by far on this subject is dedicated to Galdós but I have also published on illustrated texts by Cervantes, Leopoldo Alas, Torrente Ballester, Javier Marías and Manuel Rivas.

6 That neither *El pintor de batallas* nor *Seek My Face* is counted among the more successful novels of their authors means, based on my experience as a classroom teacher, that many readers, even those with a noteworthy literary culture, do not possess a high level of graphic culture, and, furthermore, do not care to attain such experience and knowledge. Such is our era of cultural specialization!

7 For a rather full discussion by APR of his relation with filmic versions of his work, see "Como *Un asunto de honor* se convirtió en *Cachito*." There is something "Shakespearean" in APR's attitude in these matters. But while the Bard is long gone, APR simply seems to have other things of more importance to do. He most definitely welcomes directors and producers of stage and film to buy the rights for his work and talk with him about their ideas but, in the end, he lets them do what they will.

8   Notably, the unusual surname of Olvido, which translates to "I forget" or "forgetfulness" in English, offers some insight into APR's mindset about his characterization of Falques' dilemma concerning his possible role in Olvido's death for the English-speaking reader/critic.

Bibliography

Anon., "Notice to the Abbotsford Edition," *Waverley Novels*, Vol. I: *Waverley* and *Guy Mannering*. Edinburgh and London: Robert Cadell and Houston & Stoneman, 1842, pp.3–4. Print.

Belmonte, José and J.M. López de Abiada, Co-ordinadores. *Alatriste. La sombra del héroe*. Madrid: Alfaguara, 2009. Print.

Miller, Stephen. "Los ciclos de la novela histórica de Galdós, Pérez-Reverte y Almudena Grandes: apuntes sobre semejanzas y diferencias," Seminario Galdós y la novela histórica actual," *Actas X Congreso Internacional Galdosiano 2013*. Yolanda Arencibia et al., eds. Las Palmas, Spain: Ediciones del Cabildo de Gran Canaria, 2014, pp. 596–591. E-book:http://actascongreso.casamuseoperezgaldos.com/index.php/cig/issue/current.

——. The Graphic-Lexical Palimpsest of War of Independence Narratives." *Romance Quarterly*, 59, No. 2 (2012), pp. 101–121. Print.

——. "History and Interpretation in War of Independence Narratives: Three *Episodios* of Galdós, *Cabo Trafalgar* and *Un día de cólera* of Pérez-Reverte, and Garcí's *Sangre de mayo*." *Studies in Honor of Vernon Chamberlin*. Mark A. Harpring, ed. Newark, DE: Juan de la Cuesta-Hispanic Monographs, 2011, pp. 145–163. Print.

——. "Introduction: Galdós, Pérez-Reverte and the War of Independence," [I guest edited this number] *Romance Quarterly*, 59, No. 2 (2012), pp. 67–68, 101–121. Print.

——. "Pérez-Reverte entre la ekfrasis y la ilustración del texto narrativo: *El sol de Breda* y *El pintor de batallas*." *Talentos múltiples*, eds. Carmen Becerra and Susana Pérez Pico. Vigo, Spain: Editorial Academia del Hispanismo, 2012, pp. 97–117. Print.

——. "Pérez-Reverte as Seen from a Galdosian Perspective." *Anales Galdosianos*, 42–43 (2007–2008), pp. 77–85. Print.

Pérez-Reverte, Arturo. *Un asunto de honor*. Madrid: Santillana/Punto de Lectura, 2007. Print.

——. *El club Dumas*. Madrid: Santillana/Punto de Lectura, 2007. Print.

——. "Cómo *Un asunto de honor* se convirtió en *Cachito*," in *Un asunto de honor*, pp. 87–108. Print.

——. *El habla de un bravo del siglo XVII* [Discurso leído el día 12 de junio 2003 en su recepción pública]. Madrid: Real Academia Española, 2003. Print.

——. *La Guerra Civil contada a los jóvenes*. Fernando Vicente, illustrator. Madrid: Alfaguara, 2015. Print.

——. *Una historia de España*. Madrid: Alfaguara, 2019. Print.

——. *Hombres buenos*. Madrid: Alfaguara, 2015. Print.

———. *El húsar*. Madrid: Ediciones Akal, 2007. Print.
———. *Ojos azules*. Sergio Sandoval, illustrator. Barcelona: Seix Barral, 2009. Print.
———. *Los perros duros no bailan*. Madrid: Alfaguara, 2018. Print.
———. *El pintor de batallas*. Madrid: Alfaguara, 2006. Print.
———. *Sabotaje. Una aventura de Lorenzo Falcó*. Madrid: Alfaguara, 2018. Print.
———. *La sombra del águila*. Illustrated by Anon. Madrid: Santillana/Punto de Lectura, 2007. Print
———. *Territorio comanche*. Madrid: Ollero y Ramos Editores, 1994. Print.
———. *Todo Alatriste*. Illustrated by Joan Mundet. Madrid: Alfaguara, 2016. Print.
Pérez-Reverte, Arturo and Carlota Pérez-Reverte. *El capitán Alatriste*. Carlos Puerta, illustrator. 1996. Print.
Pozuelos Yvancos, José María. "Todo empezó con la lectura, el juego más serio."
https://www.zendalibros.com/empezo-la-lectura-juego-mas-serio/. Accessed 18 June 2019. Web.
Rodríguez, José Joaquín. "Reseña. Territorio comanche," *Bibliópolis. Crítica en la red*.
http://www.bibliopolis.org. Accessed 22 June 2019. Web.
Salvador, Gregorio. "Contestación." *El habla de un bravo del siglo XVII* by Arturo Pérez-Reverte. Madrid: Real Academia Española, 2003, pp. 53–66. Print.

PART IV

Crossroads of Social, Gender, Artistic, Literary & Cinematic Time & Space, Not to Mention Tradition & Modernity, in Latin/Latino(x) America

CHAPTER
11
Time Space and Creativity

Rose Mary Salum

A dark wood bookcase, a gnawed sofa, a house in the downtown area of Mexico City, the cries of children playing football on the streets, my father's book collection. I write this on his birthday but he is no longer among us. His books are not in my childhood home, either, as some of them are hidden among the shelves of other libraries. The others, which I used to read as my mother urged me to help her in the kitchen or do my homework, remain in my house. Despite the fate of these texts, my first memory takes me back to that corner between the sofa and the bookcase that embraced my body while I traveled in the arms of Saint Exupéry or Louisa May Alcott.[1] The impression they left on me has transcended time. There was something in the arrangement of their sentences, perhaps in their literary voice, which sealed their stories in my tender mind. I was becoming a "reader" and I did not realize it. I would not recognize it for many years, until I came of age and understood without overthinking it, without decorating it with sophisticated words, that I could not be at peace without a book nearby and that in the future, I wanted to be wrapped in ideas. I did not try to convince myself with logic, nor did I tell myself that I was becoming a reader. Rather, that desire was expressed through an image. It would show me the path, that is, I was to continue studying, reading and discovering new worlds.

But things were not falling into place in a linear way; between the time I held the first book in my hands and my adulthood, there was an unexpected intermission. One day, in the middle of a class, our teacher questioned us about the future and what our plans were for life; the possibility of becoming an author flashed through my brain in an instant. The feeling was not pleasant; I felt a void when imagining a life of paralysis and boredom that would surely bring loneliness. So, I tried to immerse myself in the world of mathematics, while avoiding the realms of physics, in history, though not in its dates and conquests; I even turned fully into the visual arts. I was looking for a voice that could then be developed through imagery. I did everything to get away from books, but all roads led me to them. If I wanted to paint, I had to read about the arts, if I wanted to learn about music, I had to research its past in all the publications available on the subject, if I wanted to explore the theater, the books were again imposed on me. What course did I ultimately take? Marriage.

From that moment on, I threw myself desperately into reading, in my thirst for knowledge. Hunger was what I felt. Maybe because in my new life, I felt I had been torn away from them. That desire brought me back to my original career, to the world of humanities and ideas. I understood that the need of knowledge had been a pillar in my life, and when I moved away from it, a disquieting thirst pushed me back to literature.

That fascination cleared a path into creativity that I had not taken seriously in the first place, but that was ever present in my sheepish desire to leave a mark in the world. One could say that I was officially entering into the creative world, but it would be a disservice to the artistic expressions I developed in my childhood. However, it is true that I started writing, though I did it with distrust. Maybe it was the censor that we all have installed inside us; I certainly nurtured it without a second thought. And, although I attended workshops, I did not dare to call myself a writer because I did not possess that aura of intelligence and almost holiness that, in my perception, other writers had.

My father was my biggest critic, and as I fell into the trap in which we all fall at the beginning, of thinking that dark or deliberately intellectual writing is the best, his critiques intensified. To console myself, I used to think that he was not "up-to-date" or had not understood my text. This attitude of mine blinded me to his more acute comments. Now in the distance that time has afforded me, I thank each and every one of them. He was right. It was not necessary to convey an intellectual arrogance to be able to express an idea. When I acknowledged it, it gave free rein to my creativity and something resembling a voice of my own began to appear. It was then that I completed a brutal move to the United States.[2]

Creativity, I understood later, was fragile and needed constant care. Any wild and dangerous environment could kill it... or rather, it could misrepresent my perception of it. My life abroad silenced the newly-acquired voice. But, there was still nothing more cruel or more perverse than self-criticism. Although it is true that self-censorship has not had the power to end this endless source, it is true that it has intermittently suffocated it. The result has been a dubious self, a constant questioning of my own creative capacity.

My father died on my birthday in 2014. At the time, I was living elsewhere, and technology had been imposed on me without having the tools to defend myself against it. It had not been a personal choice. We were all surprised and fascinated by it. I turned to it with enchantment. For the first time, technology allowed me to multitask and saved me the burden of hiring a team of people. For the first time, this small device could carry the most abundant source of information anyone had ever conceived of for me. And if that was not enough, I could have an entire library on hand if I had wanted to. My dad's bookshelf was forgotten; I had everything I ever imagined in one convenient and portable way. I could carry with me most classic books or the most up-to-date *New York Times* articles. I had access to all the books from Latin American and European writers, as well as the Asian ones. If there was a paradise, there it was, in that little thing that could be held with one hand.

Nobody prepared me for what would come next. The damage caused by the technology of the 21st century caused me to perceive it as irreversible, even though in reality this has not been the case. My capacity for concentration and for deep thought were ruefully undermined. I did not dare to confess aloud that finishing a complete book now demanded self-discipline and rigor. Despite the malleability of my brain, or perhaps because of it, I could not escape the constant stimuli that the cell phone vomited at all times, syphoning my concentration meant for reading or creating. Could you say that my creativity has been affected since the beginning of the new century? Yes. And that my capacity as a reader has been undermined? Yes. Why read a complete book, I said to myself, when I could read just one part and capture in that exercise the intention, tone and history of what the author was trying to convey. This abnormality was reaffirmed when my already-affected brain tended to jump from one place to another without the possibility of placating it.

You have to meditate, my friends told me; that restores the capacity for concentration. However, the challenge was to acquire that habit when I spent most of the day glued to my cellphone's screen. And even when I had finally managed to sit down and quiet myself, I was turning to my phone as applications promised to take me to the most profound of meditative states. The original purpose was nullified.

I began to look back with nostalgia to times when we were not dependent on technology, with the certainty that, indeed, the past had been better. Other days, I questioned my creative capacity to the extent of provoking the creative paralysis I hated so much. Seemingly blocked, I consoled myself with other colleagues who echoed my state. But when creativity showed up timidly, and where I could spy the chance for a new text, I could see that all of the negative experiences had been the product of fear. The capacity to respond with creativity to the books I read was still in there somewhere. Deteriorated, perhaps beaten up, but not completely gone.

Many years have passed and the memories of that corner near my father's timid bookshelf have remained as a counterbalance between who I was in Mexico, embraced by the love of my parents, and who I am today, living in the United States, constantly bombarded by an irritating apparatus that is the absolute expression of imperialism—so hated in some of the books I read as a child. I know that the longing for those conversations with my father, his bookshelves, his wise suggestions and, above all, the absence of all these elements that distract me with such ease, intensifies. But if it is true that I allowed it into my life, there must be the possibility of modifying it in such a way that its technology can serve more as a tool than as a predator of the creative world. Maybe that attitude could give me back the space to listen to the children who play with my granddaughter when she gets to visit me. Alternatively, it will provide me with the time to rearrange, on the pale wooden shelves, my own books that I acquired when curiosity drove me. The future is still uncertain. Achieving that purpose seems impossible because the pressure is constant and the thread of thought that triggers my ideas can break at any moment. Perhaps delving into the creative process could offer a viable solution. We will have to bet on it, surrender to the process and trust that holding the tension of the opposites will bring me the solution.

Notes
1 Authors of *The Little Prince* and *Little Women*, traditionally books read by not-quite-adolescent children.
2 Mexico had become a dangerous place for those perceived to be able to pay ransoms for kidnapped family members, thus many of the so-called privileged class were sent by their families to other, safer countries.

CHAPTER
12
Why Can't a Feminist be Sexy? Sandra Cisneros' *My Wicked, Wicked Ways*

Gwendolyn Díaz-Ridgeway

In reference to the comments about the cover of her poetry collection, *My Wicked, Wicked Ways* (1987), Cisneros states:

> I'm surprised that some feminists said 'How could you, a feminist, pose like lewd cheesecake to sell your book?' After I thought about it, I said: 'So why can't a feminist be sexy? Sexiness is a great feeling of self-empowerment'. (Rodríguez-Aranda)

So why can't a feminist be sexy, I ask? By the time Cisneros published *My Wicked, Wicked Ways* in 1987, the days when feminists believed they should burn their bras and be like men were coming to an end. In *Women's Time*, Kristeva describes three stages of feminism, the first was of a political nature, the second focused on gender roles from a psychoanalytic stance and the third, her innovation, was the stage she considered androgynous or devoid of sexual difference, what she calls "demassification of the problematic of difference" (Moi 184–85). Cisneros' work begins where Kristeva's third stage of feminism ends. In fact, Cisneros portrays a fourth stage that differs from Kristeva's androgyny thesis and is closer to Jane Gallop's idea of feminine *jouissance*/enjoyment (316). In *The (M)Other Tongue: Finding the Other in the Mother*, Gallop posits female sexuality as an end in itself and constructs female identity in relation to her sexual self. To do so, she concludes that women must find the Other in the (M)other, by that she means that women have traditionally been viewed as mothers or daughters but not as individuals in their own right.

Patriarchy has limited women to their reproductive function. Thus, Gallop contends that women must appropriate their right to exist for themselves and not in function of others.

Cisneros has often reflected that she has chosen to not be a mother because she wanted to be a writer first and foremost and since she was not financially solvent as a young writer, she could not do both. She has always been fiercely independent and has rejected the idea of marriage as well. A product of the sexual revolution of the sixties, she is not afraid to depict sexual desire in her work. The very titles of her poetry collections, *My Wicked, Wicked Ways* and *Loose Woman*, defy the conventional and restrictive sense of morals and propriety expected of women by the male-dominated society.

My contention is that Cisneros relishes in debunking the myths of female propriety imposed by both the patriarchy and the Hispanic phallocentric culture and, in so doing, rebels against the prototypes of Virgin/*Malinche*,[1] Madonna/Prostitute perpetuated by the symbolic social contract. She carves out for herself, for Chicanas and for women in general, a new woman's space, free of taboos and judgments that relegate a woman to a sub-class in the social contract or to her reproductive roles.

Cordelia Chávez Candelaria posits the concept of the "Wild Zone" in Chicana literature, a paradoxical space created by the Chicana writer that both explores an unrestricted, unconquered existence, free of imposed gender roles, and challenges the existence of the restricted woman's space as defined by patriarchy (66). What is important about the exploration of this "wild zone," is that it engenders a space where Chicana expression is defined from within Chicana experience itself and not in relation to the dominant hegemonies. In her poetry, Cisneros sets out not only to re-appropriate Chicana female sexuality but also to re-appropriate and redefine religious beliefs and iconography. Doubly-marginalized, female and Chicana, she subverts the symbolic order of the hegemonic patriarchy and re-appropriates it on her own terms in a bold act of self-affirmation and empowerment, colored in brown skin tones, code-switching dirty talk, culture-crossing metaphors and daringly-erotic scenarios.

To begin with, there are the titles. Cisneros intends to be as up-front, in-your-face as possible from the start. By titling her first book of poems, *My Wicked, Wicked Ways,* and her second one, *Loose Woman*, she is making a clear statement that she intends to subvert the existing social sanctions on female sexuality by making an asset out of a sanction. She flaunts her sexual self in the face of a social structure that denies women their sexuality and in so doing, empowers herself. In this context, "wicked" and "loose" mean sexual and empowered, free and self-determined, and her poems portray both. The same is true of the book covers. In *Wicked,* the sexy, red lipstick, wine-drinking Sandra on the cover was not just a ploy to sell books, as feminists argued, it was an image that was cogent with the theme of the book: an assertive woman, who is free from patriarchal strictures, is free to assume her sexuality. In *Loose Woman,* we see a collage of Mexican iconography that prominently features a photograph of Sandra with slicked-back hair, dangling earrings, dark lipstick and a dress cut low in the back.

The poetry of *Loose Woman* portrays differing aspects of female sexuality and is reflective of Cisneros' attempt to subvert conventional morays and re-appropriate for the female that which has been denied to her. Four poems of this collection stand out as most defiant. One of my personal favorites is *I'm So in Love I Grow a New Hymen* (16). This poem manages to subvert the patriarchal idealization of virginity by suggesting that the female voice's desire for the man is so strong that she will grow a new hymen if that is what it takes to have him. Yet her sexual yearning, far from naïve, is compared to a conflagration, a terrorists' passion, an explosion, a spiritual high, a triumphant march. With imagery of the "straights" of Gibraltar,[2] Euclidean geometry[3] and "Gaudí's hammer against porcelain plates,"[4] the voice in the poem refers to the physical sensations of penetration, not as someone being possessed, but rather as the one whose role is dominant in the act of intercourse, the poetic voice guides the other in the act to the precise Euclidian geometric place of her desire (17).

In *Extreme Unction*, the poetic voice is that of a woman who has concluded that taking a husband is akin to taking her life; hence, the concept of the last rights of extreme unction (12). She wonders what it might have been like to have "braved" a marriage, or "bellied his child." But, ultimately, she concludes that a husband would be like a "balm for the occasional itch" and being a wife means a "seamed tongue." Love, she concludes, would not last as wife but rather as witch. However, by witch, she means a woman on her own, left to her own devices and not subsumed by the role of wife or Other of the man.

In *Once Again I Prove the Theory of Relativity*, the female poetic voice is that of a woman who yearns for her lover to return to her. In the monologue, she directs to him, she says "If you came back/ I'd give you parrot tulips and papayas/ laugh at your jokes/Or wouldn't say a word" (74). She worries that after she has again "savored you like an oyster," he'd grow tired and part for Patagonia or Laredo.[5] But, meanwhile, she "will have held you under my tongue/learned you by heart." And here is the punch line: "So that when you leave/ I'll write poems."

She will have what she wanted, food for thought, food for writing, experience to render into poetry. While the poem is about her desire for him, it is also about her desire of rendering experience into poetry, ultimately privileging her craft over her man.

The title poem, *Loose Woman*, is an inversion of the idea of the male on the prowl, the sexual beast whose desire conquers all (112). Here the voice is that of a woman who assumes her sexuality without guilt or shame. "They say I'm a beast/And feast on it. When all along/ I thought that's what a woman was." Like man, woman, too, is a sexual being and as such, she takes pride in her sexual prowess. She is not afraid to say what she thinks whether "Diamonds and pearls tumble form my tongue" or "toads and serpents" describe her mood (112). "I like the itch I provoke" (113), she says. Her daring attitude confronts the mob that "arrives with stones and sticks to maim and lame and do me in" (113). But, she has "built my little house of ill repute/Brick by brick. Labored/ Loved and masoned it" (113). And she is not about to shy away from the power that being sexual affords her: "I live like so./ Heart as sail, ballast, rudder, bow" (113). This self-empowered woman sails ahead, like Pancho Villa taking rightful ownership of Mexican lands.[6] As Villa defeats Porfirio Díaz, she defeats the male prerogative in sex. "By all accounts I am/ A danger to society [patriarchal society]/ I'm Pancha Villa" (113), she concludes, a revolutionary in the land of men.

Her re-appropriation of female sexuality expands into the arena of religion as well. In her essay, *Guadalupe,*[7] *the Sex Goddess*, Cisneros confronts the patriarchal construction of a sexless virgin, reinventing the image as La Lupe, a strong, sexualized woman who is God rather than the mother of God. Cisneros says that "when I see the Virgin of Guadalupe, I want to lift her dress as I did my dolls and look to see if she comes with *chones*/underwear) and does her *panocha*/vagina) look like mine" (4). For Cisneros, the sanctity of the virgin must be redefined to include her sexuality in order for modern woman to identify with her (McCracken 173). What Cisneros is doing here is re-defining the virgin in terms of what women are truly like in order for the virgin to become real to women. Thus, she re-appropriates traditionally-patriarchal religious symbols and re-defines them in women's terms by conflagrating the sexual with the religious.

According to Ellen McCracken, the publishing industry in recent years has commodified the Latina as an exotic sexual being, hence the broad commercial appeal of Latina literature in the last few years, McCracken notes that many Latina writers have played to this commodification in order to get published. However, I contend that this is not the case of Sandra Cisneros, whose poetry is all about the rejection of patriarchal constructions of the female, of *anglo* perspectives of Chicano otherness and of religious misogyny. Cisneros' poetry is about female empowerment through assuming her sexuality as woman, Chicana and religious.

To conclude, let us consider Cisneros' statement about the cover of her *Wicked, Wicked Ways*. She says that the cover portrays "a woman appropriating her own sexuality. In some ways, that is also why it's wicked; the scene is trespassing that boundary by saying 'I defy you. I am going to tell you my own story'" (Rodríguez Aranda 72) And *that*, indeed she does.

Notes

1. Malinche, originally Malinalli, then Malintzín, sold into slavery among Mesoamerican tribes, eventually came to be the intrepreter for the Spanish *conquistador* of the Aztecs, Hernán Cortés, due to her experiences and linguistic abilities. She was baptized as Doña Marina, assisted him in his efforts and bore him a son—but was "given" to another Spaniard as wife and disappeared from history. She is a figure of some controversy in Mexico for her role, variously known positively as the mother of the first so-called *mestizo* and negatively as a traitor, *la Chingada* (an obscene sexual reference for a rape victim).
2. A possibly double sexual innuendo of the homonym, "straights," most overtly refers to the geography of the Straits of Gibraltar, the narrow sea passageway between the Iberian Peninsula and Morocco.
3. Euclidian geometry, another sexual innuendo, among other aspects, deals with the intersection of lines and angles and spaces.
4. Probably not so much overt sexual innuendo as a reference to the aforementioned "Wild Zone" of the Chicana that Chávez Candelaria posits, the "hammer and plates" refer to Antoni Gaudí, Catalán architect, known for his fantastically-unusual, "wild," if you will, constructions in Barcelona, Spain. Gaudí broke apart Talavera, brightly-decorated pottery, to use as mosaic pieces in the traditional Mediterranean *trencadis*-style decorating of his creations, especially those in Güell Park. However, the hammer and plates interaction could be interpreted as the initial sex act, especially in view of Cisneros's poem, *I'm So in Love I Grow a New Hymen*.
5. Patagonia, the mostly-uninhabited plains of the Southern region of the Southern Cone of South America (Argentina and Chile), and Laredo, Texas, the desert-like area on the semi-empty northern border between Mexico and the U.S., are commonly used equivalents for distant ends-of-the-earth places.
6. Known for his revolutionary role, Pancho Villa symbolizes the revolt of the Mexican *campesinos* against dictatorship in the early 20th century. However, as a less well-known precursor of his self-appointed role as champion of the downtrodden, as a young man, he killed a landowner

who assaulted his sister, thus an appropriate source of not only sociopolitical but gender "justice" and the term, "Pancha Villa."
7 According to the Roman Catholic Church and Mexican tradition, the Virgin of Guadalupe, patron saint of Mexico, first appeared to an indigenous man, Juan Diego Cuauhtlatoatzín. He carried roses, given to him out-of-season on the hill of Tepeyac, near today's Mexico, D.F., by an indigenous-appearing Our Lady of Guadalupe, meant as evidence of her appearance to him on her fourth appearance to him, in 1531, in order to convince church officials that the original *Basílica de Guadalupe* should be built as per her request.

Works Cited

Chávez Candelaria, Cordelia. "Notes on a Chicana-identified 'Wild Zone'" of American Culture," *Trabajos Monográficos: Studies in Chicana/Latina Research* (Davis,CA: MALCS Institute, 1993). Print.

Cisneros, Sandra. *Loose Woman*. New York: Alfred A. Knopf, 199. Print.

———. *My Wicked, Wicked Ways*. New York: Random House, 1987. Print.

McCracken, Ellen. *New Latina Narrative: The Feminine Space of Postmodern Ethnicity*. Arizona: University of Arizona Press, 1999. Print.

Gallop, Jane. "The (M)Other Tongue: Finding the Other in the Mother." *Critical Inquiry*. Vol. 3, No. 2, Winter 1987, pp. 314–24. Print.

Kristeva, Julia. *New Maladies of the Soul*. New York: Columbia UP, 1995. Print.

Moi, Toril. *The Kristeva Reader*. Columbia UP, 1986. Print.

Rodríguez-Aranda, Pilar. "Interview with Sandra Cisneros." *Americas Review*. Spring, 1990, pp. 64–80. Print.

CHAPTER

13

Confrontations on All Fronts: *The War of the End of the World* by Mario Vargas Llosa

Jorge Chavarro

Translated by Debra D. Andrist

In 1981, Mario Vargas Llosa published *The War of the End of the World*, his sixth novel. The story of the town of Canudos, Brazil,[1] came out after an intermediate period occupied by Vargas Llosa's *Pantaleón and the Visitors* and *Aunt Julia and the Writer*, works characterized by humor and the subliterary,[2] but the intermediate period culminates with *The War of the End of the World*, described by critics as a masterpiece, a return to Vargas Llosa's brilliant first period of publications.[3]

The War of the End of the World is, first and foremost, a historical novel that exposes the relationship between politics and domination and the resulting circles of violence inscribed in the intertextuality of the biblical apocalyptic discourse and the texts of the *Old Testament* as the exodus. But, it is also a discourse of otherness, as in the image of Christ, which defines the saint whose initial discourse contains nothing incendiary, but is converted in such before the success of his words seeking to gather the dispossessed. The less-studied otherness is that of the figure of the woman, of silent presence and subordinated to men by the superiority of the war-like events in the text.

The scenario paints a country emerging from a monarchy and initiating a republican system led by a military establishment that does not believe in the need for legislative institutions. The text is constructed within these parameters of the military due to the need to control the insurrection and, before the failure of the first and second expeditions, and to set the stage for a final attack designed explicitly for total genocide.

Thus, it can only be assumed as a masculine world, with women inhabiting it as figures relegated to functions of helpers and victims. Most of the women in *The War of the End of the World* are invisible, sheltered by a globalizing term like "the beatas/the blessed" or as the women of the "sacred choir," accentuating their condition as biblical women, subordinated to the protective service of one Antonio Counselor but, in the same way, to Christian submission to any other of the male characters.

Case-in-point features Antonio and Honorio Vilanova and their cousins, Antonia and Asunción Sardelinha, still almost girls, who leave their village fleeing the plague that "kill[s] . . . parents, . . . sister, Luz María, a brother-in-law and three nephews" (139). They manage to reach Joazeiro, the Bahia town where Antonio decided to try his luck, and by then, "the two sisters were pregnant: Antonia by Antonio and Asunción by Honorio, "their saviors" (140).

Concurrently, a description of María Quadrado is paradigmatic of the notion of divine punishment; she is a penitent woman who dragged a wooden cross and wore a sack with holes for her arms. "'I was twenty years old but I had suffered so much that I seemed very old.' She was a woman with a broad face, bruised feet and a shapeless body with mouse-colored skin" (80). Hers was a punishment imposed by the men who took their role as executioners for violations that occurred during their wanderings without direction: a sheriff, a cowboy, two hunters and a shepherd—that explains her decision to shave her head, self-mutilation as a sign of final penance for her sins, the last one, to have felt compassion for her rapist among the last of the wanderers.

Finally, she arrives at Monte Santo and establishes herself in a cave, where she also ends up giving advice, as the *Santón*[4] did, even without knowing him. She protected the adulteresses who ran to take refuge in her cave. During the visit of the Counselor to Monte Santo, she does not leave the cave but, when he leaves, she follows him. With time, she becomes the "mother of all men" and "superior of the sacred choir," no woman closer to the Saint, and only she and Alejandrina Correa, part of the sacred choir, are saved from anonymity.

The description of Alejandrina Correa is also linked to the figure of a man who becomes her redeemer, the one who saves her from the stigma of singleness. She becomes the common-law wife of the priest, Don Joaquim, the parish priest of Cumbe, who was sent there as punishment for excesses with a minor, a pleasant fellow but, frankly, interested in the things of the world, especially in women.

Alejandrina's life had been shadowed since she was a child, when her ability to find underground sources of water during the time of the great drought was discovered, a skill that made her famous but not happy. Her supernatural faculties kept her away from both children and adults, as nobody was comfortable with her, "as if falling in love with her would have been a desecration" (206), a Marian-like desecration.[5]

Father Joaquim found her after she had left her twenties behind—and her younger sisters already had husbands. Their romance started slowly, or at least it did not become evident until the day Alejandrina hauled him out of the tavern with a forceful speech, "he came with me but it took a lot." They had three children and their relationship ended up being accepted by parents and siblings. Yet, upon the end of the last visit of the Counselor, Alejandrina leaves with him, leaving everything, which did not surprise the priest.

However, the ultimate female figures of the novel are Jurema and Estela, the Baroness. Jurema is subject to barter, a minor but nontransferable possession, without the right to discontent, credulous without objections, as when she tells the story of the image of San Antonio, in whose honor the town is called San Antonio das Queimadas. This is history to which another character, an adventurer, Galileo Gall, reacts by calling it pernicious and anti-scientific—and her own husband only reacts with a shrug. She is described as reserved, with what seems more shyness or obligation to go unnoticed as a good wife and servant, so she smiles as if she does not hear or understand, and physically, she is the opposite of María Quadrado: "She is young, with a smooth and burnished face" (161), she is barefoot, with loose hair and wearing a sleeveless tunic.

The men who support this fanatical world in which the aforementioned women move belong to two camps. On one side is the rhetorical and military confrontation between Antonio Counselor, Colonel Moreira César, a hero called to save the nation, and the anarchist, Galileo Gall, and on the other, the shortsighted journalist[6] and the Baron de Caña Brava, interlocutors in the fourth and last parts of the text. It is important to highlight them because they represent, in the case of the first, the object of vindication of the image of Jurema and, in the second, the ratification of the masculine Christian/Jewish paradigm. The Baron is a shrewd and diplomatic man, who prefers dialogue and negotiation to violence; he is oblivious to that world he has seen all his life from his social extreme as an aristocrat and favorite of the monarchy.

That is why he is seen by Republicans as dangerous. Seymour Menton compares him to the chameleon that observes and remains static in his window. The Baron is determined to agree with republicanism for the sake of social and family stability. But, Menton also proposes that "With this character, Vargas Llosa justifies the change of his own ideology" (814). However, not everything about the Baron is worthy of praise. Although Gall dies as a result of the violation that prevents him from seeing the end of Canudos, he is not the only one who exercises violence, and in the case of the Baron, paradigmatic of caste, the violation of servitude. Sebastiana, the eternal and fervent maid of Estela, his wife, is raped in her presence. Estela is mentally unhinged and perceived as unrecoverable, and "although Sebastiana's spirit and mouth had resigned to obey, her entire body continued to resist" (873). When the Baron gets "to reach her sex with his mouth . . . he felt the soft pressure of fingers on his back. He turned his head and looked, knowing what he was going to see, there stood Estela, looking at him. She did not seem scared, enraged, horrified, but lightly intrigued" (874). Then, "I can see, in the tumultuous moment when life seemed to burst between her legs, that the baroness always had both hands on Sebastiana's face, at which she looked with tenderness and mercy, while she blew slowly at him" (877). The erotic description is made between declarations of love to his wife and pretending that it serves as a new alliance between the two. At the same time, it is understood that this is happening as the result of the confession of happiness that the shortsighted journalist had made to him about his own relationship with Jurema.

The final portrait of Jurema is redemptive, not only for her, but also for the myopic journalist. Jurema ceases to be the resigned object that has been delivered to full possession by the Baron and the Baroness to Rufino. She believes that this flat world that makes her feel safe, for publicly possessing the role of companion who could choose her man, is happiness. After the death of Rufino, she faces the threat and risk of becoming Pajeú's wife, before which she decides that she would prefer to die.

Like the journalist when he confesses to the Baron his own desire to die, which is due to life without love, the Baron cannot understand that Jurema, the little girl of Calumbí, can be a source of happiness, especially for a man who seems so minimal and manifestly resigned, but not to physical death, but to life without love, "not to love, not to be loved by any woman . . . to be ugly, to be shy, to never have in my arms a woman who did not charge for it . . . excluded from love and pleasure. Condemned to whores" (818–819).

All the pain that led Jurema to Canudos and the sense of curse that accompanied her on that trip and then upon staying, suddenly transforms into happiness when she finds the journalist at the door of the sanctuary after believing him dead. "Embraced in his arms, she heard him say that he loved her and she said that she loved him, too. It was true"(840). And then, she felt happier than she had ever been in her whole childhood life of protected and comfortable servitude in Calumbí or in her marriage to Rufino.

Despite loving him, he could not cure her fear. And to love him meant overcoming shame and doing and desiring in body and thought the things that were sins; in those days, she had learned

> that love was also an exaltation of the skin, a dazzling of the senses. . . . If someone had told her that a man she was not married to would raise her skirts and take it from the view of another who was there . . . while they enjoyed and said mouth-to-mouth that they loved each other . . . and yet it happened every night since that afternoon. (843)

In *The War of the End of the World*, the apocalyptic scenario is patently obvious from the title, that is to say, the destruction of the represented universe, whose crossroads refers to the maintenance of historical contexts or of the time period to the pressures of the renovating periphery. The destruction corrresponds to the untimely arrival of these new ideas whose object is framed under the sign of progress that is synonymous with modernity, as is the secular state with the separation of church and state, the freedom of worship and the introduction of evaluative measures of the characteristics of the new state. Brazil is being born as a republic and it is not bad to acknowledge, to register, to establish a unified system of weights and measures that one wants to be the decimal one and finally, the establishment of a central tax system.

The insurrection in Canudos is explained only as the desire to maintain a feudal and Catholic system. However, the aspirations of europeanizing modernity ignore the realities of the poor and isolated regions of the north. The two sides make distorted readings of reality, which are paid forward by parallel fanaticisms that become the firewood that fuels the fire. On the one hand, figures such as Galileo Gall and militaristic philosophers like Colonel Moreiras turn the scenario into an extended and total misunderstanding, which will lead to the absolute physical annihilation of the city and its thirty thousand inhabitants.

The apocalypse is not, fortunately, the end of the text. The myopic journalist, the rag doll of the military campaign, emerges as the interpreter of the facts, the antihero made hero, who announces his decision to write about the history of the war to save it from oblivion. At the same time, he has saved himself upon discovering that he can love and be loved—and finally has lost his fear! The journalist's functional blindness doesn't keep him from registering the facts with the rest of his senses and via Jurema's eyes and those of the dwarf. The rest see but are blinded by fanaticism.

Notes

1. This plot of Vargas Llosa's novel was inspired by real-life events in Brazil: *eNotes* explains "In 1903, six years after the siege of Canudos (1897), the Brazilian engineer and journalist Euclides da Cunha, one of the two people to whom *The War of the End of the World* is dedicated, published *Os Sertões: Campanha de Canudos,* translated by Samuel Putnam as *Rebellion in the Backlands,* 1944. In Cunha's epoch-making work, called by some the Bible of Brazilian literature, are all of the facts from which Mario Vargas Llosa weaves his fiction: the charismatic leadership and revolutionary preaching of Antonio Conselheiro, the establishment of a bizarre millenarian community in the backlands (*os sertões*) of northern Brazil, the military campaigns to suppress the anti-Republican community of converted bandits and outlaws, and the opposition of Brazil's two major political forces (monarchist and republican) in a country that had recently become a republic."
2. The parodic use of the subliterary genre, evident especially in *Aunt Julia and the Writer*, allows the author to masterly convert the paraliterary into literary.
3. *The City and the Dogs, The Green House* and *Conversation in the Cathedral,* Vargas Llosa's first three Nobel Prize-winning novels, have been considered, together with *The War of the End of the World*, as his four best works.
4. Santón refers to a "big' saint," in terms of affection rather than size.
5. As in to desecrate the Virgin Mary.
6. Many Hispanists identify this character as Vargas Llosa's alter ego due to the parallels between the characterization and the author's life.

Bibliography

Arkinstall, Christine. "*The War of the End of the World*: Some Forgotten Proto (agonists)." *Antipodes I*. December 1988, 105–113. Print.

Bernucci, Leopoldo M. "Vargas Llosa and the Biblical Tradition: The *War of the End of World*." *Iberoamericana Magazine* 1987. PDF: revistaiberoamericana.pitt.edu Web.

Cornejo Polar, Antonio. "*The War of the End of the World*: Sense (and Without Meaning) of the History." *Remate Of Males*. Campinas, (13) 83–89, 1993. PDF: usfs.bo, 2012 Web.

Fight, Laura. "Apocalypse and Literature in *One Hundred Years of Solitude* by Gabriel García Márquez, *The War of the End of the World* by Mario

Vargas Llosa and *Estrella distant* by Roberto Bolaño." *Other Modernities Magazine*. Apocalypse 2012- 07/2013. PDF: unirioja.es Web.

Martínez-Fallero, Luis. "Literature and Myth: Demystification, Intertextuality, Rewrite." *Signa Magazine* 22, 481–496, 2013. PDF: revistas.uned.es Web.

Mac Adam, Alfred. "Euclides Da Cunha and Mario Vargas Llosa: Meditations." *Intertextual Iberoamericana Magazine*. 1984. PDF: revistaiberoamerica.pitt.edu Web.

Menton, Seymour. "The War against the Fanaticism of Mario Vargas Llosa. Acts of the Congress 1992." *Cervantes Virtual Center*. PDF: cervantes.es Web.

Montenegro, Patricia. "The Relativity of Perspectives in *The War of the End of the World.*" *Journal of Latin American Literary Criticism*. January 1984. pp. 311–21. PDF: Researchgate.net Web.

Schraibman, J. and Little, W. "*The War of the End of the World* and *Os Sertoes*: A Note Of Reading." *Mythologies Magazine Today*, 2017. PDF: raco.cat Web.

Vargas Llosa, Mario. *The War of the End of the World*. Ed. Penguin. Collection Pocketsize. First edition: June 2015. Print.

Villalobos Alpízar, Iván. "The Notion of Intertextuality in Kristeva and Barthes." *Rev. Filosofía*, Univ. Costa Rica. XLI (103), pp. 137–145, January–June 2003. PDF: ucr.ac.cr Web.

https://www.enotes.com/topics/war-end-world/in-depth

CHAPTER
14

The Many Homes: A Reading of Marina Perezagua's *The Story of H*

Eduardo Cerdán

Translated by Debra D. Andrist

From her first book of short stories, *Criaturas abisales/Unfathomable Babies (Creatures)* (2011), Marina Perezagua showed that hers is a literature that resists the closed categories of the publishing market. Science fiction, historical fiction, allegory, fantastic literature: labels change, distort, resignify, themselves in her work.

From the story, *Little Boy*, included in *Leche/Milk* (2013), her second book of stories, Perezagua developed *Yoro* (2015), an ambitious novel that deserved the Sor Juana Inés de la Cruz International Prize for Novels in 2016, awarded at the International Book Fair of Guadalajara. Angelina Muñiz-Huberman, one of the members of the jury, said at the award ceremony that the novel, from the title,[1] on, "proposes itself [as] a book immersed in the multiple possibilities of interpretations, in ambiguity, in irony and in transgression, in war, evil and its banality in the manner of Hanna Arendt."

Within *Milk*, the story which inspired the novel openly dialogues with the story that gives title to the book. Thus, in *Milk*, Japanese soldiers are the victimizers of a Chinese mother in the context of the second Sino-Japanese war, while in *Little Boy*, the focus is on the Japanese, not as victimizers, but as victims of the atomic bomb. With the book of 2013, it was clear, then, that Marina Perezagua is interested in the counterpoint, the multiplicity of looks and the analysis—through the fiction—of both the contradictions of violence and the already-evoked "banality of evil."

Like in her story, *Father*, *Yoro*—translated into English by Valerie Miles as *The Story of H*—takes off from the effects of the atomic bomb dropped on August 9, 1945 in Hiroshima, and features H: a hermaphrodite who is raised as a boy until his adolescence, when the explosion of the bomb strips him of his male sex and s/he begins to live as a woman, which is what he, now she, has always wanted. A transsexual character. We do not know the real name of H, the narrator-protagonist who, as we know from the first page, has committed a crime. S/he names herself "H," because, she says, "I was always denied a voice and a Spaniard told me that, in his language, "h" is the silent letter" (12). There is also, as Muñiz-Huberman pointed out, a polysemic game, i.e., multiple interpretations: "H" could be in place of Hiroshima, hermaphrodite or hibakusha, which means "person affected by an explosion," a term that was commonly used in Japan to talk about survivors and that made the quality of life of the survivors invisible. It is a word, to say "H," "that dodged not only the pain but the miracle of survival. [To say] 'an explosion' seems to refer to any outburst [but] Hiroshima was THE explosion" (34).

Paternity/motherhood is the leitmotiv of *Yoro*, divided into nine chapters, "months" plus one called "Childbirth", which narrate what happens between 1942 and 2014, between Hiroshima and the Democratic Republic of the Congo. H's capital wish is to have a child. And since she has a half-formed uterus, she realizes that the only real possibility of having that desire fulfilled had been in the male genitals that the bomb snatched from him. For that reason, the character, Jim, becomes a preponderant force. He is an American soldier who was a prisoner of war of the Japanese, and was entrusted, as part of his military duties, to raise a Japanese baby, *Yoro*, during the first five years of life. Settled in New York after being adopted by a family in the United States after her recovery, H meets Jim—17 years older—in 1960, when she is not yet 30 and they begin a romantic relationship. In the protagonist pair, once again, the victim/victimizer duality appears. H, Japanese, is a victim of the Americans; Jim, American, is a victim of the Japanese. Perezagua designs a couple that, in a kind of mirroring, complements each other, like yin and yang. There is the driving force of the novel: H and Jim are determined to find out the whereabouts of *Yoro* and with that purpose, visit New Mexico, Borneo, Queimada Grande . . . but Jim never gets to fulfill his mission, because he dies in a traffic accident in 1969.

The plot becomes bizarre. H, middle-aged and still looking for *Yoro*, gets "pregnant." With others, she recognizes that it is a psychological pregnancy but, in her confessions, she declares that the pregnancy is absolutely real. Now come some stylistic considerations of the novel, which begin by questioning a "Sir" who will judge her for her crime. "The pages that follow—the novel starts—constitute my statement" (11). From here, there is no counterpoint: the whole book is narrated from a single perspective, a single voice, a single deictic point. The narrator—we know—addresses the anonymous "Sir," but it is also clear that, with a stranger reader in mind, she allows herself some digressions:

> There are things that I want to write without thinking about you, I do not know if in order to revive them or because, deep down, deep down in my desires, I would like someone who is not involved in revenge and close to the deep feelings of people to understand me. (30)

We are, then, faced with an unreliable narrator—a technique that for modern narrative has its foundation stone, I believe, in Henry James's *The Turn of The Screw*, which opens the text to a very well achieved ambiguity, a key piece of the novel. Also, as I have already said with Muñiz-Huberman, there is an idea that threads through *Yoro*: "the banality of evil." In her 1963 book, *Eichmann in Jerusalem. A Report on the Banality of Evil,* Hannah Arendt coined this phrase, which depicts cruelty, not as a characteristic of "monsters"—not even exclusive to subjects with psychiatric disorders—but as something that can be part of normal people, anodynes, which act almost by inertia. Years after her book, Arendt clarified this idea:

> I spoke of "the banality of evil" and meant with this no theory or doctrine but something quite factual, the phenomenon of evil deeds, committed on a gigantic scale, which could not be traced to any particularity of wickedness, pathology or ideological conviction in the doer, whose only personal distinction was a perhaps extraordinary shallowness. However monstrous the deeds where the doer was neither monstrous nor demonic, and the only specific characteristic one could detect . . . was something entirely negative: it was not stupidity but a curious, authentic inability to think. (Arendt 417)

The argument that Perezagua often goes to—to present the victim and the victimizer as two sides of the same coin—serves to really show, far from the pamphlet and the manifesto, that evil crouches in unsuspected places and that it can come out to light if circumstances are aligned for it. Thus, the humanitarian catastrophe caused by the explosion of the atomic bomb, the crimes committed on board the ship *ryoku Maru* (also known as *Crucero de la Muerte*/*The Cruise of Death*) and the Burma Railway (or Death Railway), among other atrocities narrated in *Yoro*, are exposed in their absolute nonsense.

What stands out for its brutality is the passage in which H and Jim visit, in 1965, a village north of Borneo where they find Sandy, a female orangutan, prostituted and systematically raped by workers of palm oil plantations, who was lying in a bed,

> [with] painted lips, a blonde wig, a semitransparent pink top [and] totally depilated. . . . She was fastened with chains to a bed of rusty iron. Her genitals were inflamed. I've never seen anyone so sad. And I say nobody because the differences between that animal and a person were absolutely imperceptible. (118)

Marina Perezagua constantly resorts to the deformation of her characters through the use of the grotesque, as well as the disgust and the monstrous. The researcher, László Vazas, has pointed out that Spanish literature has been prodigal in texts that use the grotesque in a humorous way, especially, or also under, the register of the fantastic. A great example of grotesque humor is, of course, Cervantes' work, *Don Quixote*. And from romanticism, this resource got a "second breath," let's say, with the influence of German and French novelists. Vazas says:

> The definitions around [the grotesque] coincide in highlighting some fundamental features: distortion of the external appearance, fusion of the animal with the human, mixture of reality with dreaming, reduction of personality to mask. [The grotesque] means a radical distancing from the things that are familiar to us, it implies a tendency towards the abnormal, the insane and accompanied by an extreme radicalism, a brusqueness until dehumanization. We also know that for Bakhtin, the grotesque has a special physical quality regarding the body and its excesses. The emphasis on the physical, on the physical body, would follow a popular tradition that often manifests itself in primitive, obscene and cruel delight. The most frequent metaphor of the grotesque is the incongruity of the human and the animal. In any case, in the background there always lies the vision of an "upside-down world". (Vazas 234–35)

Perezagua, clearly a connoisseur and heir of the universal literary tradition, has used the grotesque in her narrative to articulate a discourse on and from the body but devoid of comedy.[2] In *Yoro*, the aforementioned passage about the orangutan, Sandy, is exemplary in the use of the grotesque, which also appears, for example, in the narration of the consequences that unleashed the atomic bomb on the bodies of the victims:

> In what had been a bathroom, I saw a naked bundle approaching me. She asked me for water. I was startled. Her head was so swollen that it had tripled in size. Only when the package said its name did I recognize that it was my professor. (27)
>
> When I was in what was left of the hospital, people walked with their arms extended forward. Those who had gone blind did so as not to stumble ... but also those who kept their eyes extended their burned and viscous arms in the same way, to prevent them from sticking to their trunk. (43)

In the reconstruction that H does of the suffering of those who were passengers of *ryoku Maru*, like Jim, "a group of men entertained themselves by confusing the buckets of excrement with the food buckets, which were similar, so that no one knew whether he was taking food or the last waste of a companion, or both at the same time" (26);

or about the Burma Railway:

> [Jim] told me that from time to time, a guard would pass and ask a prisoner to kneel and open his mouth. The guard spat inside. If the prisoner swallowed the spit without even making a gesture of disgust, the guard continued on his way; otherwise, he would cut his throat. (57)

Towards the middle of the novel, in the fifth chapter, "month," when Jim has already died, the character of H moves to the margins of sanity. She develops agoraphobia, suffers a depressive episode and, meanwhile, her "pregnancy" seems to accelerate and slow down according to the circumstances. H gets old, of course, but stays pregnant. In the second half of *Yoro*, Perezagua inserts two characters who are a reflection of what the protagonist lives. The first is an old female dog—whom H adopts and upon whom she relies to get out of her self-imprisonment—who is pregnant and gives birth in her apartment. Then, referring to one of the pups: "I forgot to tell it before. But I kept one of her puppies. If I mention it, it is because, as you will see later, it is important because, while holding that puppy's leash, I entered a more luminous era" (186).

Later, when the character has regained some stability, she falls in love with a man she calls "Irrational Number," who—here we enter the allegorical —loads H on his shoulders to help her out into the world. "Irrational number" has a poetic outcome, close to the *fatum* of the Greek tragedies:[3] he dies submerged in the mud, while H is saved by getting out by climbing on top of him: "Via that, I had gotten out of the trench, after which I took refuge in the kitchen, of my own sadness? . . . I cursed him for leaving me like this, [alone] again, and for taking away his (my) four paws. Then I cursed myself" (209).

A dislocated character, in the last years of H's life, she is permitted a "trip to the seed (beginning of it all)." After having so many homes, and at the same time, none, she leaves New York to spend a season in Japan. In 1977, accompanied by her dog, who, incidentally, also gives birth at an advanced age like her mother, she arrives in the town of Wagu and knows in the exercise of apnea a way of finding herself. Later she moves to Tokyo, travels briefly to Africa and returns to the capital of Japan, which she ends up leaving because she intends to live her last days in New York. There, once she returns in 1999, she finds a letter from *Yoro*, who asks Jim to save her, since she is working by force in a uranium mine in the Democratic Republic of the Congo, and she is also pregnant after being raped.

Thus, the last two chapters of the novel, which cover from 1999 to 2014, become a *tour de force* in which an elderly woman, who is over 60 years old and still pregnant, travels to the Democratic Republic of the Congo in search of *Yoro*. She does not find that particular *Yoro*, the daughter, who has already died, but the granddaughter with the same name. The novel reaches a very high climatic point, the anagnorisis[4] of which the Greeks spoke, when H finds out that the first *Yoro*, the girl that was assigned to Jim, was an experiment to investigate the scope that the radiation could have had in the descendants of those who survived the bomb. *Yoro* was the biological daughter of a *hibakusha*: H, whose sperm, before they removed his testicles, were used for the experiment. The narrator writes that Jim knew it, and that's why he looked for her; and that, although he was surely waiting to tell her the truth, his death prevented him from doing so.

The anticipated "Enlightenment" of the novel happens when H finds her granddaughter, *Yoro,* of a Japanese mother and an African father, exhibited in a zoo (again the dehumanization/animalization, the violence towards the Other). After being insulted and chained, the Giraffe, named for her long neck, elongated by five bronze rings, weakly points out to H which man tricked her in order to cage her. The outcome of *Yoro*, the crime that could be guessed from the first line, is the burning of the tent where that man is found, a soldier sustained with resources of the United Nations Organization.

As a result of reading *Yoro*, a question arises: terrible and sinister, can violence and cruelty be part of that which is beautiful? Of course not. They can, however, produce aesthetic effects that escape sensationalism and that appeal to the catharsis referred to in the classics. Immanuel Kant said so in his *Critique of the Judgment of 1790* and several thinkers since then (in the twentieth century, for example, the aforementioned Hannah Arendt, Susan Sontag or Jean-François Lyotard), have written about a category that would fit in very well with the aspirations of the novel by Marina Perezagua: the sublime. According to Emmanouil Aretoulakis, for Kant and Edmund Burke, pioneering philosophers in the subject, "the sublime is about the feeling of terror. However, it is mostly in the former that the sublime implies total helplessness and an inevitable passivity before the terrible object" (16).

In the English version of *Yoro*, Marina Perezagua tells in her "Author's Note," which does not appear in the Spanish version, that her novel is a kind of settling of accounts with, as well as tribute to, the past. "Granddaughter" of the Spanish Civil War, lulled by stories full of horror and death, Perezagua assumes her existence as something that could not have happened without the resistance of her ancestors, and says that talking about a war that is not of her homeland, as she did in *Yoro*, means accepting that any war is everyone's war. Perezagua has achieved in *Yoro* a work of great discursive force that throws her characters into extreme situations in which tenderness and vileness coexist and follow each other, vertiginously. It is remarkable, I say finally, that the structure of *Yoro* is designed as the *uroboros,* the snake that eats its tail. Rounded, dense, in a constant—and unsuspected—game of mirrors, it is a text that puts important reflections on mourning, loss, love, body, war, history and the autophagic[5] tendency of the humans under the lens. Even in the middle of the darkest haze, Perezagua seems to tell us with this novel, there is always room for light.

Notes

1 In Spanish, *Yoro*—the name of a core character in the novel—is phonetically identical to "I cry:" the first person singular of the verb "to cry." It's not gratuitous, of course. It is a game like the one Jacques Derrida (1968) played with the *différance*: a French word that varies from grammatically correct (différence) only in the plane of writing, by the spelling it with "a" instead of the "e." This is not noticeable at the phonetic level because both sound exactly the same. From this notion, Derrida proposes that at the center of the existence of things and the mental representations we have of them, what there is, is not an essence, but a différance, a constant temporalization and differentiation, since it tends to think in a binary way, in oppositions that are, also, differentiations: man/woman, sane/crazy, white/black.

2 At least until *Yoro*, humor was not an important resource in Perezagua's work. This, however, changed from her second novel, *Don Quijote de Manhattan* (2016), in which there is an obvious shift in register, as compared to her previous three titles. In this, the fourth, the author used parody, the grotesque and the laughable to "update" Cervantes' two great characters, Don Quixote and Sancho Panza, who in Perezagua's book, wander the New York City of the XXI Century.
3 According to *Wikipedia*, "Destiny, sometimes referred to as fate (from Latin *fatum* – destiny), is a predetermined course of events."
4 Wikipedia defines "anagnorisis" [as] a moment in a play or other work when a character makes a critical discovery. Anagnorisis originally meant recognition in its Greek context, not only of a person but also of what that person stood for. Anagnorisis was the hero's sudden awareness of a real situation, the realization of things as they stood, and finally, the hero's insight into a relationship with an often antagonistic character in Aristotelian tragedy."
5 *Wikipedia* defines "Autophagy (or *autophagocytosis*) [as] meaning "self-devouring" and "hollow," is the natural, regulated mechanism of the cell that disassembles unnecessary or dysfunctional components. It allows the orderly degradation and recycling of cellular components."

Works Cited

Aretoulakis, Emmanouil. *Forbidden Aesthetics, Ethical Justice, and Terror in Modern Western Culture*, London: Lexington Books, 2016. Print.

Arendt, Hanna. "Thinking and Moral Considerations: A Lecture," *Social Research*, vol. 38, no. 3, 1971, pp. 417–446. Print.

Derrida, Jacques. "La Différance," *Bulletin de la Societé Française de Philosophie*, vol. 62, no. 3, 1968, pp. 73–101. Print.

Perezagua, Marina. *Leche*. Barcelona: Los Libros del Lince, 2013. Print.

——. *The Story of H*. New York: HarperCollins Publishers, 2018. Print.

——. *Yoro*. Barcelona: Los Libros del Lince, 2015. Print.

Vasas, László. "La tradición de lo grotesco en la literatura española y los esperpentos de Valle-Inclán," Csejtei, Dezsö *et al. El 98 a la luz de la literatura y la filosofía*, Hungary: Fundación Pro Philosophia Szegediensi, 1999, pp. 232–236. Print.

CHAPTER
15
China and *Chinago*: Globalization of the Kung Fu Genre and the Interpretation of Hero and History

Hiqing Sun

In 2005, a low-budget Mexican film, *Chinago*, came onto the market, claiming itself to be "Latin America's first martial arts movie." Directed by Peter Van Lengen and starring Chilean actor and martial arts champion, Marko Zaror, this film originally caught attention and stimulated curiosity among Chinese scholars in Hispanic studies, as its release coincides with the peak time of the making of Kung Fu films by renowned Chinese directors on the world stage at the turn of the century. *The New York Times* critic, Elvis Mitchell, suggested "[that the film] attacks the screen with energy and movement and creates a placid surface that offers a new perspective and a spirituality not normally found in these pictures."

Chinago follows a plain narrative line of a *Kung Fu* fighter, Braulio Bo, who works with the Mexican police to fight drug dealers and who is constantly involved in struggles against the underground forces in local society where the criminal organizations have connections with Asian Mafias. Throughout Braulio Bo's martial arts adventure in a Spanish-speaking world, the film demonstrates a strong consciousness of emphasizing the "Chinese factors," so as to make sense of *Kung Fu* genre for this film. But, apparently it cannot rely on any historic background of "an ambitious period epic" that recent Chinese productions would usually take (Dargis). Besides the display of different *Kung Fu* fighting scenes, one notable example is the recurrence of the ghostly image of Bo's grandfather along Bo's journeys. The grandfather is also Bo's mentor, who is, naturally, a martial-art master from Shaolin Temple, one of the most famous historical sites for classical *Kung Fu* practice, and whose legacy has helped carry Bo through the difficult times.

A thorough review would eventually find that this film has more of a resemblance to the so-called Hong Kong popular *Kung Fu* genre of the 1980's, which is produced in a "fast-food" mode and focuses on display of violence and intuitive fighting/crime scenes instead of telling any sensational story with up-to-date visual techniques. Although aesthetically this low-budget film is not comparable to any of the award-winning ones from China, its plots, developed around the fate of one hero, still arguably set forth the common elements on which the success of those finely-made films on Asian screen also rely and therefore, pose the question of what makes the worldwide reception for the *Kung Fu* genre happen.

Notably, the beginning of the 21st century cinema is marked with many *Kung Fu* heroes from Chinese films, highlighted by Ang Lee's *Crouching Tiger and Hidden Dragon,* which has won several major Academy awards. These films include, in 2001, Zhang Yimou's *Hero*, also nominated for the Academy Award of best foreign picture; in 2003, Tsui Hark's *Seven Swords*, selected to be the inaugurating presentation in the 2005 Venice International Film Festival; and Stephen Chow's *Kung Fu Hustle*, a finalist for Golden Globe Award of 2006. All the above-mentioned films have shown the eagerness to illustrate essences of Chinese culture, from the realm of fine arts to its philosophy, with a backdrop of grand social-turmoil periods from the country's long history. It seems that people have realized that *Kung Fu* is not only a type of fighting show, it involves a value system rooted in a rich culture and it is the value system that stands behind the globalization of this originally popular genre in Chinese folkloric literature. However, in a thorough screening of the Mexican production, *Chinago*, the audience would find it hard to associate it with any trait of the Eastern culture, despite the reiteration of Bo's Chinese bloodline. The roughly-made storyline with a lack-of-orientation narrative puts Bo in a clueless journey—wherever he goes, there simply would be an outlaw that he must fight. The relatively-poor fighting skills (probably due to the absence of special effects) and the lack of multi-angled representations of *Kung Fu* all contribute to the failure of the overall representation of the hero's journey. Meanwhile, one can still recognize several *Kung Fu* genre elements that are displayed— skillfully or not—in this film. For example, there is representation of *Kung Fu* on a spiritual level—a Chinese master-ancestor (Bo's grandfather) who is a role model for the protagonist and also a "Zen" educator who had taught Bo the value of wisdom and peaceful mind over force or violence so as to become a hero. As Bo's mentor, the grandfather's legend would serve as a source of strength for the hero's survival. Another example is the figure of a young and beautiful female protagonist, a *Kung Fu* killer from Hong Kong, who functions as a counterpart and challenger to Bo when she allies with the evil force. The presentation of martial art fighting between the hero and his rival villains develops, along with the buildup of the superiority of the hero's *Kung Fu* skill at different levels—from the initial conflict with minor criminals to the final duel against the major mafia head. The aesthetic gaps between *Chinago* and the representative *Kung Fu* films produced in China during the same period shall not be perceived only as the differentiation due to mentalities of the directorial teams or the applications of new techniques or budget, for the filmic narrative can speak for itself on whether a story can successfully provide commonly-acknowledged values of a genre to the audience. Upon the surprise (or disappointment) of the aesthetic gap between Chinese and foreign production of the *Kung Fu* genre, the audience actually faces a question of what makes a filmic work be "authentic" or "valuable" *Kung Fu*.

The above-mentioned Chinese films all have touched upon the theme of hero and history, with their stories based on some historic periods that had truly existed in China. Yet, from the perspective of *Kung Fu* literature, there are doubtfully many "new" things in the narratives of these films. In other words, their type of success is rather recognition or resurrection of the prototypical features of *Kung Fu* arts.

Like detective fiction in the western world, *Kung Fu* or martial arts literature is considered a popular genre, welcomed by mass readers, yet excluded from the canon. Also, like detective fiction, whose original concern is reasoning and analysis instead of crimes, the original narrative intention of the *Kung Fu* genre is not about fighting, but of the construction of an art. A typical *Kung Fu* story needs to emphasize the artistic nature of *Kung Fu* force as an engagement of natural power and spiritual power, so it often recreates true historic figures and events in a fantastic realm. The long history of China and its many chaotic periods of warfare, political corruption, racial conflict and shifts of power have provided a fertile field to grow many *Kung Fu* heroes.

The *Kung Fu* heroes appeared as early as the fifteenth century in the chapter-novels of the Ming dynasty. In *The Cases of Master Bao*, for example, the prototype of a *Kung Fu* master is actually a police-detective by the name of Zhan Zhao, who fights alone against the criminals and helps his Mayor Bao secure the local society. The *Kung Fu* heroes (called "Xia" in Chinese) live a kind of simple life in their stories; they basically either pursue or escape, fight to either save or to punish. In modern versions of the genre, they also fight to love.

To access the nature of *Kung Fu* narrative, the detective genre can be taken as a reference, which depends on the narrative tension emerged from the detective-criminal-solution relationship to support its textual values. The *Kung Fu* genre may also portray a violent outlook with personal adventures. But, its early prototype and its many subgenres manifest that the life of the genre dwells in a sophisticated relationship among the hero, the enemy and the "weapon"—in a general way, including not only tools but also philosophies or doctrines, of fighting and survival. It is upon this relationship that a narrative tension, with specific ethical and aesthetic codes, can be established. In so far as fighting with martial arts, or shows of hand-to-hand violence, cannot become an index for this genre without being further exemplified by the stereotypical narrative tension, nor can the hero.

Twentieth-century film and television became a new ground for the *Kung Fu* genre to develop its fantasies into more sub-genres and for a much larger group of reader-audiences. The American audience may well recall Bruce Lee—but, if viewed through the lens of the *Kung Fu* traditions, his films constitute a "Hollywoodized" version of *Kung Fu*-gangster presentation, with American stories, American thoughts and American approaches to Eastern cultures, yet completely estranged from the historical code of the traditional *Kung Fu* genre. I mention Lee here because, although he can not be recognized as generic from the view of classic Chinese *Kung Fu* literature, his films make the successful visualization of martial art for the first time, which proceed with, if not greatly inspire, the filming of the traditional *Kung Fu* literature.

The focus of the genre study shall be on the other side of the Pacific Ocean, about the relationship between longtime *Kung Fu* literature and its visual representations. In Asia, Director Hu Jinquan was a vanguard in representing *Kung Fu* art. His *Dragon Gate Inn* (1958) is the first film that successfully translated a classical *Kung Fu* novel onto screen. Through the financial success of Hong Kong films during the 1970's and 1980's, *Kung Fu* became a name for a wide variety of films and a large number of productions featuring "violence for violence's sake" have overwhelmingly brand-named Hong Kong film. Of course, some of these films have gained huge commercial success. But, they are not actually *Kung Fu* art viewed from a generic angle. They call themselves "fighting (*Wu Da*) films," and for a moment, during which no one yet has questioned about the true aesthetic value of *Kung Fu* works, these violent features seem to be deciding the fate of the *Kung*

Fu genre. However, a direct result of the abusive mass production of the "fighting" films is that serious film artists began to feel tired and began to be less serious—which means, they began to make mockeries or spoofs of "fighting films." In a frivolous way, these artists reveal that "fighting" is too weak to replace the aesthetics of *Kung Fu* art. Just like that not every murder story can be detective genre, fighting is not the core of the *Kung Fu* genre but rather its most extended base through which other values can touch down in the narrative. That is to say, fighting is indispensable for the *Kung Fu* narrative but it is not equivalent to the genre. Using detective genre again as example, a murder mystery may be solved in a crime story but the narrative is not to show people how to solve a case; likewise, fighting may be the most impressive scene of *Kung Fu* genre but it is not the ultimate value the audience is to expect.

In latter years, significantly since *New Dragon Gate Inn* (by Tsui Hark 1991) and *The Knife Carrier from Shuangqi Town* (by He Ping, 1993), some major generic factors originated from classical *Kung Fu* novels were reiterated through representations of history and hero. These new presentations bring up a question about the "vehicle" that carries the development of the genre: is it the hero or the history? The two films respectively by Ang Lee and Zhang Yimou seem to have diverse inclinations: Lee's *Crouching Tiger* uses history to mold a hero and Zhang's *Hero* examines a history through a hero's journey. Zhang's 2002 film inspired a broad discussion, not concentrating only on its artistic values, but also on the director's audacious modification of a true history—a failed assassination of a famous tyrant and a discussion of who the real hero is—the assassin or the tyrant. Since Zhang is a world-renowned director, many Chinese critics strongly question the motive of such "irrational change" and the cultural value (not entertainment value) of a film with twisted images of hero and history. Zhang's supporters have argued, not so strongly, that it is merely a film "for fun," as if all "films for fun" could pass the censorship in China, no matter how much history or hero be twisted. One may criticize the film as a flattery for the tyrant and may even say that he means to please the current Chinese government which also came into power after a civil war and who used to rule the country with high-pressure methods. Such criticisms apparently ignore the representations of the cruelty of the tyrant and the suffering of the common people as a basic tone in the illustration of the history. *Crouching Tiger*, based on a classical *Kung Fu* fiction, is free from such questioning, even though it also bears untrue images of China in the Qing Dynasty. For example, no individual was allowed to store weapons at home and there was no cross-state pursuit of criminals. *Dragon Gate*

Inn sets its story in a desert area that actually did not belong to China in the Ming dynasty (it was included in China's territory in Qing Dynasty), plus, the major evil character presented as a *Kung Fu* master in this film is actually a civil official in history. Yet no audience has shown much interest in these "little" problems. By "little," I mean that they allow little possibility for the audience to associate it with current social-political issues in China. Therefore, in this case, the interpretation of hero and history is extended by the audience's critical consciousness, without which the interpretation may be incomplete, while with which, the interpretation can be endless or over-interpretation. This is because the narrative form of this genre leaves enough space or blanks in depictions of many cultural factors aside from *Kung Fu* art. As to Zhang's *Hero*, to observe the aesthetics of the film as a genre, one may notice that it is not the modification of hero or history that has marked the success of this work.

Tzvetan Todorov once indicated that a genre means one cannot write further, otherwise, it will become literature, instead of a genre (43). The difference dwells in the ethical code and the aesthetic code that a generic narrative carries, which would be brief and even cancel any wider scope of reception. Thinking reversely, one may ask if the reader also needs to "not read further" in order to enjoy a genre. The same can be suggested for the *Kung Fu* genre. For Zhang Yimou's *Hero*, the sense of *Kung Fu* art will stop at the point when one tries to access a new interpretation of the historic function of Qinshihuang (the first emperor of China). The genre does not interpret the emperor. The emperor is not represented but encoded in the generic scope, in the representation of the *Kung Fu* heroes. He may be a historic sign, a dramatic sign, or an ethical one, but his significance is manifested from beyond the construction of the genre. He is a "reader" of a mystery, who finally figures out the trap set for him by the "hero," and therefore, helps curtain the *Kung Fu* drama from the textual level. Aesthetically, the army of Qin Country, unpredictable nature and the tragic fate of the six nations conquered by Qin speak for the film better than the emperor in the *Kung Fu* narrative, since together they shape a legend of the enemy (the Qin emperor) in a more challenging way for the construction of hero, for the center of values in the mystery of fighting, romance of killing and art of conflicting.

In historic studies, people may often argue who makes our history—the hero or the mass—is it the hero who makes history or some specific historic conditions that create the hero? However, in the *Kung Fu* genre, hero and history function within the narrative structure and immediately under the ethical code provided by the tension among hero-enemy-weapon. So, what is a *Kung Fu* hero? Despite the aesthetic gaps between the Mexican *Chinago* and the Chinese *Hero* or the American *The Matrix*[1] in the generic narrative of *Kung Fu*, the interpretation of hero is carried out through legends that may or may not touch upon any theme from reality. The narrative of the *Kung Fu* genre usually consists of a legend of a weapon—it may not simply be a killing tool but something special to assist the hero on the way to his final success (a sword or a spirit bears no difference in the core of martial art), a legend of duel (a manifestation of a matured hero with matured martial arts), a legend of love, and sometimes, a legend of a master or mentor—in this last one, Bo's grandfather in *Chinago* and Master Li in *Crouching Tiger* are meant to have a similar function, despite the huge difference in fame between the two works. These legends construct the aesthetics of the genre, which sublimate the beauty of a human kind from out-of-dark violence and infamy. History and hero are interpreted within the development of these legends. In other words, the basic narrative purpose of the genre is not to stun the audience with violent scenes (although some samples of production tend to prove so when they actually deviate from the genre). The purpose is to show how much beauty and harmony can be endured over the tension of conflicts and hostility. Any figure that can afford such beauty and harmony can be a hero.

Also, a director of *Kung Fu* genre would be very cautious when using violent scenes, as it may blur the neat and lofty image of the hero. For the *Kung Fu* genre, being a hero does not mean that one has to be a skillful fighter or possess a lethal weapon, but be one who can overcome those and one who only fights when it is very necessary. In some *Kung Fu* films such as *Shaolin Temple* (starring Jet Li, 1985) and *The Knife Carrier in Shuangqi Town*, the hero only fights once, in the final duel against the evil figure; the rest of time, he has been involved in all kinds of mischief until the death of his master. The interpretation of hero and history is made through the thin and often shifting border between peace and war, civilization and barbarism. Not all heroes are represented as neat and lofty at the same level, as one can see from the figure of Bo in *Chinago* and Neo in *The Matrix*, but they are mostly peace lovers, passive fighters. They follow an ethical code much clearer than a historical one.

But, after all, the core value of *Kung Fu* is not about how to kill but how to survive. It is not about rebellion but loyalty. It is not about fighting skills but about the way of being—being the one as being for all. It is not about force of violence but power of mind, as we see in traditional *Kung Fu* literature, as well as in the films based it. The protagonist does not succeed due to a skill or weapon more powerful than his enemy's but due to justice and faith. For example, in *New*

Dragon Gate Inn, the superior weapon(s) are two swords; one is male and the other is female, and they will merge into one super-powerful weapon when their owners are true lovers and are using them at the same time—a symbol of love that defeats the symbol of evil. In Zhang Yimou's *Hero*, the consideration of peace for the nation overpowers the personal desire for retaliation when the *Kung Fu* master decides to spare the emperor's life. On the other hand, of course, one must face the reality that most of the *Kung Fu* films, low-budgeted, with limited marketing resources, like *Chinago*, may not embrace a broad social or historic setting but let the story develop in a rather limited space and time and heroes like Bo would have to fight rivals inside a building rather than throughout a vast forest.

The revival of the *Kung Fu* genre in recent years is due to the directors' grasp of the non-violent nature in representing the martial art as an art in literature. It is comparable to, although loftier than, the detective/criminal fiction genre, as it does not have to depend on meticulous reasoning and modern *modus operandi*. Yet its revival reminds the reader of the "metaphysical detective stories" written by writers such as Jorge Luis Borges and Italo Calvino during the middle of last century, which form counterparts to the American hard-boiled subgenre. That is to say, these writers sought the original wisdom and cool manner of precursors such as Edgar Allan Poe during a time when Dashiel Hammett and Raymond Chandler were selling very well. One cannot say the genre of crime mystery and the one of *Kung Fu* are comparable in many ways, but observing their history and contemporary works may indicate that, in both cases, some retroactive efforts occur to reiterate the values of the traditions when certain factors such as violence and grotesqueness tend to overwhelm the composition of the genres.

Hero and history are two factors whose weights may not have changed much through the development and the "globalization" of the *Kung Fu* genre. The concurrence of films like *Chinago* and their masterpiece counterparts reminds us that the *Kung Fu* films may not have a mission to interpret hero or history for the audience. The interpretation is rather dependent on the audience's own feeling of familiarity or strangeness with the hero's journey. Hero and history belong to a metaphysical scope in which all narrative factors can be marked by symbols—not realistic objects, the action can be set anywhere, of any type (devastating desert, immense bamboo forest, ancient college, cyberspace, imagined palace, imagined fighting, there is no show of consistency in the change of the settings). In *Hero* and *The Matrix*, it is even directly stated that the imagined and the false sensation are parts of the route toward the final duel and the final revelation. History is actually processed to become a fuzzy zone within the setting of the story. The descriptions of settings are part of the hero's journey but not necessarily part of the history: this is another aspect of the aesthetics of the *Kung Fu* genre: its many beautiful ways to represent conflicts, death and life.

The hero, with an experience of becoming "the one" in the story, functions as a connection between the type of history and the form of narrative in these films but he does not constitute the core of the aesthetics of the genre. The core is a fantasy that the audience may not enjoy in any other textual or narrative level. This reminds us of the American Western film genre, in which great nature and kind souls make heroes; meanwhile, history is something too familiar to be the focus.

The genre carries a legend that bridges over the diversity of aesthetic or cultural criteria from Asia to the Americas, carrying on the essential value of the martial arts representation. In all the above-mentioned films, the interpretations of specific historical events in their narratives continue the tradition of the *Kung Fu* genre, in which history is rewritten to allow for maximum need of a hero and the performance of *Kung Fu* action.

Although dealing with different historical backgrounds, in all these films, the format of *Kung Fu* narrative prevails at the cost of the loss of some truth from a historical or realistic perspective, as they all contain a manipulation of certain pre-existing texts in order to carry out the major deeds of their heroes and the biggest shows of martial art fantasy. Like genre films in general, some values are diluted for others to be enriched.

Note

1 *Wikipedia* explains why this film is cited in this chapter's context, "*The Matrix* is a 1999 science fiction action film[3][4] written and directed by the Wachowskis [whose] approach to action scenes was influenced by Japanese animation[7] and martial arts films, and the film's use of fight choreographers and *wire fu* techniques from Hong Kong action cinema influenced subsequent Hollywood action film productions. . . . While some critics have praised the film for its handling of difficult subjects, others have said the deeper themes are largely overshadowed by its action scenes."

Works Cited

Chinago. Dir. Peter Van Lengen. Perf. Marko Zaror, Susana González. Mandrill Films, 2006.
Crouching Tiger, Hidden Dragon. Dir. Ang Lee. Perf. Chow Yun Fat, Ziyi

Zhang and Michelle Yeoh. Pegasus Media, China Film Group Corporation, and the Weinstein Company, 2000.

Dargis, Manohla. "Crouching Tiger: Hidden Truths in the Court of a King Who Would Be Emperor." *The New York Times.* <http://www.nytimes.com/movie/review?res=9503E5DF103EF934A1575BC0A9629C8B63&mcubz =1> Aug. 27, 2004. Web.

Hero. Dir. Yimou Zhang. Perf. Jet Li, Tony Leung, and Maggie Cheung. Miramax and Beijing New Picture Film, 2002.

Kung Fu Hustle. Dir. Stephen Chow. Perf. Stephen Chow, Yuen Wah, Yuen Qiu. Columbia Pictures Asia, 2004.

Mitchell, Elvis. "Action Fans, Be Prepared For Heart and Feminism" Film Review. *The New York Times.* <http://www.nytimes.com/movie/review?res= 9503EFD7133CF93AA35753C1A9669C8B63&mcubz=1> Oct. 9, 2000. Web.

New Dragon Gate Inn. Dir. Raymond Lee. Perf. Brigitte Lin, Tony Leung Ka-fai, and Maggie Cheung. Film Workshop and Seasonal Film Corporation, 1992.

Seven Swords. Dir. Tsui Hark. Perf. Leon Lai, Donnie Yen. Weinstein Company, 2005.

The Matrix. Dir. the Wachowskis. Perf. Keanu Reeves, Laurence Fishburne, and Carrie-Anne Moss. Warner Brothers, 1999.

Todorov, Tzvetan. "The Typology of Detective Fiction." *The Poetics of Prose.* Ithaca (NY), Cornell UP: 1997, pp. 42–53. Print.

Conclusions

While the fifteen chapters by thirteen contributors (three of us appear twice each) to this collection vary rather widely in work(s) examined and critical approach to the specific content, those seeming dissimilarities are eclipsed by the contributors' overriding dedication to the real, invented and virtual phenomena of the Hispanic worlds. The multiplicity of the aforementioned grids of intersections, crossroads, if you will, actually tie the chapters together, segueing from one grouping to another rather than disconnecting them.

As the editor of, and contributor to *Crossroads: Time & Space/Tradition & Modernity in Hispanic Worlds,* I had the unique opportunity to study these essays at length and categorize them in four groups according to general overlaying types of re and intersections. These groups or types correspond to the part-divisions of the book, which shift from the physical to the social, artistic, religious and political, from the social and literary and space, not to mention tradition and modernity, in Spain, contrasted with the social, gender, artistic, literary and cinematic time and space, not to mention tradition and modernity, in Latin/Latino(x) America.

Reviewing the book's title, the four other considerations besides Hispanic worlds, time and space/tradition and modernity, the passage of time as harbinger of change, i.e., tradition versus modernity, is a constant throughout all the essays. Space, however, is both physical and intellectual—and now expanded in different directions. Two particularly distinctive essays, while each fits into one of two of the aforementioned "geographic" third and fourth book divisions dedicated to space, represent additions to the definitions of Hispanic worlds, as formerly defined in previous books I have edited. One chapter pioneers the crossroads of the real world of art productions and the virtual world of critical research methods and the other plumbs the intersections of personal experience and memory and their effects on intellectual (and career) dedication and development.

This current book, the fifth collaboration by several of us among the authors/scholars, with variations among other contributors from book to book, follows *The Body: Subject & Subjected*; *Insult to*

Injury: Violence in Spanish, Hispanic American and Latino Art & Literature; *S/HE: Sex & Gender in Hispanic Cultures*; and *Family, Friends & Foes: Human Dynamics in Hispanic Worlds*. *Crossroads* represents my active decision as an editor/scholar to expand beyond the, however well-developed, single-author studies to incorporate differing specific subjects of study and differing perspectives and research methodologies. This collaborative approach to publishing, rather than continuing with only my own scholarly efforts alone, not only allows me to personally expand my investigative realms but to learn and relate to those of my colleagues.

May this approach herald the same for the readers!

The Editor and Contributors

Debra D. Andrist, PhD, Professor of Spanish/formerly Chair of Foreign Languages (seven+ years) at Sam Houston State University, Huntsville, TX, was formerly department Chair and Cullen Endowed Chair holder at University of St. Thomas/Houston (11+ years) and Associate Professor at Baylor University, Waco, TX (14+ years). She earned a BA/Fort Hays Kansas State University in sociology and Spanish, an MA/University of Utah in Spanish and the PhD/State University of New York/Buffalo in Spanish, as well as was awarded a Mellon summer post-doc in magical realism at Rice University/Houston, TX. She is a sociologist who deals with gender and/or medicine in art & literature; her scholarly works include international presentations, books, translations, articles, reviews, interviews and movie guides. Her most recent books as editor, in which she is also a chapter author, are *The Body: Subject & Subjected. The Body Itself & Its Functions, Illness, Injury, Treatment and Death in Spanish, Indigenous & Hispanic American Art & Literature, Insult to Injury: Violence in Spanish, Hispanic American & Latino Art & Literature, S/he: Sex & Gender in the Hispanic Worlds* and *Family, Friends & Foes: Human Dynamics in Hispanic Worlds,* published by Sussex in 2016, 2017, 2018 and 2019, respectively. Many of her published articles and (inter)national presentations deal with life, art & literature by and about women, both visual (painting, especially) and in created societies (literature in all genres.) She has won grants, as well as awards for teaching, service and administration. She has led numerous study abroad experiences in Mexico, Spain, Ireland and Costa Rica and was an exchange professor in Chile and Canada, as well as doing a Fulbright Hayes stint in Morocco. She belongs to many professional organizations and has been an officer in most, besides being a museum docent and on the boards of various community organizations.

John Francis Burke, Ph.D, teaches political theory, religion and politics, US Latinx politics, comparative politics and US American politics at Trinity University in San Antonio, Texas. He is an interdisciplinary scholar who has published articles especially on political theory, intercultural relations, social justice and religion & politics in several journals and periodicals including *The Review of Politics* and *Commonweal*. He is the author of *Mestizo Democracy* (College Station, TX: Texas A&M Press, 2002), a text on democracy and multiculturalism in the U.S. Southwest and *Building Bridges Not Walls: Nourishing Diverse Cultures in Faith /Construyamos puentes, no muros: Alimentar a las diversas culturas en la fe* (Collegeville, MN: Liturgical Press, 2016), a text on integrating diverse cultural spiritualties constructively in faith-based communities. He has also appeared as a political commentator on many Texas media outlets, both in English and Spanish. In addition to his scholarly work, he has coordinated social justice institutes and programs at the University of St. Thomas in Houston, TX and Cabrini University in Radnor, PA. He has also served on several committees and conducted workshops in Indiana, Pennsylvania and Texas dealing with social justice and intercultural issues. Finally, he has extensive experience in church liturgy and has earned a "reputation" for cultivating vibrant multilingual choirs.

Eduardo Cerdán (Xalapa, México, 1995), writer and essayist, holds a BA in Hispanic Language and Literatures from the National Autonomous University of Mexico, where he has given classes in literary research since 2015. He is editor-in-chief of *Punto de partida,* a literary magazine. He has won prizes in national story competitions, has collaborated on collected writings and on periodical publications like *Confabulario, La Jornada Semanal, Literal: Latin American Voices, Letras Libres* and *La Palabra y el Hombre*. He has participated in collections of stories by Mexican and Latin Americans (*UV, BUAP, UAM-X and Ediciones Cal y Arena*), as well as with essays about Hispanic literature (Sussex Press). Part of his work has been translated into English and French.

Jorge Chavarro, MD, MA in Spanish, was born in Colombia in a village with jungle heat and sun. The natives called it Tora; it is now known as Barrancabermeja. However, he lived in Bogota from the age of ten months. He graduated from medical school in the turbulent seventies, met and married his wife, Marthica. Their first child is now a physician in the U.S. Chavarro's medical degree came after his children, including a specialization in urology in the eighties. His cherished daughter was a gift born during his urologist degree and is now a Spanish teacher in Texas. He practiced his specialty in Colombia and taught urology at his alma mater, the National University of

234 | *The Editor and Contributors*

Colombia. In early 2002, he was a victim of kidnapping by the Colombian Self-Defense, the reason for his immigration to the U.S., which led to starting over professionally in the surgery field in the U.S. His avocation and dream to become a writer and teach literature led him to an MA in Spanish at Sam Houston State University in 2014 and to currently pursue a PhD at Texas A & M University.

Elizabeth White Coscio, PhD, teaches Spanish language, literature, culture, clinical conversation and other Spanish applied-language courses at the University of St. Thomas in Houston, Texas. She holds the Cullen Endowed Chair of Spanish, was Chair of the Modern and Classical Languages Department 2007–17, and also led study abroad experiences. Although she has also worked in marketing and sales, an area that provided experience in budgeting, staff development, and influencing clients, she has always taught language courses at all levels. Past experience includes many years of teaching secondary level French, university Spanish courses including practical-language application courses (translation, business, media, for the medical professions and English as a Second Language at Rice University, University of Houston, and other institutions. As collaborator on a Spanish middle school text, she wrote and edited games and projects and has produced critical articles on a variety of both peninsular and Latin American topics, as well as books, translations, international presentations, reviews, interviews, and other. She is a past vice president and president of the South Central Modern Language Association, Director of the Latino Studies Program and sponsor for Sigma Delta Pi Spanish Honor Society, both of the latter at UST.

Gwendolyn Díaz Ridgeway, PhD, originally from Buenos Aires, Argentina, is professor of English and director of the graduate program in literature at St. Mary's University in San Antonio, TX., where she teaches World Literature and Literary Theory. She earned a BA from Baylor University and the PhD from the University of Texas/Austin and did a post-doc on Latin American magical realism at Rice University. Díaz co-founded and directs the *Las Americas Letters* Series in Literature and the Arts, an annual conference held at St. Mary's. She is frequently invited to speak abroad on the topics of her research. Fluent in Spanish, English, French and Portuguese, Díaz has published six books in both Spanish and English on topics of Argentine literature. Her latest are *Women and Power in Argentine Literature* (Univ. Texas Press, 2009); *Mujer y poder en la literatura argentina* (Emece, 2009); *Texto, Contexto y Postexto en la obra de Luisa Valenzuela* (Univ. of Pittsburgh, 2010) and a collection of her own short stories, *Buenos Aires Noir*. Díaz also has published articles on Latin American literature, literary theory and U.S. Latino literature, as well as on works by Sandra Cisneros, Cristina Garci and others. Her awards include a Fulbright that took her back to her native Buenos Aires where she finished the book on women and power, a Carnegie Mellon Fellowship, the St. Mary's University Distinguished Professor Award for both undergraduate and graduate teaching and an Honorary Professorship at the *Universidad Católica de Salta* in Argentina.

Montse Feu, PhD, is an Associate Professor of Spanish at Sam Houston State University. She is the co-advisor of the Spanish M.A. program and advisor of Latinx student organizations. She serves on the CHSS Diversity and Inclusion Committee. She has taught Spanish, Gender Studies and Humanities courses at Hood College, the University of Houston and UH-Downtown; she was a research assistant in the Recovering the U.S. Hispanic Literary Project. Feu recovers the literary history of the Spanish Civil War exile in the United States, US Hispanic periodicals and migration and exile literature at large. With her students, she has examined and translated such recovered texts. Feu has presented her research at academic conferences and her articles have appeared in peer-reviewed journals and publishers in the United States and in Spain. Her article, "The U.S. Hispanic Flapper: *Pelonas* and *Flapperismo* in Spanish-language Newspapers 1920-1929," won the Research Society for American Periodicals Prize (2015). She is the author of *Correspondencia personal y política de un anarcosindicalista exiliado: Jesús González Malo (1943-1965)* (Universidad de Cantabria, 2016) and co-editor with Christopher Castañeda of *Writing Revolution: Hispanic Anarchism in the United States* (University of Illinois Press, 2019). Her manuscript, *Fighting Fascist Spain*, examines the antifascist activism and culture of workers and anarchists (University of Illinois Press, 2020). She is board member for the Recovering the U. S. Hispanic Literary Heritage and for the Research Society for American Periodicals. She is a fellow of the Cohort #2 of the Texas Academic Leadership Academy (TALA). She was recently awarded the 2019 Western Social Science Association Outstanding Emerging Scholar. She can be reached at mmf017@shsu.edu.

Kimberly A. Habegger, PhD, is Professor of Spanish and chair of languages at Regis University in Denver, Colorado, where she teaches language, literature, culture and interdisciplinary courses. She graduated from Ohio State University with a doctorate in Romance

Languages and Linguistics with an emphasis on historical theater from the Post-war period. Participation in several seminars and institutes such as an NEH Summer Teaching Institute have afforded her the opportunity to connect her research interests with the needs of the curriculum. In past years, her research has produced several presentations and publications that explore the iconography and semiotics of the traditional arts of the American Southwest and of Spain. Of late, she has been investigating the phenomenon of the contemporary iconic wineries of Spain designed by widely renowned architects. Recent professional and personal trips to Spain, the Dominican Republic, Costa Rica, and Peru have informed her awareness of the cultural aesthetics of the Hispanic world.

Enrique Mallen, PhD, is Professor in the Department of World Languages & Cultures at Sam Houston State University. He completed his Ph.D. at Cornell University. Dr. Mallen has published extensively on linguistics, literature, and art history. The titles of some his books are: *Con/figuración Sintáctica, The Visual Grammar of Pablo Picasso; La Sintaxis de la Carne: Pablo Picasso y Marie-Thérèse Walter; Poesía del Lenguaje: De T. S. Eliot a Eduardo Espina; A Concordance of Pablo Picasso's Spanish Writings; Antología Crítica de la Poesía del Lenguaje; A Concordance of Pablo Picasso's French Writings; La Muerte y la máscara en Pablo Picasso; Pablo Picasso: The Interaction Between Collectors and Exhibitions, 1899–1939*; and *Eduardo Espina: Poesía del Deslenguaje*. He has published in journals like *Linguistische Berichte, Studia Linguistica, Theoretical Linguistics, Studies in Language, Interdisciplinary Journal for Germanic Linguistics & Semiotic Analysis, Revista de Estudios Hispánicos, NewWorldPoetics, National Geographic, Avant-Garde Studies, Arts, Athens Journal of Humanities & Arts*, and *The Conversation*. He has contributed to encyclopedias such as the *Enciclopedia de lingüística hispánica* and the *International Encyclopedia of the First World War*. Interviews with him have appeared in *The New York Times, El País, ABC, El Observador, The Guardian, Artnews, Forbes Magazine* and *Revista Literal*. Dr. Mallen is a recognized expert on Pablo Picasso, being director and general editor of the Online Picasso Project, an encyclopedic digital archive and catalog of the works and life of the Spanish artist, which he created in 1997. He has won research grants, as well as awards for his teaching and research. He has led study abroad programs in Spain for Texas A&M University (1996-2006) and Sam Houston State University (2009-2017); and he was Adjunct Professor at *Heinrich-Heine Universität*, Düsseldorf from 2013 to 2016.

Luis Meneses, PhD, is a Postdoctoral Fellow and Assistant Director (Technical Development) of the Electronic Textual Cultures Lab at the University of Victoria (Canada). He is a Fulbright scholar, and currently serves on the board of the *Text Encoding Initiative* (TEI) Consortium and on the *IEEE Technical Committee on Digital Libraries*. His research interests include digital humanities, digital libraries, information retrieval and human-computer interaction. His current research focusses on the development of tools that facilitate open social scholarship.

Stephen J. Miller, PhD, is Professor of Hispanic Studies at Texas A&M University. Among his research fields are Nineteenth-Century through Contemporary Narrative with special emphasis on Spanish Peninsular and American narrative. He is the author of the following volumes: *El mundo de Galdós: teoría, tradición y evolución creativa del pensamiento socio-literario galdosiano* (1983); *Del realismo/naturalismo al modernismo: Galdós, Zola, Revilla y Clarín (1870-1901)* (1993); *Galdós gráfico (1861-1907): orígenes, técnicas y límites del socio-mimetismo* (2001). He is co-editor and contributor to these volumes: *Critical Studies on Gonzalo Torrente Ballester* (1988; with Janet Pérez); and, *Critical Studies on Armando Palacio Valdés* (1993; with Brian J. Dendle). In 2001, he did the introductions to his facsimile editions of three Galdosian graphic narratives: *Gran teatro de la pescadería*, *Las Canarias*, and *Atlas zoológico*, and to two of Galdós's sketchbooks: *Álbum arquitectónico* and *Álbum marítimo*. For the last decade, he has been doing short book reviews for *Choice* of critical studies, biographies and collected letters of Hemingway, Bellow and Updike. As contributor and co-editor with José Pablo Villalobos, he published *Rolando Hinojosa's "Klail City Death Trip Series:" A Retrospective, New Directions* in 2013. He is presently working on an original book-length critical study of Hinojosa's *Klail City Death Trip Series*.

Rose Mary Salum, MFA, is founding editor of the bilingual literary magazine, *Literal: Latin American Voices* and *Literal Publishing*. She has authored *The Water that Rocks the Silence*, translated by C.M. Mayo and the winner of the International Latino Book Award and the prestigious Panamerican Award Carlos Montemayor, *Delta de las arenas, cuentos árabes, cuentos judíos* winner of the International Latino Book Award) and *Entre los espacios /Spaces in Between*, translated by Debra D. Andrist. She was the guest editor for *Hostos Review* for the issue, *Almalafa y Caligrafía, Literatura de origen árabe en América Latina*. Her awards and recognitions include Author of the Year 2008 for the Hispanic Book Festival, four Lone Star Awards, two Council of Editors of Learned Journals Awards, St. Thomas University's Classical Award, and a recognition from the U.S. Congress among others. She is a member of the Academia Norteamericana de la Lengua.

Haiqing Sun, PhD, Texas Southern University, is Professor of Spanish, with research focus on Latin American narrative and comparative study of Latin American and Chinese film and literature. She has published research on Latin American detective fiction, on writers, Jorge Luis Borges, Mario Vargas Llosa, Roa Bastos, Rodolfo Walsh, encyclopedic entries, and Chinese translations of works by Octavio Paz, Gabriela Mistral, and Luis Buñuel. She currently serves as editor for journals, *Caribbean Vistas* and *Yangtze River Academic*, and is Invited Guest Professor of Pingdingshan University. She has also worked as principal investigator in literature and culture projects funded with grants of National Endowment for the Humanities (NEH), and Humanities Texas (HTx).

Index

Fictional characters are listed within single quotes, with the name of the film/book/play/story in brackets. In most cases the character is indexed under the first name e.g. 'Jim' (Perezagua's *Yoro*).

Page numbers in italics refer to figures, plates or tables.

a priori knowledge, 50
ABC newspaper, 189*n*
"absent object", 75, 76, 78, 83
"the abyss" (domain of rhetoric), 75, 76, 77
Academia di San Luca, 73
Adams, Peter J., 74
'Adelantado' (Carpentier's *Los pasos perdidos*), 63, 64
affirmative action initiatives, 110
Agee, William C., 39
ALA (American Literary Agency), 162–163, 167–168, 172, 173*n*
'Alatriste, Diego' (Pérez-Reverte's *Alatriste* series), 180, 181, 186
Alcott, Louisa May, 195
'Alejandrina Correa' (Vargas Llosa's *The War of the End of the World*), 206–207
Alfarache, Progreso, 164
allegory
   ambivalence in, 49
   ancient Greek and Roman scholars, 49
   applied to diverse forms, 49, 54
   as a brief trope, 49
   Carpentier's *Los pasos perdidos*, 47, 57, 59
   changing concept of, 49–50
   defined, 49
   Latin American postmodernism, 54–55
   relationship to sacred texts, 49
   varying degrees of expression, 49
Allen, Augustus Chapman, 88, 103*n*

Allen, John Kirby, 88, 103*n*
Alonso, Jaime, 25
Alurista, 169, 176*n*
'Amado' (Sender's "Manuela en Copacabana"), 166–167
American Literary Agency (ALA), 162–163, 167–168, 172, 173*n*
anagnorisis, 217, 219*n*
Analytical Cubism, 140
Anderson, Stanford, 64
Andrist, Debra D., ix–x
anglos, 88, 103*n*
Ansto, 141
'Antonia Sardelinha' (Vargas Llosa's *The War of the End of the World*), 206
'Antonio Counselor' (Vargas Llosa's *The War of the End of the World*), 206, 207
'Antonio Vilanova' (Vargas Llosa's *The War of the End of the World*), 206
Anzaldúa, Gloria, 113, 115, 117
Aragón Wine Museum, 5
Aranda, Emilio, 90
Aranda, José F., Jr., 89
arch-writing, 53
archilexeme, 148
archiphoneme, 148
archisememe, 148
architecture
   and the avant-garde, 61
   Bauhaus movement, 61
   Heidegger's definition, 59
   Hispanic Postmodern Project, 46–66

240 | Index

architecture *(continued)*
   Latin America building projects, 47–48
   Le Corbusier, 61, 62, 63
   Los pasos perdidos (Carpentier), 47, 57, 58, 59
   and the poetic, 46
   polarization of practice, 60
   postmodernism, 47
   purpose of, 46
   reciprocal relationship with literature, 46
   of resistance to universalization, 46–47, 57
   Spanish wine museums, 3–17
   see also Museum of Fine Arts/Houston (MFAH); Valley of the Fallen
d'Arenberg Cube, McLaren Vale, 5
Arendt, Hannah, 60, 212, 214, 218
Aretino, Pietro, 72
Aretoulakis, Emmanouil, 218
Arias, Constantino, 43
Aristotle, 49–50
art, and divination, 75
The Art Institute of Chicago, 79
artefacts, Spanish wineries, 3, 5, 7
Artismuño, Ignacio, 48
Asociación para la Defensa del Valle de los Caídos, 25–26
assimilation, 113, 114
Asturias, Miguel Ángel, 57
'Asunción Sardelinha' (Vargas Llosa's *The War of the End of the World*), 206
Atzlán, 114
Aubry, Eugene, 39
Audinet, Jacques, 116
Austin, Texas
   diocese established (1947), 92
   St. Julia's Catholic Church built, 93
   Sociedades Guadalupanas, 93–96
autophagy, 218, 219*n*
Ávalos, Juan de, 22
avant-garde, 33, 61
Ávila, Sta.Teresa de, 71, 73
Aznar, José María, 25
Aznar Zubigarary, Manuel, 25

Bacchus, 6, 7
back-turned figures, El Greco's paintings, 71, 78, 81, 83
Bakhtin, Mikhail, 215

Baldassari, Anne, 128
'Bao' (*The Cases of Master Bao*), 222
Barayón, Amparo, 166, 168
'Doña Bárbara' (Gallegos's *Doña Bárbara*), 55
Barcala, Diego, 24, 27
Barcelona, Güell Park, 48
The Barnes Foundation, 81
'Baron de Caña Brava' (Vargas Llosa's *The War of the End of the World*), 206, 207–208
Barragán, Luis, 48
Barreiro, Javier, 164
Basque Country, separatist movements, 188
Bataille, Georges, 77
Baudelaire, Charles, 47
Bauhaus movement, 61
Baxandall, Michael, 72
BBC News, 25
Beck, Audrey Jones, 40
Beck, John A., 40
becoming, "*Chora*", 76
Beethoven, Ludwig van, 55
being, "*Chora*", 76
Bellah, Robert, 113
bereavement, languages of, 28–29
Bernadac, Marie-Laure, 128, 131
Bibliópolis website, 182
Bing Search, 32
Bismarck, Otto von, 111
'Black Panther' (Sender's "Pantera negra/Black Panther"), 170–171
Blaffer Foundation, 40
Blaffer, John H., 38
Blaffer, Robert Lee, 38
Blake, William, 154
Blei, D.M., 143, 145
'Bo' (*Chinago*), 220–222, 226, 227
'Bob' (Sender's "Adiós pájaro negro/Goodbye Black Bird"), 169–170
bodegas, 3–5
   artefacts, 3, 5, 7
   Dinastía Vivanco winery, 5–8, *11*, 16
Bodegas Antión, 6
Bodegas Darien, 5, 6
Bodegas Fariña, 5, 10–15, *14*, 16
Bodegas Irius, 6
Bodegas Marqués de Riscal, 5
Bodegas Otazu, 5
Bodegas Portia, 5
Bodegas Protos, 5

Bodegas Vega Sicilia, 8
Bodegas Vivanco, 5
Bodegas Ysios, 5
Borges, Jorge Luis, 227
Botero, Fernando, 33
Botta, Mario, 63
'boulevardier', 173*n*
Bourgeois, Louise, 40
Brasilia, 48
Bremmer, Ian, 108, 112
Breton, André, 128
Brexit, 109
Brillembourg, Tanya Capriles de, 33
Briones, Rioja, 5
Brokaw, Galen, 62, 63
Brooks, David, 121
The Brown Foundation, Inc., 39
Brown, George R., 39
Brown, Herman, 39
Bruguera, Tanya, 34
Bubley, Esther, 44
Buentello, Fr. Michael, 97, 98
Buggelin, Gretchen, 16
Buonarroti, Michelangelo, 30*n*, 72
Burke, Edmund, 218
Burke, John Francis, xv, 108, 113, 114, 116, 121
Burke, Kenneth, 75, 76
Burl Marx, Roberto, 48

Caesar, 181, 183
Calandria, Juan José, 35
Calatrava, Santiago, 3, 16
Calderón de la Barca, Pedro, 180
Calle, Johana, 34
Calvino, Italo, 227
Candela, Félix, 47–48
Cantera, Santiago, 27
Cantú, Federico, 35
Canudos, siege of (1897), 210*n*
Capote, Yoan, 34
Caracas University City, 48
Caram, Dorothy Farrington de, 100, 101
Carlos I, King of Spain, 21
Caroline Wiess Building, 37
Carpentier, Alejo
  architectural influence, 61
  article about Le Corbusier, 61
  Tientos y diferencias, 56
  see also Los pasos perdidos (Carpentier)
Carroll, Lawrence, 44

Casagemas, Carles, 79
The Cases of Master Bao, 222
Casqueiro, Javier, 27
Castilla y León, 8, 10
Castillo, Sergio, 98
Catalonia, separatist movements, 188
Catholicism *see* Hispanic Roman Catholicism
Caudet, Francisco, 163
cell phones, 197
Centro de la Cultura del Rioja, 6, 9–10, *13*, 16–17
Cerdán, Eduardo, xii
Cervantes, 186, 215
Chandigarh, Punjab, 62
Chandler, Raymond, 227
Chavarro, Jorge, xii
Chávez Candelaria, Cordelia, 200, 203*n*
Chávez, Hugo, 110
Chávez, Nelly, 98
Chávez, Roberto, 98
Chessman, Caryl, 171
'Chessman' (Sender's "Chessman"), 171–172
Chicana literature, 200
Chicano/Chicana, defined, xiii
Chicanx studies, 114, 115
Chilean Wine Museum, 5
Chillman, James, Jr., 37
China
  Ming dynasty, 222, 225
  Qing Dynasty, 224, 225
  see also Kung Fu films
Chinago film (Van Lengen), xii, 220–222, 226, 227
Chinese language, 52
"*Chora*", 75, 76, 77, 78
Chow, Stephen, 221
Cigales DO (*denominación de origen*), 8
Cisneros, Sandra
  Extreme Unction, 201
  female sexuality, 199, 200–201
  feminism, 199
  Guadalupe, the Sex Goddess, 202
  I'm So in Love I Grow a New Hymen, 201, 203*n*
  Loose Woman collection, 200, 201–202
  Loose Woman poem, 202
  My Wicked, Wicked Ways, xi–xii, 199, 200, 201, 203

Cisneros, Sandra *(continued)*
    Once Again I Prove the Theory of Relativity, 201
    poetry, xi–xii, 199, 200–203
"the city" (domain of rhetoric), 75, 77
civil republicanism, 113
Clark, Lygia, 33
Clark, Robert, 43
CNT México, 164, 165
Coatlicue state, 115
Cohen, David, 16
collage, 129, 138–139, 140
Comunidad Ibérica, 164
concentration, 197
Concrete art movement, 33
consciousness
    Derrida's grammatology, 52, 54
    and mysticism, 71, 74
Conselheiro, Antonio, 210*n*
conservative nationalism, 111–112
construction, "fictional" projects, 46
Cordeiro, Waldemar, 33
Cortés, Hernán, 203*n*
Coscio, Elizabeth, x
cosmopolitanism *see* elitist cosmopolitanism
Cossio, Manuel B., 82
Cowling, Elizabeth, 134
creativity
    of language, 53
    Picasso, 139–140
    Salum's experience, 196–198
Crespin, Elías, 33
Crimea, Russian expansionist nationalism, 112
"crisis of legitimacy", 46, 65
critical regionalism, 46, 47, 48, 57, 65
Crouching Tiger and Hidden Dragon film (Lee), 221, 224, 226
Crow, John, 19–20, 29
Cruz-Diez, Carlos, 34, 36
Cruz, San Juan de la, 71, 73
Cubism, 82, 128, 140, 142
cubist collage, 129, 138–139, 140
Cuelgamuros, 20
Cullen, Hugh Roy, 39
Cullen, Lillie, 39
Cullinan, Nina J., 38
cultural dynamism, 112
cultural identity, 112
Cunha, Euclides da, 210*n*

Dacosta, Milton, 33

Daix, Pierre, 128
Dallmayr, Fred, 116
Dargis, Manohla, 220
Darié, Sandú, 33
"dasein", 59
Davies, David, 73
Davis, Camilla, 38
Day of the Dead celebration, 90, 103*n*
de la Renta, Oscar, 37
De León, Arnoldo, 101
De Man, Paul, 49
de Montebello, Philippe, 39
deconstruction, 50–51, 53
deformations, El Greco's paintings, 71, 78, 83
Deleuze, Gilles, 133, 142
"demand", "the Imaginary", 76, 77
Derrida, Jacques, 50–54, 59, 218*n*
"desire", "the Symbolic", 77, 129
detective fiction, 222–223, 227
El Diario de Nueva York, 163
Díaz, Gwen, xi–xii
Díaz, Porfirio, 88, 202
Dickens, Charles, 185
Diego. San Juan, 97, 104*n*, 204*n*
différance, 53
differential sign, 51
Digital Humanities, 142
Dinastía Vivanco winery, 5–8, *11*
disegno, 73
divination, and art, 75
divinization, 75
Divisare website, 6
Dixon, Mildred, 35
Doggett, Lloyd, 94
dolmens, 59
Don Quixote (Cervantes), 215
Dragon Gate Inn film (Hu Jinquan), 223, 225
dualism, 53
Dumas, Alexandre, 179, 184

Eagleton, Terri, 48
ecstasy, 71, 74, 78
ego, 76
elitist cosmopolitanism
    as "anywheres", 108
    characteristics of, 108–109
    cultural identity, 112
    global vision of, 108–109
    inclusion of migrants and refugees, 109
    lateral vision of *mestizaje*, 116–122

personal autonomy, 108
political centrists, 109
self-reliance, 108
separation of "us" from "them", 112
threat to liberal democracies, 106, 107
transnational communities, 109, 114
Elizondo, Fr. Virgilio, 91, 113, 116, 117
enganchadores (labor agents), 88
Escorial, 21
Escudier, Carlos, 24, 25
España Libre, 164, 165
Esparza, Jesús Jesse, 89
'Estela' (Vargas Llosa's *The War of the End of the World*), 207, 208
Euclidean geometry, 201, 203*n*
EUR, Rome, 21
Europa Press Nacional, 29
evil, banality of, 212, 214
Exiled Writers' Committee, 165
expansionist nationalism, 112
Extensible Markup Language (XML) files, 150

fantasies, 77
Farrington, Curtis, 101
fascist architecture, 21–22
fatum, 216, 219*n*
'Faulques' (Pérez-Reverte's *El pintor de batallas*), 187–188, 190–191*n*
female sexuality, 199–201
feminism, stages of, 199
Fernández, José Gabriel, 34
Fernández, Magdalena, 34, 37
Feu, Montse, x
Fichte, Johann Gottlieb, 141
Ficino, Marsilio, 72
Figari, Pedro, 35
flânerie, 162, 163, 166, 167, 173*n*
flaneur, 162, 168, 173*n*
Flores, Archbishop Patricio, 95
Foster, Hal, 47
Foster, Norman, 3
Foucault, Michel, 4
Frampton, Kenneth
  architecture of resistance, 46, 57
  autonomy of the arts, 61
  civilization's concern with instrumental reason, 65
  critical regionalism, 47, 57
  natural light, 63

"polis" space, 55–56
tectonics, 64
universalization tendencies, 46, 60
vanguard as a liberal movement, 61
Franco, Carmen, 25
Franco Foundation, 25
Franco, Francisco
  criticism of government prohibited, 19
  death (1975), 19, 20
  fondness for Phillip II, 21
  regime condemned, 26
  Sender's opposition to, 165
  Valley of the Fallen decree (1940), 19, 20, 23
  Valley of the Fallen tomb, 20, 22, 23, 25, 26, 27, 29
Frank, Robert, 43, 44
Franzheim, Kenneth, 38
Frazer, James, 50
Freud, Sigmund, 50, 53
Fuentes, Carlos, 47, 54–55
Fundación Gego, 34–35
Fusi Aizpúrua, Juan Pablo, 25

'Galileo Gall' (Vargas Llosa's *The War of the End of the World*), 207, 208, 209
Gallegos, Rómulo, *Doña Bárbara*, 55
Gallop, Jane, 199–200
Galston, William, 107, 108
Gálvez, Bernardo, 87
García Márquez, Gabriel, 57
Gaudí, Antonio, 48, 201, 203*n*
Gaulle, Charles de, 111
Gego (Gertrud Goldschmidt), 34–35, 36
Gehry, Frank, 3, 15, 16
Generation of 1898, 172
Germany
  centrist political parties, 109
  see also Nazi Germany
gestures, El Greco's paintings, 71, 78, 83
Gibraltar Straits, 201, 203*n*
Gironès, Toni, 16
Glassell, Alfred, Jr., 39
global economy, 107, 109, 110
Goethe, Johann Wolfgang von, 55
Goldberg, Jonathan, 72
Goldberger, Paul, 39
Golden Globe Award, 221
Golding, John, 138, 139

Goldschmidt, Gertrud (Gego), 34–35, 36
González Echeverría, Roberto, 55, 57, 58, 60
Goodhart, David, 108, 109, 110, 111
Gorski, Philip, 113
Gossage, John R., 43
Gottman, Jean, 55
Gracia, Jorge, 116, 118
Graham, Dan, 40
grammatology, 50–54
Grand Central Art Galleries, New York, 37
Grassi, Ernesto, 75
Gray, Christopher, 81
Great Depression, 89–90
El Greco (Doménikos Theotokópoulos), 72–73
   back-turned figures, 71, 78, 81, 83
   beholder in real space, 83
   Burial of the Count Orgaz, 79
   Greek Orthodox roots, 72
   human gestures and deformation, 71, 78, 83
   influence on Picasso, 71, 78–83
   late paintings, 78
   The Martyrdom of Saint. Maurice, 81
   mysticism, 71, 73–74, 78
   The opening of the Fifth Seal of the Apocalypse, 81–82
   Picasso's passion for, 78–79
   pictorial rhetoric, 77–78
   religious paintings, 79, 80, 81–82
   in Rome, 73
   St Joseph and the Christ Child, 81
   in Spain, 72, 73
   The Trinity, 80
Greenberg, Clement, 61
Groisman, Adriana, 44
Gropius, Walter, 61
grotesque, concept of
   Perezagua's *Yoro*, 215–216
   Sender's *Relatos fronterizos*, 162, 165–166, 168, 171, 172–173
Guadalupana Association, 96, 97–98
Guadalupana Papers, 91–92
guadalupanismo, 90, 91, 93, 96
   defined, 87n
Guadalupe, Treaty of, 87
Guggenheim Museum, Bilbao, 15, 16
Guggenheim Museum, New York, 38

Gulliver's Travels (Swift), 60
Guzmán, Pablo, 97, 98, 99

'H' (Perezagua's *Yoro*), 213–214, 215, 216–217
Haaf, Susanne, 157
Habegger, Kimberly A., ix, 4
Habermas, Jürgen, 46
Hadid, Zaha, 3
Halle, Bruce, 36
Halle, Diane, 36
Hammett, Dashiel, 227
Hansen, Victor Davis, 115
Harland, Richard, 51, 52, 53
Harney, Lucy D., 60
HATFL (Houston Area Teachers of Foreign Language), 101
Hawhee, Debra, 75
He Ping, 224
Heidegger, Martin, 51, 59, 65
Hellenism, 59, 60
Hemingway, Ernest, 182, 190n
Henderson, Ray, 169
Hero film (Zhang Yimou), 221, 224, 225, 226, 227–228
heterotopias, 4–5
Heywood, Anthony, 108, 109, 111, 112
HHF (Houston Hispanic Forum), 100–101
Hinojosa, Rolando, 190n
Hispanic, defined, xii, xiii
Hispanic American, defined, xii–xiii
Hispanic Roman Catholicism, 90, 91, 92, 93
   see also Guadalupanismo; *Nuestra Señora de Guadalupe*; *Sociedades Guadalupanas*
Hitler, Adolf, 112
Hobby Center for the Study of Texas, 102
Hogg, Ima, 41
Holl, Steven, 39
Holmes, Ann, 38
home
   concept of, ix, 41–44
   defined, 32
'Honorio Vilanova' (Vargas Llosa's *The War of the End of the World*), 206
Houston Area Teachers of Foreign Language (HATFL), 101
Houston Chronicle, 38, 96
Houston Heights, 89

Houston Hispanic Forum (HHF), 100–101
Houston History magazine, 89
Houston Ship Channel, 89
Houston, Texas
  Bayou Bend Collection and Gardens, 41
  Encuentro Hispano de Pastoral, 96
  ethnic/linguistic diversity, 102–103
  Foley's department store, 38
  founding of the city, 88, 103*n*
  Great Depression period, 89–90
  guatemaltecos, 102
  Hispanic population, 41, 102
  Immaculate Heart of Mary Catholic Church, 90
  Lorenzo de Zavala Elementary School, 99
  Magnolia Park, 89, 90, 99
  Mexican Catholic churches, 90, 91, 96
  Mexican illegal immigrants, 100
  Mexican "immigrant era" ends (1930s), 89–90
  Mexican immigrants (1970s and 1980s), 99–100
  Mexican immigrants (1990s), 101–102
  Mexican median household income, 101
  Mexican population (19th c.), 88
  Mexican population (early 20th c.), 88–89
  Mexican students, 99
  Our Lady of Guadalupe Catholic Church, 90, 91, 96
  Rienzi, 41
  Rusk Elementary School, 99
  salvadoreños, 102
  Second Ward, 89
  settled by *anglos*, 88
  Sociedades Guadalupanas, 90–92
  Ward system, 89, 103*n*
  see also Museum of Fine Arts/Houston (MFAH)
Hu Jinquan, 223
Huarte construction firm, 24
Hudson, William, 119
Hugo, Victor, 166
human ego, 76
Humble Oil & Refining Co, 38
Humboldt, Alexander von, 58
Huntington, Samuel P., 116

Husserl, Edmund, 51–52

illusion, transcendental art, 72–73
"the Imaginary", 76, 77
Indian language, 52
"inverted millenarianism", 46
Iribarren, Juan, 34
'Irrational Number' (Perezagua's *Yoro*), 216–217
Italy
  defeat in WWII, 22
  monumental classicism architectural style, 21
  Spanish Civil War (1936–1939), 22

Jackson, J.B., 4
James, Henry, 214
Jameson, Fredric, 46, 166
Jencks, Charles, 61
Jesus of Nazareth, 97, 117
'Jim' (Perezagua's *Yoro*), 213, 215, 216, 217
Jiménez, Carlos, 40
'Joaquim' (Vargas Llosa's *The War of the End of the World*), 206, 207
Saint John the Evangelist, 82
Johnson, Eastman, 43
Jordan, M.I., 145
Joris, Pierre, 132, 133
'the journalist' (Vargas Llosa's *The War of the End of the World*), 206, 207, 208–210
Joyce, James, 140
Judis, John, 108, 110
Jung, Carl, 50
Jung, Hwa Yol, 116
'Jurema' (Vargas Llosa's *The War of the End of the World*), 207, 208–209, 210

Kahlo, Frida, xi, 36
Kahn, Louis, 16
Kant, Immanuel, 218
Kennedy, John F., 92
Kertész, André, 43
Kierkegaard, Sören, 54
Kimbell Museum, 16
Kinder Institute, 102
King, Charles L., 163
The Knife Carrier from Shuangqi Town film (He Ping), 224, 226
Koshar, Rudy, 28
Krauss, Rosalind, 48, 49

Kristeva, Julia, 199
Kung Fu films, 220–228
   Chinago, xii, 220–222, 226, 227
   Crouching Tiger and Hidden Dragon, 221, 224, 226
   Dragon Gate Inn, 223, 225
   "fighting (*Wu Da*) films", 223–224
   genre elements, 221–222
   Hero, 221, 224, 225, 226, 227–228
   hero and history theme, 222, 224–228
   The Knife Carrier from Shuangqi Town, 224, 226
   Kung Fu Hustle, 221
   New Dragon Gate Inn, 224, 226–227
   Seven Swords, 221
   Shaolin Temple, 226
   value systems, 221, 226–227
Kung Fu Hustle film (Chow), 221
Kung Fu literature, 222–223, 226

Lacan, Jacques, 76, 77, 129, 141
Lam, Wifredo, 33
language
   Husserl's phenomenological theory of, 51–52
   mystical discourse, 74, 75
   "the Symbolic", 77, 129
langue, 50, 53
Laredo, 201, 203*n*
Latent Dirichlet Allocation (LDA), 145
lateral universality, 116
Latin American, defined, xiii
Latin American Boom, 48, 55, 56–57
Latino, defined, xiii
Latinx, defined, xiii
Latinx studies, 113, 114, 115, 116
Latinx world, 113
Latinxization, 113, 122*n*
LDA (Latent Dirichlet Allocation), 145
Le Corbusier, 61, 62, 63
Le Pen, Marine, 111
Leach, Neil, 46, 59
League of American Writers, 165
Lee, Ang, 221, 224
Lee, Bruce, 223
Leiris, Michel, 140
Leirner Collection, 33, 36
Leo XIII, Pope, 97
Leonardo da Vinci, 72
Leser, Tina, 43
Lévi-Strauss, Claude, 51

Levine, Suzanne Jill, 57
Li, Jet, 226
liberal democracies
   elitist cosmopolitanism threat, 106, 107
   individual and minority liberties and rights, 106
   legitimate problems within, 121
   populist threat, 106, 107
   redistribution of resources, 106–107
   revitalizing of, 113
liberal nationalism, 109, 111
literary criticism, 49, 50
literary Realism, 47
literary regionalism, 54–55
literature, reciprocal relationship with architecture, 46
Lizars, William Home, 43
Llewellyn, Marc, 5
logos, 50, 54, 75
Logroño, 6, 9
Long, Bert L., Jr., 42
Long, Huey, 110
'Lorenzo Falcó' (Pérez-Reverte's novels), 187, 190*n*
Los Angeles County Museum of Art, 42
Los Carpinteros, 34
The Lost Steps see Los pasos perdidos (Carpentier)
'Lucas Corso' (Pérez-Reverte's *El club Dumas*), 181
Lucian, 60
Luke, Gospel of, 97
'Luz María' (Vargas Llosa's *The War of the End of the World*), 206
Lyotard, Jean-François, 218

Maar, Dora, 42
McCracken, Ellen, 202
McLaren Vale region, 5
McQuillan, Thomas, 61
Magic Realism, x–xi, 47, 56, 57
Mainer, José-Carlos, 163
Maiztegui, Fr. Juan, 91, 93
Malinche, 200, 203*n*
Mallén, Enrique, x
Las Mañanitas, 96
Mannerism, 72, 81
'Manuela' (Sender's "Manuela en Copacabana"), 166–167
Marcuse, Herbert, 61
'María Quadrado' (Vargas Llosa's *The*

War of the End of the World), 206, 207
Marino Pascual, Jesús, 3, 5, 6, 9, 10
Markovsky, Bishop John, 96
Márquez, José Luis, 182
martial arts movies *see Kung Fu* films
Marzio, Peter C., 39, 40
Masterson, Carroll Sterling, 41
Masterson, Harris III, 41
materialism, 54
Matisse, Henri, 40
The Matrix, 226, 227–228, 228*n*
Matta, 33
Maurín Julià, Joaquim, 163, 166
melting pot concept, 114
La memoria viva website, 24
Méndez, Diego, 19
menhirs, 58–59
Menton, Seymour, 207–208
Merriam-Webster Dictionary, 32
mestizaje
    as a democratic ethos, 107
    Latinx heritage of, 116
    original meaning, 113
    past historical renderings, 112–116, 120
    privileging of European culture, 113–114, 120
    resistance rending of, 114–116
    unity-in-diversity, 113, 117–118, 122
mestizaje (lateral vision of), 116–122
    commodification of human relationships, 118–119
    consensus and conflict factors, 120
    culture transformations, 118
    ethos of openness and persuasion, 119
    global mixing of cultures, 118
    no privileging of heritage, 117
    places and their heritages, 120
    unity of diverse cultures, 117
    unity and diversity as integral, 117–118
Metropolitan Museum of Art, New York, 81
Mexican Cession (1848), 87
Mexican Revolution (1910), 88
Mexico
    Day of the Dead celebration, 90, 103*n*
    racial classification, 113–114
Mexico University, 47–48

MFAH *see* Museum of Fine Arts/Houston (MFAH)
Michaël, Androula, 140
Mies van der Rohe, Ludwig, 38, 39, 40, 61
migrants
    elitist cosmopolitanism, 109
    lateral *mestizaje*, 118, 119
    Mexican immigrants in US, 88–90, 96, 99–100, 101–102
    nativist populists, 110, 111
Miles, Valerie, 212
Miller, Marilyn Grace, 113
Miller, Stephen, x
Milwaukee Art Museum, 16
mind
    aware of itself as an entity, 76
    "Chora", 75
    a signified ascribed to the brain, 54
    unconscious, 53
    understanding of reality, 73
    univocity, 53
Mitchell, Elvis, 220
modernism
    architecture, 38
    Latin American literature, 46, 47
    Los pasos perdidos, 65–66
modernity
    as an incomplete project, 46, 57
    defined, 47
    as a state of alienation, 80
    Vargas Llosa's *The War of the End of the World*, 209
Modotti, Tina, 36
Moi, Toril, 199
Monasterio de San Lorenzo, El Escorial, 81
Moneo, Rafael, 3, 40–41
monoliths, 58
Montenegro, Roberto, 35
Montesquieu, Charles de Secondat, Baron de, 165
monument, defined, 48–49
Morales, Armando, 33
More, Thomas, 60
'Moreira César' (Vargas Llosa's *The War of the End of the World*), 206, 207
'Colonel Moreiras' (Vargas Llosa's *The War of the End of the World*), 207, 208, 209
Most, John, 140

248 | Index

'Mouche' (Carpentier's *Los pasos perdidos*), 58, 59, 64
mourning, languages of, 28–29
Muguruza, Pedro, 19
Muller, Jan-Werner, 108, 111, 121
Mundet, Joan, 185
El Mundo newspaper, 23
Muñiz-Huberman, Angelina, 212, 213, 214
Muñoz, Óscar, 34
Musée d'Art Moderne de la Ville de Paris, 79
Museo de la Cultura del Vino, 5–8, 16–17
Museo de Santa Cruz, Toledo, 81
Museo del Prado, Madrid, 80
Museo del Vino de Valladolid, 5, 8–9, 12, 16–17
museum, defined, 5
Museum of Fine Arts/Houston (MFAH), 32–44
  additional wings (1926), 37
  Adolpho Leirner Collection of Brazilian Constructive Art, 33
  Beck Building, 40–41
  Blaffer Memorial Wing, 38
  Brillembourg Capriles Collection of Latin American Art, 33
  Brown Auditorium Theater, 39
  Caribbean Art Fund Collection, 34
  Caroline Wiess Law Building, 37, 38, 39, 40, 41
  concept of "home", 41–44
  Cruz-Diez Foundation, 34
  Cullen Sculpture Garden, 39–40
  Cullinan Hall, 38, 39
  Fundación Gego Collection, 34–35
  galleries expansion, 38
  Glassell School of Art, 39, 40
  Hispanic exhibitions, 35–37
  Home–So Different, So Appealing exhibition, 32–33, 41–42, 44
  Intersecting Modernities: The Brillembourg Capriles Collection, 33
  Junior School, 40
  The Light Inside, 41
  lighting, 38, 41, 63
  original building, 37
  permanent collections, 38
  Wilson Tunnel, 41
The Museum of Modern Art, New York, 38, 81

Mussolini, Benito, 21
MySQL relational database, 142
mystical discourse, 74–75
mysticism
  and consciousness, 71, 74
  enhanced rhetorical expression, 71
  and El Greco, 71, 73–74, 78
  and Picasso, 71–72
  and rhetoric, 75–76
  Spanish Golden Age, 71

Nast, Thomas, 42, 43
National Gallery of Art, Washington, 80
nativist populism *see* populism
Navarro, José, 91
Nazi Germany
  architectural styles, 21
  defeat in WWII, 22
  expansionist nationalism, 112
  Spanish Civil War (1936–1939), 22
'Necessary Angel' (Sender's "Pantera negra/Black Panther"), 170–171
The Necessary Angel (Stevens), 170–171
"need", "the Real", 76, 77
'Negro' (Pérez-Reverte's *Los perros duros no bailan*), 186
'Neo' (*The Matrix*), 226
neo-classical fascist architecture, 21
Neo-Concrete art movement, 33
Neoplatonism, 73
New Dragon Gate Inn film (Tsui Hark), 224, 226–227
The New York Times, 39, 220
New York Times magazine, 42
Nieto, Margaret, 96
Nietzsche, Frederick, 51
Noble, Greg, 7
Noguchi, Isamu, 39–40
Nolen Willis, R., 39
North American Committee to Aid Spanish Democracy, 165
Nuestra Señora de Guadalupe, 90, 91, 92, 93, 95, 97–99, 117, 204*n*

objet petit a, 141
Obrascón-Huarte-Laín (OHL), 24
Obregón, Roberto, 34
O'Brian, Patrick, 79–80
Oedipus complex, 77
O'Gorman, Juan, 47–48

Oiticica, Hélio, 33, 36
Ojeda, Alberto, 25
'Olvido' (Pérez-Reverte's *El pintor de batallas*), 187–188, 189, 190–191*n*
La Opinión, 163
Ordaz Romay, M. Ángeles, 165
Orozco, José Clemente, 35
otherness, Vargas Llosa's *The War of the End of the World*, 205
Our Lady of Guadalupe *see Nuestra Señora de Guadalupe*
Ouspensky, P.D., 75
oxymoron, 76

painting, postmodern aesthetic, 48
'Pajeú' (Vargas Llosa's *The War of the End of the World*), 208
papiers collés, 128, 129, 139, 141
parole, 50, 53
Parrot, Louis, 129
particularism, 116
Los pasos perdidos (Carpentier), 55–60, 61–66
　allegorical journeys, 62
　as an allegory for Latin American culture and identity, 57
　architectural allegorical subtext, 47, 57, 58, 59
　"bookish journeys" description, 61
　city buildings from the air, 61–62
　descriptions of columns, 64–65
　descriptions of light, 63
　Hellenism, 59, 60
　modernism/tradition paradox, 65–66
　synopsis, 56
　time perspective, 62–63
　travel trope, 57
　window references, 63–64
Patagonia, 201, 203*n*
patriarchy, 200, 201, 202–203
Patrimonio Nacional, 27
Peñafiel, 8
La Peregrina, 95, 99
Pérez Galdós, Benito, 182, 184, 185, 189, 190*n*
Pérez-Reverte, Arturo
　Alatriste series, 180–181, 182, 183, 184–185, 186, 188
　Un asunto de honor, 186
　El capitán Alatriste, 180
　El club Dumas, 179–180, 181, 184–185
　devotion to pictorial art, 181, 184–186
　"El habla de un bravo del siglo XVII", 180
　film versions of his work, 186, 190*n*
　La Guerra Civil contada a los niños, 188
　Una historia de España, 183, 188
　Hombres buenos, 190*n*
　El húsar, 179, 186
　as a life-long reader of fiction, 181, 184
　El maestro de esgrima, 179
　marginal characters, 181, 186–187
　Ojos azules, 184–185
　Los perros duros no bailan, 186
　El pintor de batallas, 182, 185, 186, 187–188, 190*n*
　quest for the meaning of everything, 182, 187–188
　Sabotaje, 190*n*
　La sombra del águila, 182, 184–185, 186
　Spain's future, 188–189
　Spanish literary critics, 180
　Spanish Royal Academy of the Language (RAE), 179, 180, 181
　La tabla de Flandes, 179, 184–185
　Territorio comanche, 182, 184, 186
　Todo Alatriste, 185
　translation work as a schoolboy, 181, 183–184
　war reporter, 179, 181, 182–183
　writings on violence, war and death, 182–183
Pérez-Torres, Rafael, 114
Perezagua, Marina
　Criaturas abisales/Unfathomable Babies (Creatures), 212
　Don Quijote de Manhattan, 218–219*n*
　Father, 212
　Leche/Milk, 212
　Little Boy, 212
　The Story of H (Yoro), xii, 212–218
　use of the grotesque, 215–216
　Yoro (The Story of H), xii, 212–218
Pettoruti, Emilio, 33
Philip the Great, 183
Philip IV, King of Spain, 180
Phillip II, King of Spain, 21
phonetic languages, 52
Piacentini, Marcello, 21

Picasso, Pablo
  addition and accumulation processes in his writings, 139–140
  adjunctive poetry, 134–138, 140
  artistic genres, xi
  backturned figures, 83
  beholder in real space, 83
  Blue Period, 80
  combinatorial poetry, 127, 129–134, 141
  complex poetry, 139–142
  Composition: Les paysans, 81
  connectors in his poetry, 131–133
  creativity concept, 139–140
  Cubism, 82, 128, 140, 142
  cubist collage, 129, 138–139, 140
  Les demoiselles d'Avignon, 81–83
  Digital Humanities analysis of his poetry, 142
  Dinastía Vivanco winery, 7
  distortions of the body, 79–80, 81, 139
  Evocation (L'enterrement de Carles Casagemas), 79
  La famille de saltimbanques (Lesbateleurs), 80–81
  graphic elements in his writings, 134, 154–156, 157
  graphic poetry, 138–139
  El Greco's influence, 71, 78–83
  hand-written poems, 128
  hyphens in poetry, 134–135
  indeterminacy in his poetry, 141
  interest in verbal communication, 128
  Lengua de fuego abanica, 130, 132, 133, 135, 136, 137–138
  links between writings and pictorial works, 128, 134
  mysticism, 71–72
  Nature morte à la chaise cannée, 138–139
  no máshacer que cuidado, 155–156, 155, 156
  papiers collés, 128, 129, 139, 141
  passion for El Greco, 78–79
  poems in French, 127, 131, 132, 133, 135, 136–137, 150, 157
  poems in Spanish, 127, 129–130, 132, 133, 134, 135–136, 137–138, 150, 157
  Le radeau de laméduse, 131, 132, 133, 135, 136–137
  Real Academia de San Fernando, 78–79
  Recogiendo limosnas, 129–130, 132, 134, 135–136
  revisions and alterations in poetry, 137, 140
  Rose Period, 80
  semantic categories, 127, 143–148, 157
  semantic distinctions, 127–128, 149–150
  semantic domains, 127, 148–149
  semantic networks, 127
  texts as Visually Complex Documents, 154, 157
  transition into poetry, 127, 128, 156
  use of gerunds, 138
  Le vieux guitariste aveugle, 79–80
  visual poetry, 127
  words and concepts, 127, 143, 146–150, 156–157
pictorial rhetoric, 77–78
pietá
  defined, 30n
  Valley of the Fallen, 22, 23
Pilgrim Virgin (*Virgen Peregrina*), 95, 99
Piper, Adrian, 44
place, "sense of place", 4, 120
Plato, 50, 53, 76
Plotinian dogma, 74
Poe, Edgar Allan, 227
Pollock, Jackson, 185
Popular Party (Spain), 23, 29
populism
  characteristics of, 109–112
  cultural identity, 112
  growth of, 106
  lateral vision of *mestizaje*, 116–122
  left-wing, 110
  political disaffection, 121
  "real people" concept, 111
  right-wing, 110–111
  rooted to specific places, 109–110, 111
  separation of "us" from "them", 112
  as "somewheres", 110
  threat from immigrants and asylum seekers, 110, 111
  threat to liberal democracies, 106, 107
  values of, 110–111

postmodern, as contradictory, 48
postmodernism
  architecture, 47
  beginnings of, 55
  Latin America, 47
  Latin American literature, 46, 47, 54–55
  paradox of, 54
  sculpture and painting, 48
postmodernity, defined, 47
Pozuelos Yvancos, José María, 189*n*
Premio Planeta, 164
La Prensa, 163
Primo de Rivera, Antonio, 20, 22, 23
PSOE (Spanish Socialist Workers' Party), 29
psyche, 76, 77
Puerta, Carlos, 185
Putin, Vladimir, 112
Putnam, Robert, 113
Putnam, Samuel, 210*n*
Python programming language, 145, 150

Qin dynasty, 225
Qinshihuang, 225
Quevedo, Francisco de, 180

RAE (Spanish Royal Academy of the Language), 179, 180, 181
Rainsford, Sarah, 25
Ramírez, Mari Carmen, 33
reading, 195–196, 197
"the Real", 76, 77
Real Academia de San Fernando, 78–79
real maravilloso, 56
reality, transcendental art, 72–73
recibiéndose ceremony, 92
Redman, Samuel J., 28
refugees, 109, 118
regionalist novels, 54–55
Reid, Tom, 102
Remington, Frederick, 185
Renaissance Neoplatonism, 73
Restrepo, José Alejandro, 34
Revelation, Book of, 82
Reverón, Armando, 33, 35
rhetoric, and mysticism, 75–76
Ribera del Duero DO (*denominación de origen*), 8, 9
Ribera del Duero region, 5, 8
Rice University, 102

Richardson, John, 72, 78–79, 82
Ricoeur, Paul, 47, 60–61
Rio de Janeiro, Concrete and Neo-Concrete movements, 33
Rioja region, 5–6, 9–10
Rivera, Diego, xi, 33, 35, 36
Robinson, Zev, 7
Rodin, Auguste, 40
Rodríguez, José Joaquín, 182
Rodríguez, Nestor, 88, 89, 101
Rodríguez Spiteri, José, 27
Rodríguez-Aranda, Pilar, 199, 203
Rogers, Richard, 3
Rojas, Carlos, 33
Rojas, Miguel Ángel, 34
Roman architectural traits, 21, 22
Roman Catholic Church *see* Hispanic Roman Catholicism
Romanticism, 47, 55, 215
Rosado Seijo, Chemi, 36
Rothenberg, Jerome, 132
Rueda DO (*denominación de origen*), 8
'Rufino' (Vargas Llosa's *The War of the End of the World*), 208, 209
Ruíz, Elenita, 96
Russia
  expansionist nationalism, 112
  pan-Slavism, 21

S. I. Morris and Associates, 39
Sabartés, Jaime, 134
Sabbatini, Innocenzo, 21
Saint Exupéry, Antoine de, 195
Saldívar, José David, 169
Salguero Rodríguez, José-María, 164
Salum, RoseMary, xi
Salvador, Gregorio, 179–180, 181, 183, 184, 189*n*
San Antonio, Texas
  Federation of *Guadalupanas*, 95
  Our Lady of Guadalupe Chapel, 91, 93
  Our Lady of Guadalupe Church, 91
  La Serenata a la Virgen Morena, 95
  Sociedades Guadalupanas, 91, 93
San Lorenzo de El Escorial, 19
Sánchez, Pedro, 27
Sánchez-Albornoz, Nicolás, 24
Sanders, Bernie, 110
'Sandy' (Perezagua's *Yoro*), 215
'Santos Luzardo' (Gallegos's *Doña Barbara*), 55

252 | Index

São Paulo, Concrete and Neo-Concrete movements, 33
Sanzio, Raphael, 72
Sarmiento, Domingo Faustino, 62
Saussure, Ferdinand de, 50, 51, 53
Schanuel, Tony, 44
Schendel, Mira, 33
Schiller, Friedrich, 55
Schlegel, William von, 54
Schoemann, Kendall, 64
Scholger, Martina, 156
Schumacher, E.F., 121
Schwartz, Michael, 83
Scott, Walter, 185
sculpture, postmodern aesthetic, 48
'Sebastiana' (Vargas Llosa's *The War of the End of the World*), 208
Segui, Antonio, 33
Seguin, Our Lady of Guadalupe Church, 96
Sender, Manuel, 166, 168
Sender, Ramón J.
  "A bordo de un avión/On Board", 167
  "A pseudo", 167
  "Adiós pájaro negro/Goodbye Black Bird", 169–170
  American Literary Agency (ALA), 162–163, 167–168, 172
  "Aquel día en El Paso/That Day in El Paso", 167
  articles in anarchist exile periodicals, 164–166
  "Aventura en Texas/Adventure in Texas", 168–169
  "Chessman", 171–172
  "La cultura y los hechos económicos", 164
  "Despedida en Bourg Madame/Farewell at Bourg Madame", 171
  "Los días y las horas" literary column, 163
  "El español 'fronterizo'", 165
  "En el Grand Canyon/In the Grand Canyon", 168
  En la vida de Ignacio More, 164
  Ensayos de otro mundo, 163
  exile in Mexico (1939), 162
  exile in United States (1942), 162
  FBI investigation, 165
  flânerie, 162, 163, 166, 167
  flaneur, 162, 168
  frontier quality of exiles, 165–166, 174*n*
  "Germinal", 167
  grotesque-sublime notion, 162, 165–166, 168, 171, 172–173
  "Manuela en Copacabana", 166–167
  "Montesquieu y el español fronterizo", 165
  national archetypes usage, 167–168
  Nocturno de los 14, 164
  "Pantera negra/Black Panther", 170–171
  publications, 163–164
  Relatos fronterizos/Border Stories, 162, 163, 166–173
  Siete domingos rojos, 164
  Spanish Republican Army officer, 162, 168
  Les tres sorores, 164
  Valle Inclán y la dificultad de la tragedia, 165–166
  "Velada en Acapulco/Night in Acapulco", 167
"sense of place", 4, 120
"sense of time", 4
separatism, 113
separatist movements, 188
La Serenata a la Virgen Morena, 95
Seró village, 16
Seven Swords film (Tsui Hark), 221
Shaolin Temple, 220
Shaolin Temple film, 226
Sheikh, Fazal, 43
Shelley, Percy Bysshe, 55
Shields, Daniel, 73
Shiner, Larry, 15, 16
Shrag, Calvin, 116
sign
  arbitrary nature of, 50
  Derrida's grammatology, 52, 54
  differential, 51
  distinction between human and natural, 51
signified, Derrida's grammatology, 52–53, 54
signifier
  Carpentier's *Los pasos perdidos*, 55
  Derrida's grammatology, 50, 51, 52–53
  transcendental, 50
Siqueiros, David Alfaro, 33, 36
'Sir' (Perezagua's *Yoro*), 213–214

Smith, David, 40
socialism, 61
Sociedad Mutualista Obrera Mexicana, 90
Sociedades Guadalupanas, 90–96
Soldevilla, Loló de, 33
Solidaridad Obrera, 164
Somontano, 6
Sontag, Susan, 218
Soto, Jesús Rafael, 37
Spain
  Constitution (1978), 188
  establishment of democracy (1978), 23, 26, 29
  Law of Historical Memory (2007), 26
  "Pact of Forgetting", 26
  separatist movements, 188
  see also Valley of the Fallen
Spanish Civil War (1936–1939), 19, 20, 22, 25, 26, 27, 28
Spanish Civil War diaspora, 165
Spanish Golden Age, 71
Spanish Inquisition, 180
Spanish Royal Academy of the Language (RAE), 179, 180, 181
Spanish Socialist Workers' Party (PSOE), 29
Spanish wineries *see* bodegas
speech, Derrida's grammatology, 50–52
Speer, Albert, 21
Spiess, Jessie, 44
Spinoza, Baruch, 52
SQLite database, 149–150
Standard Query Language (SQL), 142
Stendhal, 184
Steven Holl Architects, 39
Stevens, Wallace, 170–171
Stevenson, Robert Louis, 184
Stonehenge, 48
structuralism, 50, 51, 53
sublime, concept of
  Perezagua's *Yoro*, 218
  Sender's *Relatos fronterizos*, 162, 165–166, 168, 171, 172–173
Sudek, Josef, 44
Sun, Haiqing, xii
Sunday, Elisabeth, 43
supplement, 51
Surrealism, 47, 56, 157
Sweeney, James Johnson, 38–39
Swift, Jonathan, 60
"the Symbolic", 77, 129

Tallet, Olivia P., 97–99
Tamayo, Rufino, 33, 35
Támez, Amada, 97
'Tapia' (Sender's "Velada en Acapulco"), 167
Taylor, David, 37
technology, 197
tectonics, 64
TEI (Text Encoding Initiative), 154–156, 157
Téllez, Arthur, 94
Téllez, Gilbert, 94
Téllez Girónsu, Don Pedro, 8
Telléz, Javier, 34
Téllez, Nellie Pérez, 93–94
Téllez, Sipriano, 93, 94
tempranillo grape, 5
Terkenli, Theano, 42
terza maniera, 72
Texas State Historical Association, 90
Text Encoding Initiative (TEI), 154–156, 157
Thackeray, William Makepeace, 185
Thatcher, Margaret, 111
Theotokópoulos, Doménikos *see* El Greco (Doménikos Theotokópoulos)
Thomas, Christian, 157
Thomson, John, 43
Thought Catalog, 32
Tierra de León DO (*denominación de origen*), 8
time
  Derrida's grammatology, 53
  heterotopias of, 4
  "sense of time", 4
Tiresias, 80
Todorov, Tzvetan, 225
Toltec ball courts, 48
Topic Modeling, 143–146
Topoi, 76
Toro DO (*denominación de origen*), 5, 8, 10
Toro town, 5, 10
Torres-García, Joaquín, 33, 35, 36
Torrús, Alejandro, 25
transcendental art, 72–73
transcendental signifier, 50
transnational communities, 109, 114
transversal philosophy, 116
Treviño, Robert R., 88, 89, 96
Trubetzkoi, Nikolai, 148
Trump, Donald, 111

254 | Index

truth, disclosure of, 116
Tsui Hark, 221, 224
Turrell, James, 41
Twain, Mark, 185

UCLA Chicano Studies Research Center, 42
Ukraine, Russian expansionist nationalism, 112
Ulmer, Gregory, 75, 76, 77, 78
unconscious mind, 53
United Kingdom
  Brexit, 109
  centrist political parties, 109
United Nations, 27
United States
  centrist political parties, 109
  Democrat Party policies, 110
  discrimination against Mexicans, 169
  impact of wealth in political campaigns, 121
  Latinx studies, 114
  manifest destiny notion, 114, 120
  Mexican immigrants, 88–90, 96, 99–100, 101–102
  migrants, 118, 119
  racism, 169–171
universality, 116
universalization, 46–47, 49, 57, 60–61
univocity, 53
Updike, John, 185
utopianism, 46, 61, 65

Valladolid, 5, 8–9
Valle Inclán, Ramón, 165–166, 172
Valle, Roberto, 8
Valley of the Fallen, 19–30
  architectural influences, 21–22
  Catholic symbolism, 22
  change of meaning of the monument, 19–20
  Christian cross, 22
  as commemorative monument, 19, 20, 25–26, 28
  completed (1959), 19
  conflicting meanings, 20
  design values, 20
  divisiveness, 27–28
  entrance fees, 23, 27
  exhumation and relocation of victims, 20, 23–24
  Franco's decree (1940), 19, 20, 23
  Franco's tomb, 20, 22, 23, 25, 26, 27, 29
  meaning for the contemporary public, 23
  multiple functions of, 20
  opposition to the monument, 19, 23, 24, 26–27
  pietá, 22, 23
  "political events" prohibited, 26
  political meaning, 19, 21–22, 23, 29
  Primo de Rivera's tomb, 20, 22, 23
  similarities to EL Escorial, 21
  statuary, 22, 23
  supporters of, 25–26, 27
  use of forced labor of Republican prisoners to construct, 20, 23, 24–25
Van Lengen, Peter, 220
vanguard, 47, 58, 61
Vargas Llosa, Mario
  Aunt Julia and the Writer, 205, 210n
  The City and the Dogs, 210n
  Conversation in the Cathedral, 210n
  The Green House, 210n
  Magic Realism, 57
  Pantaleón and the Visitors, 205
  The War of the End of the World, xii, 205–210
Vasconcelos, José, 114
Vazas, László, 215
Veach, Grace, 75
Velázquez, Diego, 180
Vélez Catrain, Antonio, 59, 61
Venezuela, left-wing populism, 110
Venice International Film Festival, 221
Vico, Giambattista, 50
Villa, Pancho, 202, 203–204n
Villa Savoie, 62
Villanueva, Carlos Raúl, 48
Vinos de la Tierra de Castilla y León, 8
Virgen Peregrina (Pilgrim Virgin), 95, 99
Vitruvius, 72
Vivanco, Pedro, 7
Vivanco, Santiago, 7
Volpi, Alfredo, 33

Walker, Challis, 35
Wall Street Occupy Movement, 110
WalletHub, 102–103
Walton, Kendall, 83
Warhol, Andy, 185
Washington Post, 32, 42

Watkin, William Ward, 37
White nationalists, 116
wine museums
    Aragón Wine Museum, 5
    architecture, 3–17
    d'Arenberg Cube, McLaren Vale, 5
    Bodegas Fariña, 5, 10–15, *14*, 16
    Centro de la Cultura del Rioja, 6, 9–10, *13*, 16–17
    Chilean Wine Museum, 5
    Museo de la Cultura del Vino, 5–8, 16–17
    Museo del Vino de Valladolid, 5, 8–9, *12*, 16–17
wine tourism, 3–5, 15–17
    Bodegas Fariña, 5, 10–15, *14*, 16
    Centro de la Cultura del Rioja, 6, 9–10, *13*, 16–17
    Dinastía Vivanco winery, 5–8, *11*, 16–17
    Museo de la Cultura del Vino, 5–8, 16–17
    Museo del Vino de Valladolid, 5, 8–9, *12*, 16–17
Winn, Robert K., 35
Winter, Jay, 28–29
Wordsworth, William, 54
writing
    Derrida's grammatology, 50–52, 53, 54

Salum's experience, 196
Wyers, Frances, 57, 59, 65

Xenophon, 181, 183
XL Semanal, 183
XML (Extensible Markup Language) files, 150
Xul Solar, Alejandro, 36

Yanguas family, 9
'Yannes' (Carpentier's *Los pasos perdidos*), 58
Yo Soy 132 movement, 102
Yoro, meaning in Spanish, 218*n*
'Yoro' (Perezagua's *Yoro*), 213, 217
Yugoslav Wars (1991–2001), 182
Yunus, Muhammad, 121

Zamora, Jorge, 5
Zaror, Marko, 220
Zelaya Kolker, Marielena, 163
Zhang Yimou, 221, 224, 225, 227
Zuccaro, Federico, 73
Zuloaga, Ignacio, 82